ON TELEVISION

"Till the eyes tire, millions of us watch the shadows of shadows and find them substance; watch scenes, situations, actions, exchanges, crises. The slice of life, once a project of naturalist drama, is now a voluntary, habitual, internal rhythm; the flow of action and acting, of representation and performance, raised to a new convention, that of a basic need."

—Raymond Williams

RAYMOND WILLIAMS ON TELEVISION

SELECTED WRITINGS

Edited by Alan O'Connor

Routledge

London   New York

Preface and articles © Estate of Raymond Williams 1989
Introduction © Alan O'Connor 1989
First published in 1989 by:

> Routledge
> a division of Routledge, Chapman and Hall
> 29 West 35th Street, New York NY 10001
> and
> Routledge
> a division of Routledge, Chapman and Hall
> 11 New Fetter Lane, London EC4P 4EE

Cover design by Goodness Graphics, Toronto, Ontario, Canada
Photograph by Camera Press Ltd., London, England
Printed in Canada
We gratefully acknowledge permission to reprint the following
articles:
"Drama in a Dramatised Society," Cambridge University Press;
"Distance," *London Review of Books*; "Television and Teaching:
An Interview with Raymond Williams," Society for Education in
Film & Television Limited; all others, *The Listener*.
Alan O'Connor thanks Dinah Forbes and Robert Clarke of Between
The Lines (Toronto), without whom this book would not exist in its
present form.

British Library Cataloguing in Publication Data

Raymond Williams on Television *1921-1988.*
1. Society. Effects of Television
I. Title II. O'Connor, Alan
302.2′345

ISBN 0-415-02627-X

Library of Congress Cataloging in Publication Data

applied for

ISBN 0-415-02627-X

Contents

Preface

It was a busy and fortunate time. Before I began writing about television I had been an active occasional participant. The first time I appeared was on the lively magazine programme *Tonight,* in the late 1950s. I was there to question the author of an educational report. An enthusiastic producer asked me to begin the discussion by taking the printed report and tearing it up. "That would be real television", he said. "It would also be vandalism", I had to reply. Soon afterwards I was learning the extraordinary experience of answering an interviewer's questions—still by habit speaking to him rather than to the actual audience—while in fact he, off camera, had his head bowed over his clipboard, rehearsing his next question. Or there was the uncertain passage between the informality of the hospitality room and the relative formality of the studio. I was booked to engage in a fierce head-to-head discussion with the Chairman of a large newspaper group. It was all smiles and chat until we were seated knee-to-knee under the lights and he leaned over and said "No holds barred, right?" I saw none of all this on the screen, since most discussions were live, but I was beginning to understand the atmosphere of this rapidly expanding institution.

Before the end of the 1960s I had taken part in innumerable discussions, live and recorded. For some years the BBC used to send a car to take me from Cambridge and return me in the small hours. I went on location in Wales to film my play *Public Inquiry*. I attended as author the live transmission, still then practised "to give the immediacy of theatre", of another play, *A Letter from the Country*. In the late Sixties I worked for many weeks with Nicholas Garnham on a personal documentary in the series *One Pair of Eyes*.

Most though not all of that work has now gone into thin air.

Yet what interests me most, looking back, is that though I was involved in these ways in the new medium almost all my writing about communications was still about print. There is one incidental reason. My book *Communications,* written in 1961, was almost entirely based on work done in adult education classes while I was still an extra-mural tutor. But then also in 1961 I had moved to internal university teaching at Cambridge and there was no room on any available course for work of this kind in any medium. By the end of the Sixties I was giving courses on film but these were not part of the syllabus. Large numbers of students attended but could not use any of this work in examinations.

The invitation to write about television came from Karl Miller, then editor of the BBC journal *The Listener.* I was to write every four weeks but had no obligation to review any particular productions. It seemed an ideal opportunity to try to make sense of the more general television experience. Yet though the invitation was welcome, I was extraordinarily busy with other work. I was in the middle of writing *The Country and the City* and an early draft of the novel which became *The Volunteers.* I was heavily engaged in teaching in the English Faculty and also in the fierce arguments just then beginning about student representation and syllabus reform. I was also more involved than at any other time in political work. In 1967 and again in 1968 I had edited the *May Day Manifesto* of a group of socialist intellectuals, opposing current Labour Government policies over the spectrum from Vietnam to the economy. I became Chairman of the National Convention of the Left which came out of the *Manifesto* and which lasted until it split over policy in the General Election of 1970.

It is then obvious that when the week for my television article came up it was a matter of finding a few hours on a Sunday to write as it came. Of course I had been watching television assiduously but the commentary had, in effect, to be taken on the wing. It seems to me now, looking back, that this sense of immediacy turned out to be important in understanding the television experience. I took many opportunities to collect my thoughts on certain types and forms of television production, and I was always prepared to write something more like a short book-review of particular work which seemed to demand it. But through all this what was really being explored was the unprecedented integration of this large and varied body of broadcasting with a busy everyday life to which, in its own ways, it referred.

As it turned out I wrote these monthly articles for more than four years. I broke off when I went as visiting professor of Political Science at Stanford University in late 1972. By this time I wanted to write more systematically about television, and my book *Television: Technology and Cultural Form* was mainly written in California. Indeed, though I taught two classes and went on a protest march in San Francisco on Nixon's inauguration, life was extremely slow and quiet there. We sat in our flat in Escondido Village and often watched American television almost round the clock. I collected my impressions of it in an article for *The Listener* after I had returned ("Impressions of U.S. Television"). The book itself was of course a different kind of writing, but it is interesting that one of its most frequently discussed concepts, that of television "flow", seems to have crystallised from the earlier kinds of experience and response. The other useful thing which happened at Stanford was contact through its Department of Communications with the newly emerging technologies of satellite and cable transmission.

Back in Britain, though they were difficult to interpret, there were many signs of change. The openness of the 1960s was already visibly limited. The argument about television institutions was stuck in an old rut. Until well into the 1980s I could get hardly anyone to listen to what I wanted to say about the problems and opportunities of the new technologies. I wrote a few more occasional pieces, but then the editorship of *The Listener* changed. The only occasional piece I have since written was for the same Karl Miller, now the editor of the *London Review of Books*. I was doing an article about a couple of new publications when the crisis of Falklands/Malvinas blew up. This crisis at once had a significant television dimension. We agreed on the phone that I would include some brief reference to it but it eventually took over the whole article "Distance".

I still watch television as often but it is ironic, looking back at the 1960s, to read myself defending television against the complaints of intellectuals all over Europe and North America. What I said then was possible, and in some cases actual, was true, but I have to face the fact that their descriptions of it are now, with only a few exceptions, remarkably accurate about current British television. Nevertheless, because of the way it went, what we have seen is not some essential and inevitable destiny of the medium. The true process is historical. The changes were politically willed and managed. The exciting burst of new work in the Sixties was very consciously and deliberately restrained. What took its place, against the best efforts of many still working in it, was the steady establishment of what must be called a mediocracy. Hardened professional controllers have constituted a new agenda of pastimes and instant celebrities. The wide and regular search into other areas of public knowledge and skill—including the universities—was effectively narrowed to the self-confident worlds of journalists and intermediaries. What had been the best kind of work was still occasionally done, but now more often as the "prestige production" rather than the steady ambition of innovation and excellence.

Yet it is all again changing. The new technologies are coming through, though in the worst hands and on the most unfavourable terms. The steady national routines will inevitably be upset. On the other hand there are now actually more young radical professionals in television and video, and in teaching and analysis of the media, than in the days of expansion and innovation. It is to them, in their diversity, fully sharing a sense of what they are up against, yet sharing also their confidence in new work waiting to be done, that these reflections are dedicated.

Raymond Williams

Cambridge, december 87

Introduction

Alan O'Connor

Although Raymond Williams has become known as one of the century's most important radical theorists on culture and literature, people who knew him firsthand say that they always thought of him above all as a writer. As a boy in Wales he aspired to be a writer and later on he combined academic work with a prolific output of books and articles intended for a readership that extended well beyond the university.

It is not surprising, therefore, that some of Williams's most sustained investigation and analysis of television appeared in the form of a regular television column written from 1968 to 1972 for *The Listener*, a weekly magazine published in England by the BBC. As well as this regular column, Williams also wrote articles on occasions when he had something to say about television coverage of Northern Ireland, violence and the Olympic Games, the Falklands war, or his impressions of American television. Because these articles have never been published as a book they have tended to be forgotten, even by specialists in television criticism. It is an omission that has resulted in a distorted image of what Williams had to say about television. In these articles as a group we have missed out on the best working example of his unique approach to popular communication.

Final preparations for *Raymond Williams on Television* took place in summer 1987 and Williams sent his Preface after a slight delay because of illness, in December. Several weeks later came the news of his sudden death on 26 January 1988. The widespread shock of this news, even among people throughout the world who knew him only through his writing, is a tribute to the importance of his serious, sometimes austere, yet personal written voice. Williams had always refused the idea of autobiography, on the grounds that social and political life is multidimensional and should not be focused through any single point of view. This argument did not exclude personal intentions, which are present in all of Williams's work. Especially during *The Listener* years what w have is something close to a diary of a writer.

In *The Listener* articles, here is Williams building a dry stone wall in preference to watching the investiture of the Prince of Wales, or kept inside because of bad October weather. Here he is watching television when he is overburdened with work at the end of term, or sitting with his nephews whom he had to fetch from ten miles away because they were stranded without a set. Here he is watching children's programmes with his granddaughter, watching television after visiting a student in prison. Here is Williams in Killarney and Naples and California.

The years of Williams's columns on television for *The Listener* are also those of the Prague Spring of 1968, of anti-Vietnam war demonstrations in Grosvenor Square, of fighting in Cambodia and in Northern Ireland, of hope for McGovern in the United States, and of the last years of the Wilson government in England. *The Listener* columns contain commentary on all of these topics.

It is a sign of the development of the communications industry and of national television systems that Williams should comment on politics through television. (Though he also wrote directly political essays, notably for the U.S. weekly, *The Nation.*) Unlike many intellectuals who say they never watch television, are uninterested, Williams insists again and again on the contemporary importance of the medium. More and more, he would argue, we see the world through television. But equally Williams rejects technological slogans. His articles about television in California contrast the high tech of the area with the institutional organization of TV, which has resulted in almost no money for independent production. He says too that one has to wait for the *New York Times* to arrive late to discover what happened in the general election in Chile.

Even more important is Williams's argument in "Drama in a Dramatised Society" that the internal development of the form of serious European drama called for something like film (or television) to make the desired moving image a technical possibility. What Strindberg called for in some of his scripts at the turn of the century—moving sculpture or moving sets—was technically impossible on the stage. The development of film, therefore, cannot be understood only as a development in technology. Indeed, the later development of television served partly as a direct continuation of the form of serious European drama—actors on stage in a room, waiting for news from outside that will affect their lives. It is also part of an observed historical process by which literacy and the availability of culture and communication were extended, though on their own terms, to more and more of the population. Now, as Williams points out, we see more drama of one kind or another in a month of television than our ancestors could ever have imagined seeing in their whole lives. Williams calls this qualitative change in everyday experience living "in a dramatised world".

These two themes—the conventions of naturalistic drama and the extension of drama to a majority form—are linked by a motif that is central to Williams's thought, and that is the idea of an only partly *knowable world*. The conventions and forms of television drama, now raised to an everyday need, the continual dramatic flow that attempts to link viewers—and sometimes does—also involves the dramatisation of state power, the advertising of commodities, and, most critically, the dramatisation of political representation, as in political speakers who "speak for Britain". It is against this dramatisation of consciousness that Williams speaks out.

The articles on the events at the Munich Olympics and the television coverage of the Falklands/Malvinas war are explorations in this vein. For in both cases television was not a passive observer but was partly responsible for what happened, actively shaped how the event unfolded. Both articles describe conventions of television (the maps and diagrams, the use of military metaphors in sports commentary), the temporality of the flow of television (the long wait of six weeks, the countdown), and the claims to representation that are built into the forms of television.

According to Williams, "What was shocking at Munich was that an arranged version of what the world is like was invad by an element of what several parts of the world are actually like." The arranged, televised version of sporting competition between national teams at the Olympic games created a pressure point for a battle of political wills. There were then seventeen immediate victims. Williams's point is about this complex political situation, but also about the normal television representation which in this way was momentarily thrust aside.

Writing ten years after the Munich events, on English television coverage of the Falklands/Malvinas war, Williams's prose carried a "sadder recognition" that the culture of distance is now running deep. Indeed, in this case the blanket coverage of the war is ripped aside only in a small number of television programmes that reported alternative views and were met by an "angry, loose-mouthed reaction". Williams's own final rejection of the television coverage comes in a private moment, when he is reminded by a bonfire in the village about his own war experience, and of what actual engagement in fighting really means. The Falklands/Malvinas article was itself a public intervention, not only about the particular crisis, but also to pose the question: If this push-button war is a rehearsal, will there then be a performance? For what other kind of push-button war are we being rehearsed?

Much of Williams's writing on television as institution also has to do with issues of representation. British public bodies such as the BBC and the Arts Council (on which Williams served a term) have appointed boards of governors. Williams repeatedly rejected the claim that these "honorary mandarins" are in any way representative. He argues this not only because the governors are unelected, but also because he sees that there are in fact many publics in post-war Britain and the claim to speak "for Britain" will no longer stand up. His growing sense of his Welsh origin is important here. Williams also argued for many years for the separation of production from the distribution of television programmes. In his book *Communications* (1962), again in *Towards 2000* (1983) and in many talks and articles, Williams calls for the establishment of genuinely independent television production companies and groups and for the organization of distribution of their programmes as independent non-commercial carriers. This plan would offer encouragement to many more local and regionally operated television services.

The most innovative aspect of Williams's columns in *The Listener* is their description of *cultural forms* of television. In his book on television Williams argues that what needs attention is not so much individual programmes as the overall "flow" of a day's programming—an idea that has been highly influential in television studies. Yet he was equally interested in describing what he called television's cultural forms. Although he did not consolidate this project into another book, its outlines are clear enough from the *The Listener* columns. An important and sustained element in these articles is the development of concrete studies of such television forms as travelogues, westerns, comedy, science programmes, childrens' programmes, sports, light entertainment, police series, spy stories, educational television, documentaries, detective series, gardening, antiques and crafts shows, science fiction, serials, and advertisements.

If there is one common theme running through the treatments of these diverse cultural forms of television it is the critique of professional commentary. This is a critique of the existing cultural forms and also a critique of the largely metropolitan, largely upper-class perspectives that come through the production, scripting, and writing. The column on sports, for instance, describes a pattern for more general processes in other forms. Williams frequently contrasts the television image, which can show us things in new ways, with television sound, which is all too often a commentary that attempts to limit the meaning of what we see. What we hear in television sports is an experience of doing something being continually translated into the language of commentary. The commentators' box attempts to substitute for the action. Except, of course, that we have to be *shown* the action and this, at least sometimes, breaks through the imposed frames of the professional commentators. Very similar is Williams's repeated criticism that we see so much of ordinary life through the frames of police or hospital series. What we get again is experience written by and through professionals: a discursive formation in which professional scriptwriters are describing the world through the work of other professionals, such as doctors or police or lawyers.

Television frequently contradicts the fundamental patterns of the popular cultural forms upon which it so much relies. A talk show depends upon our everyday interest in meeting and listening to people; yet unlike our ordinary experience the programmes themselves have exclusive power over selecting who talks and how they may talk. Television also frequently contradicts itself, especially in its flow of programming. Williams's best example of this is in the column "Combined Operations" in which he contrasts programmes about a Transatlantic airplane race, a publicity stunt that seems to have been connected with the sale of British military aircraft, and a documentary in which a pilot in West Africa is attempting to save a harvest from destruction by locusts. It isn't often that a single evening's television dramatises so visibly, as Williams puts it, "the conflicts and contradictions of a politically intolerable world".

The analysis of television collected in this book is part of a projet, now cut short by Williams's death, to continually show such intolerable conflicts and contradictions as they are mediated, in ways not at first obvious, through the complexity of televised cultural forms. It is important that this kind of cultural analysis continue.

Part I

Television: Cultural Form and Politics

Drama in a Dramatised Society

Drama is no longer coextensive with theatre; most dramatic performances are now in film and television studios.* In the theatre itself—
national theatre or street theatre—there is an exceptional variety of
intention and method. New kinds of text, new kinds of notation,
new media and new conventions press actively alongside the texts
and conventions that we think we know, but that I find problematic
just because these others are there. Dramatic time and sequence in a
play of Shakespeare, the intricate rhythms and relationships of
chorus and three actors in a Greek tragedy: these, I believe, become
active in new ways as we look at a cutting bench or an editing
machine, in a film or television studio, or as we see new relations
between actor and audience in the improvised theatre of the streets
and the basements.

Again, we have never as a society acted so much or watched so
many others acting. Watching, of course, carries its own problems.
Watching itself has become problematic. For drama was originally
occasional, in a literal sense: at the Festival of Dionysus in Athens or
in medieval England on the day of Corpus Christi when the waggons
were pulled through the streets. The innovating commercial theatres
of Elizabethan London moved beyond occasion but still in fixed
localities: a capital city, then a tour of provincial cities. There was to
be both expansion and contraction. In Restoration London two patent theatres—the monopoly centres of legitimate drama—could
hardly be filled. The provincial theatre-building of the eighteenth
century, the development of variety theatres and music-halls, the
expansion of London's West End theatres in the second half of the
19th century: all these qualified occasion but in the light of what was

*Williams's introductory remarks on the occasion of this public lecture are omitted
here.

to come were mainly quantitative changes. It is in our own century, in cinema, in radio and in television, that the audience for drama has gone through a qualitative change. I mean not only that *Battleship Potemkin* and *Stagecoach* have been seen by hundreds of millions of people, in many places and over a continuing period, nor only that a play by Ibsen or O'Neill is now seen simultaneously by ten to twenty million people on television. This, though the figures are enormous, is still an understandable extension. It means that for the first time a majority of the population has regular and constant access to drama, beyond occasion or season. But what is really new—so new I think that it is difficult to see its significance—is that it is not just a matter of audiences for particular plays. It is that drama, in quite new ways, is built into the rhythms of everyday life. On television alone it is normal for viewers—the substantial majority of the population—to see anything up to three hours of drama, of course drama of several different kinds, a day. And not just one day; almost every day. This is part of what I mean by a dramatised society. In earlier periods drama was important at a festival, in a season, or as a conscious journey to a theatre; from honouring Dionysus or Christ to taking in a show. What we now have is drama as habitual experience: more in a week, in many cases, than most human beings would previously have seen in a lifetime.

Can this be merely extension: a thing like eating more beef muscle or wearing out more shirts than any ancestor could have conceived as a widespread human habit? It certainly doesn't look like a straight line extension. To watch simulated action, of several recurrent kinds, not just occasionally but regularly, for longer than eating and for up to half as long as work or sleep; this, in our kind of society, as majority behaviour, is indeed a new form and pressure. It would of course be easy to excise or exorcise this remarkable fact if we could agree, as some propose, that what millions of people are so steadily watching is all or for the most part rubbish. That would be no exorcism: if it were true it would make the fact even more extraordinary. And it is in any case not true. Only dead cultures have scales that are reliable. There are discernible, important and varying proportions of significant and trivial work, but for all that, today, you can find kitsch in a national theatre and an intensely original play in a police series. The critical discriminations are at once important and unassumable in advance. But in one perspective they pale before the generality of the habit itself. What is it, we have to ask, in us and in our contemporaries, that draws us repeatedly to these hundreds and thousands of simulated actions; these plays, these representations, these dramatisations? It depends where you ask that question from. I ask it from watching and from contributing to the extraordinary process itself. But I can hear—who can not?—some familiar voices: the grave merchants whose apprentices and shopboys slipped away to Bankside; the heads of households whose wives, and the heads of colleges whose students, admitted to read English, would read novels and comedies in the morning. These sober men would know what to say about contemporary California, where you can watch your first movie at six-thirty in the morning and if you really try can see seven or eight more before you watch the late movie in the next recurrent small hours. Fiction; acting; idle dreaming and vicarious spectacle; the simultaneous satisfaction of sloth and appetite; distraction from distraction by distraction. It is a heavy, even a gross catalogue of our errors, but now millions of people are sending the catalogue back, unopened. Till the eyes tire, millions of us watch the shadows of shadows and find them substance; watch scenes, situations, actions, exchanges, crises. The slice of life, once a project of naturalist drama, is now a voluntary, habitual, internal rhythm; the flow of action and acting, of representation and performance, raised to a new convention, that of a basic need.

We cannot know what would have happened if there had been, for example, outside broadcasting facilities at the Globe. In some measure, at least, we must retain the hypothesis of simple extension of access. Yet I would argue that what has happened is much more than this. There are indeed discoverable factors of a probably causal kind. We are all used to saying—and it still means something—that we live in a society which is at once more mobile and more complex, and therefore, in some crucial respects, relatively more unknowable, relatively more opaque than most societies of the past, and yet which is also more insistently pressing, penetrating and even determining. What we try to resolve from the opaque and the unknowable, in one mode by statistics—which give us summaries and breakdowns, moderately accurate summaries and even more accurate breakdowns, of how we live and what we think—is offered to be resolved in another mode by one kind of dramatisation. Miner and power worker, minister and general, burglar and terrorist, schizophrenic and genius; a back-to-back home and a country house; metropolitan apartment

and suburban villa; bed-sitter and hill-farm: images, types, representations: a relationship beginning, a marriage breaking down; a crisis
of illness or money or dislocation or disturbance. It is not only that
all these are represented. It is that much drama now sees its function
in this experimental, investigative way; finding a subject, a setting, a
situation; and with some emphasis on novelty, on bringing some of
that kind of life into drama.

Of course all societies have had their dark and unknowable
areas, some of them by agreement, some by default. But the clear
public order of much traditional drama has not, for many generations, been really available to us. It was for this reason that the great
naturalist dramatists, from Ibsen, left the palaces, the forums and the
streets of earlier actions. They created, above all, rooms; enclosed
rooms on enclosed stages; rooms in which life was centred but inside
which people waited for the knock on the door, the letter or the
message, the shout from the street, to know what would happen to
them; what would come to intersect and to decide their own still
intense and immediate lives. There is a direct cultural continuity, it
seems to me, from those enclosed rooms, enclosed and lighted
framed rooms, to the rooms in which we watch the framed images of
television: at home, in our own lives, but needing to watch what is
happening, as we say, "out there": not out there in a particular street
or a specific community but in a complex and otherwise unfocused
and unfocusable national and international life, where our area of
concern and apparent concern is unprecedentedly wide, and where
what happens on another continent can work through to our own
lives in a matter of days and weeks—in the worst image, in hours
and minutes. Yet our lives are still here, still substantially here, with
the people we know, in our own rooms, in the similar rooms of our
friends and neighbours, and they too are watching: not only for public events, or for distraction, but from a need for images, for representations, of what living is now like, for this kind of person and
that, in this situation and place and that. It is perhaps the full development of what Wordsworth saw at an early stage, when the crowd
in the street (the new kind of urban crowd, who are physically very
close but still absolute strangers) had lost any common and settled
idea of man and so needed representations—the images on hoard-
ings, the new kinds of sign—to simulate if not affirm a human identity: what life is and looks like beyond this intense and anxious but
also this pushed and jostled private world of the head.

That is one way of putting it; the new need, the new

exposure—the need and exposure in the same movement—to a flow of images, of constant representations, as distinct from less complex and less mobile cultures in which a representation of meaning, a spectacle of order, is clearly, solidly, rigidly present, at certain fixed points, and is then more actively affirmed on a special occasion, a high day or a festival, the day of the play or the procession. But there is never only need and exposure: each is both made and used. In the simplest sense our society has been dramatised by the inclusion of constant dramatic representation as a daily habit and need. But the real process is more active than that.

Drama is a special kind of use of quite general processes of presentation, representation, signification. The raised place of power— the eminence of the royal platform—was built historically before the raised place of the stage. The presentation of power, in hierarchical groupings, in the moving emphases of procession, preceded the now comparable modes of a represented dramatic state. Gods were made present or made accessible by precise movements, precise words, in a known conventional form. Drama is now so often associated with what are called myth and ritual that the general point is easily made. But the relation cannot be reduced to the usual loose association. Drama is a precise separation of certain common modes for new and specific ends. It is neither ritual which discloses the God, nor myth which requires and sustains repetition. It is specific, active, interactive composition: an action not an act; an open practice that has been deliberately abstracted from temporary practical or magical ends: a complex opening of ritual to public and variable action; a moving beyond myth to dramatic *versions* of myth and of history. It was this active variable experimental drama—not the closed world of known signs and meanings—that came through in its own right and in its own power; significantly often in periods of crisis and change, when an order was known and still formally present but when experience was pressing it, testing it, conceiving breaks and alternatives; the dramatic possibility of what might be done within what was known to have been done, and each could be present, and mutually, contradictorily potent, in specific acted forms. We need to see this especially now, when myth and ritual, in their ordinary senses, have been broken up by historical development, when they are little more, in fact, than the nostalgia or the rhetoric of one kind of scholar and thinker, and yet when the basic social processes, of presentation, representation, signification have never been more important. Drama broke from fixed signs, established its permanent distance from myth and ritual and from the hierarchical figures and processions of state; broke for precise historical and cultural reasons into a more complex, more active and more questioning world. There are relativities within its subsequent history, and the break has been made many more times than once. Any system of signs, presenting and representing, can become incorporated into a passive order, and new strange images, of repressed experience, repressed people, have again to break beyond this. The drama of any period, including our own, is an intricate set of practices of which some are incorporated—the known rhythms and movements of a residual but still active system—and some are exploratory—the difficult rhythms and movements of an emergent representation, rearrangement, new identification. Under real pressures these distinct kinds are often intricately and powerfully fused; it is rarely a simple case of the old drama and the new.

But drama, which separated out, did not separate out altogether. Congruous and comparable practices exist in other parts of the society as in the drama, and these are often interactive: the more interactive as the world of fixed signs is less formal. Indeed what we often have now is a new convention of deliberate overlap. Let me give the simplest example. Actors now often move from a part in a play, which we can all specify as dramatic art, to deploy the same or similar skills in the hired but rapturous discovery of a cigar or a facecream. They may be uneasy about it but, as they say, it's better than resting. It's still acting after all; they are no more personally committed to that cigar than to the character of that bluff inspector, for which they were also hired. Somebody wrote it, somebody's directing it: you're still in the profession. Commercials in Britain have conventional signs to tell you they're coming, but the overlap of method, of skill and of actual individuals is a small and less easily-read sign of a more general process, in which the breaks are much harder to discern.

Our present society, in ways it is merely painful to reiterate, is sufficiently dramatic in one obvious sense. Actions of a kind and scale that attract dramatic comparisons are being played out in ways that leave us continually uncertain whether we are spectators or participants. The specific vocabulary of the dramatic mode—drama itself, and then tragedy, scenario, situation, actors, performances, roles, images—is continually and conventionally appropriated for these immense actions. It would moreover be easier, one can now often feel, if only actors acted, and only dramatists wrote scenarios.

But we are far past that. On what is called the public stage, or in the public eye, improbable but plausible figures continually appear to represent us. Specific men are magnified to temporary universality, and so active and complex is this process that we are often invited to see them rehearsing their roles, or discussing their scenarios. Walter Bagehot* once distinguished between a real ruling class and a theatrical ruling show: the widow of Windsor, he argued, in his innovating style of approving and elegant cynicism, is needed to be shown, to be paraded, before a people who could never comprehend the more complex realities of power. I watched this morning the televised State opening of Parliament. It is one thing to say that it was pure theatre; it is harder to see, and to say, that beyond its residual pageantry was another more naturalised process which is also in part a cousin of theatre. Monarchs, of course, have always done something like this, or had it done for them. Those who lasted were conscious of their images even if they called them their majesties. Moreover, like many actors, people find roles growing on them: they come to fit the part, as he who would play the King. What is new, really, is not in them but in us.

It is often genuinely difficult to believe in any part of this pervasive dramatisation. If we see it in another period or in or from another place, it visibly struts and frets, its machinery starts audibly creaking. In moments of crisis, we sometimes leave this social theatre or, as easily, fall asleep in it. But these are not only roles and scenarios; they are conventions. When you can see a convention, become really conscious of it, it is probably already breaking down. Beyond what many people can see as the theatricality of our image-conscious public world, there is a more serious, more effective, more deeply rooted drama: the dramatisation of consciousness itself. "I speak for Britain" runs the written line of that miming public figure, though since we were let in on the auditions, and saw other actors trying for the part, we may have our reservations; we may even say "Well I'm here and you don't speak for me." "Exactly," the figure replies, with an unruffled confidence in his role, for now a different consciousness, a more profound dramatisation, begins to take effect; "you speak for yourself, but I speak for Britain." "Where is that?" you may think to ask, looking wonderingly around. On a good day from a high place you can see about fifty miles. But you know some

*Walter Bagehot (1826-77). English writer and political scientist. Author of *The English Constitution*.

places, you remember others; you have memories, definitions and a history.

Yet at some point along that continuum, usually in fact very early, you have—what? Representations; typifications; active images; active parts to play that people are playing, or sometimes refusing to play. The specific conventions of this particular dramatisation—a country, a society, a period of history, a crisis of civilisation; these conventions are not abstract. They are profoundly worked and reworked in our actual living relationships. They are our ways of seeing and knowing, which every day we put into practice, and while the conventions hold, while the relationships hold, most practice confirms them. One kind of specific autonomy—thisness, hereness—is in part free of them; but this is usually an autonomy of privacy, and the private figure—the character of the self—is already widely offered to be appropriated in one or other of these dramatised forms: producer or consumer, married or single, member or exile or vagrant. Beyond all these there is what we call the irreducible: the still unaccommodated man. But the process has reached in so far that there are now, in practice, conventions of isolation itself. The lonely individual is now a common type: that is an example of what I mean by a dramatic convention, extending from play to consciousness. Within a generation of that naturalist drama which created the closed room— the room in which people lived but had to wait for news from outside—another movement had created another centre: the isolated figure, the stranger, who in Strindberg's *Road to Damascus* was still actively looking for himself and his world, testing and discarding this role and that image, this affirming memory and that confirming situation, with each in turn breaking down until he came back, each time, to the same place. Half a century later two ultimately isolated figures, their world not gone but never created, sat down on the road waiting for what?—call it Godot—to come. Let's go, they said, but they didn't move. A decade later other more radically isolated figures were seen as buried to their necks, and all that was finally audible, within that partial and persuasive convention, was a cry, a breath. Privacy; deprivation. A lost public world; an uncreatable public world.

These images challenge and engage us, for to begin with, at least, they were images of dissent, of conscious dissent from fixed forms. But that other miming, the public dramatisation, is so continuous, so insistent, that dissent, alone, has proved quite powerless against it. Dissent, that is, like any modern tragic hero, can die but no more. And critical dissent, a public form you can carry around to lectures or even examinations: it too comes back to the place where it started, and may or may not know it for the first time. A man I knew from France, a man who had learned, none better, the modes of perception that are critical dissent, said to me once, rather happily: "France, you know, is a bad bourgeois novel." I could see how far he was right: the modes of dramatisation, of fictionalisation, which are active as social and cultural conventions, as ways not only of seeing but of organising reality, are as he said: a bourgeois novel, its human types still fixed but losing some of their conviction; its human actions, its struggles for property and position, for careers and careering relationships, still as limited as ever but still bitterly holding the field, in an interactive public reality and public consciousness. "Well yes," I said politely, "England's a bad bourgeois novel too. And New York is a bad metropolitan novel. But there's one difficulty, at least I find it a difficulty. You can't send them back to the library. You're stuck with them. You have to read them over and over." "But critically," he said, with an engaging alertness. "Still reading them," I said.

I think that is where we now are. People have often asked me why, trained in literature and expressly in drama, making an ordinary career in writing and teaching dramatic history and analysis, I turned—*turned*—to what they would call sociology if they were quite sure I wouldn't be offended (some were sure the other way and I'm obliquely grateful to them). I could have said, debating the point, that Ruskin didn't turn from architecture to society; he saw society in architecture—in its styles, its shaping intentions, its structures of power and of feeling, its façades and its interiors and the relations between them; he could then learn to read both architecture and society in new ways. But I would prefer to speak for myself. I learned something from analysing drama which seemed to me effective not only as a way of seeing certain aspects of society but as a way of getting through to some of the fundamental conventions which we group as society itself. These, in their turn, make some of the problems of drama quite newly active. It was by looking both ways, at a stage and a text, and at a society active, enacted, in them, that I thought I saw the significance of the enclosed room—the room on the stage, with its new metaphor of the fourth wall lifted—as at once a dramatic and a social fact.

For the room is there, not as one scenic convention among all the possible others, but because it is an actively shaping environment—the particular structure within which we live—and also, in continuity, in inheritance, in crisis—the solid form, the conventional declaration, of how we are living and what we value. This room on the stage, this enclosed living room, where important things happen and where quite another order of importance arrives as news from a shut-off outside world; this room is a convention, now a habit, of theatre; but it is also, subtly and persistently, a personage, an actor: a set that defines us and can trap us: the alienated object that now represents us in the world. I have watched, fascinated, as that room has broken up; the furniture got rid of, a space cleared; people facing each other across an emptiness, with only the body, the body as object or the body as rhythm, to discover, to play with, to exhaust itself. But more important than this has been a dynamic process when the room is dissolved, for scene is no longer external and yet is still active, and what we see is a projection of observed, remembered, and desired images. While Strindberg at the turn of the century was writing a new drama of moving images—a wall papered with faces; aspects of character and appearance dissolving, fragmenting, fusing, haunting; objects changing literally as you look at them; while Strindberg was writing this, beyond the capacity of the theatre of his time, other men, in quite different ways, were discovering means of making images move; finding the technical basis for the motion picture: the new mobility and with it the fade, the dissolve, the cut, the flashback, the voice-over, the montage, that are technical forms but also, in new ways, modes of perceiving, of relating, of composing and of finding our way.

Again I heard, as if for the first time, what was still, by habit, called dramatic speech, even dialogue; heard it in Chekhov and noticed a now habitual strangeness: that the voices were no longer speaking to or at each other; were speaking with each other perhaps, with themselves in the presence of others. But there was a new composition, in which a group was speaking, yet a strange negative group; no individual ever quite finishing what he had begun to say, but intersecting, being intersected by the words of others, casual and distracted, words in their turn unfinished: a weaving of voices in which, though still negatively, the group was speaking and yet no single person was ever finally articulate. It is by now so normal a process, in writing dramatic speech, that it can be heard, any night, in a television serial, and this is not just imitation. It is a way of speaking and of listening, a specific rhythm of a particular consciousness; in the end a form of unfinished, transient, anxious relationship, which is there on the stage or in the text but which is also, pervasively, a structure of feeling in a precise contemporary world, in a period of history which has that familiar and complex transience. I don't think I could have understood these dramatic procedures as *methods*—that is to say, as significant general modes—if I had not been looking both ways. I could have seen them, perhaps, as techniques: a professional viewpoint but in my experience not professional enough, for it is where technique and method have either an identity or, as now commonly, a significant fracture, that all the hard questions of this difficult discipline begin.

I am here to profess no more and no less than the questions of this discipline. That is to say, I profess the questions, but would then stand aside and argue, without benefit of title, for my own more particular answers.

Inaugural Lecture, University of Cambridge, 29 October 1974

Distance

The most arresting image on television, in recent weeks, has been the stylish map of the world which introduces *Newsnight*. It does not show the Falkland/Malvinas islands.

The problems of television during this crisis* can be referred to familiar frames: the issues of control and independence; of the quality of reporting; of access and balance in discussion. All are important, but underlying them are some more difficult questions: latent for many years but made very sharp and specific by these events and their representation. They can be summarised as problems in the culture of distance.

The central technical claim of television is that it can show us distant events. The hybrid name selects this quality, following *telescope, telegraph, telephone, telepathy,* with *tele* as the combining

---

*The Argentinian military occupied the Falkland Islands on April 2, 1982. Williams's article would have been written before they surrendered on June 14 to the British taskforce of some 30 warships and 6,000 troops.

form, from the Greek for "afar", related to *telos,* "end". Yet in most everyday television, distance, in any real sense, is not the leading factor. We are in one place, usually at home, watching something in another place: at variable distances, which however do not ordinarily matter, since the technology closes the gap to a familiar connection. The familiarity can be an illusion, but the qualitative change when we see really distant events is usually obvious. We have been shown men walking in space and on the Moon. We have seen our whole planet from outside. And from time to time, indeed often, we have seen men fighting in wars.

The strangest quality of these last weeks has been an absence. That is why the incidental omission of the now famous islands from *Newsnight's* diagram map sticks in the mind. Certainly it reminds us how selective, and then how differently selective, the television picture of the world can be. But what is much more significant is the revealed distance between the technology of television, as professionally understood, managed and interpreted, and the political and cultural space within which it actually operates.

Of course from the beginning there were two linked factors which changed what had been understood as the ground rules of television news. The great distance of the islands from Britain, and the fact that in all its early stages this was a naval and long-distance air campaign, led to almost insuperable logistical problems. At the same time there were genuine security requirements: disclosure of the identities and positions of various forces could have exposed them to attack. Yet these factors were then extended. The Ministry of Defence, which has more press and information officers than any other government department, produced a spokesman of such stunning formality that televising him seemed in itself a new form of communication. Deprived of its actualities, television stood its reporters in the streets outside closed doors, constructed models and panels in its studios, and showed film from Argentina.

This strange and protracted sequence was in itself a novel representation of the culture of distance. It has led to much impatience, but then it may eventually be seen that the systematic exhaustion of patience has been part of the inner history of these events. The long, slow approach to the islands was a material reality. But then: to go all that way and do nothing? To hear those discussions night after night, as in an unusually extended pre-match analysis? To want at least something to happen, as in the ordinary rhythms of television?

"We have been discussing this now for six or seven weeks." The Zimbabwe negotiations lasted six or seven months. Behind both issues there had been argument and attempted negotiation for many years. But then, in the absence of more familiar rhythms, a new and particular rhythm was eventually established. Its principal elements were slowness and inevitability. Its supporting factors were that for many different reasons, and enclosing many different opinions, most capacities for long-term attention and for any substantial patience were indeed exhausted. The slow movement reached its bloody climax. "Let's get it over with," many were saying and had been effectively rehearsed to say.

Yet this is still only part of the culture of distance. Suppose, for contrast, that this had been an American operation. There can be little doubt that the film would have been got back, quickly, and would have filled our screens. But film of what? It is said that what was eventually the nightly exposure of ground fighting, and of fires and corpses, turned public opinion, in the United States and elsewhere, against the war in Vietnam. There is no certainty that this is true. That war lasted so long that patience was exhausted with quite other political consequences than the present action is likely to give rise to. But it was in any case the representation of a close-up war: physically distant on the earth but physically close in the lens. What has been happening in the South Atlantic, up to the point where British troops went back on the islands, has been a war of technical distance: of buttons pressed and missiles fired from distances often beyond the range of normal vision; moreover, in many cases, of missiles programmed to direct themselves to their targets. It is the kind of destruction which many of us have been trying to think about in a nuclear exchange, but with two effective differences: that it is on a comparatively small scale, and that it is (as the long slow rhythm had assured us) at a very safe distance.

At a reputedly safe distance, but the precise images of this war of distance had been strongly built into the culture. In every games arcade we can press buttons and see conventionally destructive flashes on targets: "the invaders". Television already has, in its library footage, film of excitingly named missiles—sidewinders, rapiers, sea wolves—streaking towards exercise targets, which flash and disintegrate and fall. If (but more strictly when) the film of the South Atlantic fighting gets back, it will be important to ask what difference there is, what difference is represented, when the flash of a hit can be remembered to contain and to be destroying a man. Deprived of actuality film, television has been inserting film of these exercises, intermittently subtitled. Is it second best? Who can say? The representation of spectacular destruction may already, in many minds, have blurred the difference between exercise and action, rehearsal and act. For it is one of the corroding indulgences of the culture of distance that to the spectator the effect at least offers to be the same.

Some of us will therefore be cautious in supporting the merely professional complaints of some people in television. Already the language of certain reporters indicates an impatience for colour and action, the prepared modes of filing a war story. Then can any of us be sure there is no television director waiting to say "Cue Harrier," "Cue Marines"? Watching the studio war-games has already indicated that this is more than a technical problem. There has been a model of the islands with ships and planes on stalks surrounding it. The proportional size of the ships and planes, and of the dark shadows they cast under the studio lights, has been so exaggerated that it is obvious that the discussion is being controlled by the culture of distance, and indeed at times reaching its morbid last phase, in the culture of alienation. The television professionals, in these constructions, have been so deeply integrated with the out-of-action military professionals they have been interviewing that it felt like suddenly entering another country. Yet it was already there in the flow: programmes such as *Sailor* and *Fighter Pilot* had laid in the view that war is a profession. The Army's own advertising slogan had been taken over, as routine, when troops were used in a labour dispute: "with dustcart drivers still on strike, Glasgow Corporation called in the Professionals" (23 March 1975). In these and other ways there were the elements of an integrated viewpoint: a good clean shot; well-ordered sequences; professionals understand professionals.

It happens that I came in on the current run a little late, after the programme had started. When the Argentines invaded, I was in Ireland at the Festival of Film and Television in the Celtic Countries. I heard the first House of Commons debate on a transistor above Killarney. Distance in that form had particular effects. Every contradiction seemed heightened. The invasion had been ordered by a brutally repressive military regime to which Labour and Conservative governments had supplied advanced weaponry. The use of force to resolve a long-standing problem was being countered by the threat or use of force to resolve it back again. The rhetoric of an expedition against a fascist military government did not exclude the possibility of active co-operation with Chile. An enterprise to restore the democratic rights of the islanders was being launched with the means and symbols of old imperialist actions. The cynical culture of late capitalism, which had used a national flag for underwear or for carrier bags, switched, as it seemed overnight, to an honorific fetishism which at the same time, though in different colours, was on the streets in Buenos Aires. In a culture which had celebrated *Monty Python*, heroic stances and ripping yards were being played or at least offered for real.

While I still read the cool and informative Irish newspapers, and watched Irish television, I got some supporting sense of the real complexity of the events. These seemed to hit every contradiction at its most exposed point, making any simple opinion or position impossible. In this peripheral problem which had suddenly become central, everything was off-balance. The House of Commons debate confirmed rather than recognised this. It was only when I got back to Wales, and saw the English papers, that I heard the screeching. Turning away to cool, low-voiced television, I found the long slow rhythm—the professional presentation of a dragging but limited time, the long march to the models—that I have been trying to describe. After several days of it, feeling the rhythm soaking in, I happened to pass a bonfire of rags and oil in the village and suddenly, in an overwhelming moment, I was in a field in Normandy and the next tank, with my friends in it, was burning and about to explode. I think I then understood the professional culture of distance. Its antiseptic presentation of the images of war was skilled but childish. This sense was deepened by the fact that, in the perspective of my generation, the professionalism being offered was not of fighting but of exercises and models. Throughout the crisis, across different opinions, I have not heard any talk of that distant calculating kind from friends who had been in actual battles.

This seems to me the determining issue. There have been some genuine attempts to present some kind of balance in discussion. It is too early to offer any precise account: that will come later. But such interviewing of dissenters and doubters as there has been has taken place within the general unreality of the presentation of war.

Moreover even the important and sustained discussion of negotiating positions and possibilities, which in the early weeks played in counterpoint to the war-games, was vitiated by the absence of hard information. Did a television reporter fly to Peru to interview its President on the precise terms of his proposals, and to question him and then others back home? If so, I missed the report. Speculation flourished in the absence of precise terms. When at last some were finally published, and the opposed positions seemed to some of us no more irreconcilable than in most serious international disputes, including many which eventually get settled, it was already the eve of the climax of that long slow rhythm. The patience of all those who, to be frank, had never sounded particularly patient was said to be exhausted.

Was said to be. One permanent element of our kind of press and television came very clearly into view during these weeks. We can call it the Corps of the Briefed. "The feeling in Whitehall". "Sources close to Ministers". The steady feed of these official/unofficial indications occurred alongside numerous official interviews and recordings. It is then necessary to ask what function they serve. Is it only a discreet nudging, beyond attributable public statements? Or is it also a way of enrolling parts of the media, on mutually acceptable terms, in a sense of being inside, being privy? Hopes might rise from some report of a rewording of a formula, but before the details, and before even the opportunity to consider the report with any care, "it is felt in Whitehall that this in no way meets Britain's requirements" (my italics). "It is understood that the basic problem is one of the credibility of the people we are trying to deal with." Indeed.

Yet some people in television, as in a few newspapers, did more than sit up and beg to be privy. One of the most ominous moments of the crisis was the angry, loose-mouthed reaction to such programmes as Panorama and other BBC reporting of alternative views. It is interesting that subsequent inquiry, by opinion poll, showed this reaction as the view of a minority. But it takes its place in a lengthening history of such incidents, most of which have hitherto concerned reporting and discussion of the conflict in the North of Ireland. It is as if, each time, the basic terms of an understanding of programming independence have to be reinvented. Yet the film from Argentina, and the television clips, which were also complained about, were showing quite clearly what a "patriotic" model of television looked like. Galtieri* spoke, on a triptych of stone-faced generals. Flags and leaders were paraded. Authorised voices interpreted and exhorted. Or, later, when fighting started, favourable news was rushed, unfavourable news delayed or discounted. Can this be really what anyone openly wants? Yet several of the incidental arguments apply. When our boys are in danger, can we tolerate voices which doubt what they are doing?

This problem also is affected by the culture of distance. If those crowds in Buenos Aires are only a flag-waving mob, looking remarkably like the rougher kinds of football crowd, if that nation and that people are only that uniformed Junta, perhaps it is not really *patriotism*. There was at least one telling interview with a mixed Argentine-British family, in which the son was just going to military service. For a moment the conflict became real, past the coarse official confrontations. Yet when David Frost repeated one of his characteristic programme models, with a British studio audience and several Argentines present by satellite, no communication of any value occurred. There was jeering from some in the British audience, before arguments were fully out, while the mainly Anglophile Argentinian bourgeois at the far end of the line offered familiar national arguments in the accents of misunderstood old friends. For that was another of the contradictions which came out so painfully in the gyrations of American government spokesmen. These Argentinians were and plainly felt themselves to be "our kind of people". To excitedly patriotic British members of that audience this didn't apply. From a different class level they were seeing enemies engaged in doubletalk. Meanwhile, for myself, the official Argentinians I kept seeing on the screen were the enemies of my Argentinian friends: friends who at the same time would not for a moment accept the official British presentation of the dispute and of the war.

The war. But is it a war? At the time of Suez a government spokesman said we were not at war: we were in a state of armed conflict. All that is happening again. It permits the obliqueness of British television reporters still speaking from Buenos Aires, even since the fighting began. It allows legal loopholes for what can still be said and done at this end, beyond the more general arguments for

*General Galtieri was President of the military government of Argentina during the Falklands conflict. He fell from power after the surrender of the Argentine forces.

the free expression of opinion in any crisis; the worse the crisis, the more the need for free information and opinion, subject only to direct security concerns. Yet it is not only in this respect that it may be necessary to consider this crisis and its modes of presentation as a rehearsal: a rehearsal which then demands detailed appraisal.

The distancing of war has been the central mode: indicated by the physical distance but confirmed and developed by a specific culture. The absence of any return fire, except at those directly exposed on our official behalf, distorts the imagination and permits the fantasies of models and of convictions without experience. But beyond the specific circumstances there is a more general question of what is being rehearsed. It is a direct question about the culture of contemporary democracy. Parliament is debating and we listen. Yet none of the representatives, it seems safe to say, could have been *directly* given the views on this unforeseen crisis of those they offer to represent. This is especially true of that decisive first debate, which inaugurated the whole sequence. What then followed was the unique modern combination of a Cabinet with absolute sovereign powers, acting within a complex of Parliamentary parties, opinion polls and television. It has been extremely powerful. On a neglected problem and an unforeseen crisis it has been able to set the agenda and the terms of public response and argument. The attempts of some television programmes and some Members of Parliament and others to express alternatives, to broaden the agenda, come already placed as dissident. The sovereign power to order war operates within the cultural power to distance. General discussion and voting are replaced by television discussion and opinion polls. The modes interact, for the war is fast or is made to appear fast, and there can be no hanging about when the threat is urgent and the blood is roused. Modern systems, in television and opinion-polling, alone correspond to this induced urgency. It is a new political form, latent for many years but now at least temporarily made actual. Its name is constitutional authoritarianism.

If it is a rehearsal, will there be a performance? That threat hangs heavier than even these bloody events. And that perhaps is the real shock. Certain assumptions about the political culture of Britain, which has been seen since the Sixties as relaxed, tolerant, peace-loving, sceptical, contemporary, have been shown to fail to hold. The distance between either the most serious or the most fashionable bearers of these attitudes and a latent and organisable majority of our people has been quite suddenly shown to be very wide, on issues that matter. In the early weeks dissidents claimed to be speaking for a majority. The opinion polls, within the whole operation, relentlessly refuted them. Volatility of opinion, the prospect of the morning after, may be cited for comfort. But there is very little that is tangible to give any reassurance. An unnecessary war has been arranged and distanced within a culture that had already distanced mass unemployment. The sinking of a ship shocks and grieves, but is then sealed over by the dominant mood. The argument about this war is difficult enough, and will of course continue. But the larger argument that now needs to be started, with a patience determined by its urgency, is about the culture of distance, the latent culture of alienation, within which men and women are reduced to models, figures and the quick cry in the throat.

London Review of Books, 17-30 June 1982

What Happened at Munich

Is terrorism becoming a spectator sport? The bitter question had to be put during the extraordinary events at Munich.* It isn't often that an estimated third of the world's population is watching, on television, what is happening in a stadium in a single city. The available publicity must have been a factor in the planning of the raid. It was also a factor in the physical and emotional responses to it. In Mexico City, before the last Olympic Games, there were demonstrations designed to attract world attention to a political situation. They were hurriedly and bloodily repressed so that the arranged events might occur.

---

*Seventeen people including 11 members of the Israeli Olympic team were shot dead on September 5, 1972. They had been taken hostage for the release of 200 Arab commandos imprisoned in Israel. The hostage-takers, Palestinian guerrillas of the Black September movement, negotiated a plane to Cairo but at a military airport outside Munich German riflemen reportedly opened fire. In the subsequent confused battle some of the Israeli athletes may have been killed by their rescuers. At least two of the slain Israeli hostages were Israeli security agents posing as team members.

Live coverage. The phrase had its ironies as the character of the competition changed. At five o'clock on the Tuesday afternoon the television cameras were showing the Israeli hostel and the familiar voice of a sports commentator was counting off the seconds as the time of a reported attack by the police came and went. In the end, of course, it didn't happen like that. The cameras caught the helicopters flying out, and next day there was film of a different quality: the obscurity of darkness and distance across the military airfield; the undramatic, inferential flashes of a repeating rifle.

Most people then said that the events contrasted, tragically, with the spirit of the Games. That is an understandable reading, and that the events were tragic is in no possible doubt. But there had been a rhetoric of competition which the shooting came to throw into relief. There had been happy commentaries about battles of wills, and about learning, by training, to drive oneself beyond pain. Some of this is only a sporting convention, like the use of such words as "tragedy","catastrophe" and "disaster" to describe an athlete falling or even failing to qualify for a final. For most of the time the convention is well understood. But I'm not sure how far a culture can go on using such a rhetoric, in any kind of good faith, while events to which such descriptions would be relevant are in any case and all the time taking place.

In any case and all the time. This also has to be stressed as we try to understand the events and the responses. Everyone was bound to be shocked by the sudden change of level. For more than a week we had been watching intense physical competition within sets of rules which the commentators explained, with clear starting and finishing points, and with a computer system to show us, in great clarity and detail, exactly what had just happened. Not the least of the ironies of that night was that the essential information, on what happened at the airfield, not only took hours to come through but was actually misreported, on television, in a way that turned out to be directly contrary to the truth. The contrast with the total visibility of the other kind of competition and communication made a necessary if bitter point.

But this reflects, in turn, on the character of the world that was being conventionally presented. Politics, they were telling us, have no place in sport. But this meant, in context: we have decided to exclude your kind of political question. For nobody could have been watching and not seen the conventional politics. Of the nation state, above all: the flags, the delegations, the *chefs de mission*. Everyone says that the medals table between states is unofficial and virtually everyone compiles and broadcasts or prints it. The victory ceremonies are submilitary, with national anthems and the raising of flags. At the official opening, in and through the marching columns, there was often a pleasant lightness of touch: people waving and smiling; the dancing and the pigeons. But when Vince Matthews and Wayne Collett took their medals in much the same spirit—talking during the anthem, Matthews happily and delightfully swinging his medal, the winner making the sporting gesture of having the runner-up come alongside him on his ritually raised piece of wood—they were banned for life. All the time, in fact, behind these marvellous young men and women, were the posses of appointed and self-appointed people who derive a right to control them. At the memorial service for the dead Israeli athletes, where it was difficult to find any form of proper solemnity because of the multiplicity of religions and nonreligions, one of the elements was a speech by Brundage* which with its coarse reference to the Rhodesian issue was directly political. There was also a speech by the President of the Federal Republic which more smoothly but equally controversially drew a line in the world, not between north and south or between east and west, but, in effect, between terrorists and all those things which make life worth living.

I looked round, while this was being said, at the national flags. I soon lost count of the number which represented states which had come into existence, or had been powerfully assisted, by acts of terrorism or armed revolt. Is this one of the effects of conventional, rule-contained competition: that every moment is a starting-point, with all previous history forgotten? Were there no irregulars of a score of honoured revolutions, no Narodniki, Mau Mau, Stern Gang and a thousand others, before Black September? I knew I could only mourn the 17 dead if I remembered the history which had made them victims: a continuing history, without rules, which by the end of the week had greatly added to their number and which as so often before had included women and children killed in their villages by attack from the air. We have even, in our time, had live coverage of that kind of killing, so we have no real excuse for forgetting it.

---

*Avery Brundage. US amateur sportsman and President of the International Olympic Committee from 1952-72.

One wrong doesn't excuse another wrong. I believe that is true and that it needs to be generally applied. What was shocking at Munich was that an arranged version of what the world is like was invaded by an element of what several parts of the world are actually like. It happened, with a certain inevitability, because the act of arranged presentation had created a point of political pressure. There was then a battle of political wills, and 17 men were its immediate victims.

A spectator sport? The jibe is too terrible, but the question it raises is persistent. A friend said recently that the viewer turns his switches and chooses his nightly war. But more and more I meet people who have virtually stopped watching the News, with its continuing reports of killing and destruction. Often they say that the world never used to be like this: a sad reflection that is very different from the opportunist commentaries and political statements which make apparently the same point. The true change, as exceptionally at Munich, is increased visibility, and none of us really knows how to respond. If the spectator of terrorism or bombing is culpable, so, in this kind of world, is the deliberate non-spectator, the man who will not look. Or if we try to be more than spectators, to become participants, we may some of us be lucky in the available political processes, but many millions of people are not, and some of them, in extremity, become what the rest of us call terrorists. And when that has been said, it is still necessary to remember that the terror is real: is not a rhetoric or only a strategy, but is killing.

Who has not felt a wish to see the world as the Olympic Games show it? Blanket television coverage, most of it enjoyable, some of it very exciting. The extraordinary physical performances, past all the petty chauvinism and rituals. But then the blanket coverage is ripped aside.

The Listener, 14 September 1972

Impressions of U.S. Television

California's television programmes begin at six in the morning. At breakfast time you can watch the first movie. Picking your way through the day, you can watch six more movies before one o'clock the next morning, when the late movie comes on. Not so much television, in contemporary California, as telemovie.

But there we were, south of San Francisco, in one of the two or three richest regions in the world, and in the place where the future is supposed to be happening. Just down the road, De Forest had invented the radio valve and the phonofilm. Just up the road, they had invented the transistor. Just across the road, a young engineer had designed a domestic receiver for television from satellites. In this heartland of technology, we were watching old films on a small flickering box. The predominance of social over technical forces could not anywhere be more clearly shown.

We received six channels easily, though none well. It seems to be true that the simple quality of the television picture is in general inferior in the United States. But this seemed a minor point. San Francisco is a beautiful city, probably the most genuinely and actively cosmopolitan in the world. In its Bay Area there are two world-ranking universities and half a dozen others. About half the age group gets higher education. Yet with the broadcasting institutions so terribly and hopelessly inadequate and wrong, you might think, if you depended on television and radio, that you were in a very small town: a small town with knobs on. Only the Berkeley independent FM radio station, and the struggling San Francisco Public Television station, KQED, suggest anything of the extraordinary cultural and intellectual resources of these five million people.

It is an instructive experience for our own "modernisers". Advertising has crippled networks and local stations to an extent that is really astonishing, even when the fact is generally known in advance. You pick up the detail very quickly. A film has barely started before it is interrupted for commercials. They keep coming at a rate of between six and nine minutes an hour. The habit of interruption has become so strong that most stations also include, within the film you are watching, two or three trailers for films they are showing later. This produces, on occasion, some surrealist effects. Since there is usually no conventional sign for a break to commercial or trailer, a sequence can run from the dinosaur loose in Los Angeles to the deep-voiced woman worrying about keeping her husband with her coffee to the Indians coming over the skyline and a girl in a restaurant in Paris suddenly running from her table to cry. Or you can get more conventionally significant sequences. The news bulletins are also regularly interrupted for commercials. One night there were harrowing pictures of crippled men coming out of the tiger cages in Vietnam and the next pictures in the sequence were of children running in a New England garden to a song about a cereal.

But this is only the surface. The deepest failing is in the very structure of the institutions. If you read back to the Twenties, you can see how broadcasting was seen almost exclusively as transmission. The material to be transmitted was supposed to exist already: state occasions, sporting events, concerts and theatres. In Britain, almost by accident, it seems, we got a transmitting authority which was guaranteed funds for independent production. In the United States this has only occasionally happened, and the structural consequences are now being deeply felt. You have to make an effort to remind yourself that you are in a country which in film, in popular music, in investigative reporting has for two generations led the world. You have to struggle to remember that if the Bay Area were an independent republic, its intellectual and literary achievements, in this century, would be very clearly seen as remarkable. But in and through the broadcasting institutions, as in some other social ways, you do not feel you are in a rich country, materially or culturally. Indeed, you feel you are in a deprived area.

No, the intellectuals told me (as they do everywhere but in Britain), we don't watch television. Yet they did. They were emotionally involved in a *ciné-vérité* series, *An American Family,* in which a Californian family was followed about by the cameras. In the middle of the filming, for other reasons, the wife filed for divorce: it was a new close way of watching and talking about the neighbours. The most admired programme, which would even empty parties, is called *Masterpiece Theatre* and turned out to be a selection of BBC-2 classic serials. This is on the Public Television network. When I left, they were just starting *The Roads to Freedom,* which had, however, been refused Public Television funding because, as it had delicately been put, it was "too adult". But in San Francisco, with the officially forbidden street signs blazing "Topless" and "Bottomless", the series had been separately bought and you could get paperbacks of Sartre's novels as a gift with a membership subscription. To keep going, this public station, KQED, has to run auctions and membership drives, with hundreds of young volunteers, and even then it can only just survive as a transmitting station. The fatal flaw, in the whole structure, is the lack of money for production. The few things KQED produces are admirable. There is *Newsroom,* a relaxed hour of news and discussion. There is *World Press,* a very simple idea, in which four people from neighbouring university departments come in and say what has been in the papers of various foreign countries that week.

There are good programmes for teachers and for the ethnic minorities—Chinese, Blacks, Chicanos. But you go into rich, glittering San Francisco and you find KQED in a small building under the freeway, and the *Newsroom* reporters are at their desks and telephones in a single room, chasing their stories. Most of the material KQED transmits comes in on the Public Television network: *Sesame Street* and *The Electric Company*; the public affairs programmes *Firing Line, Bill Moyers' Journal, Washington Week in Review*. When I was in the KQED office, they had just had a memorandum that all three of these public affairs programmes were not being funded for the next year: there was a new majority on the Commission which makes allocations. Even *Newsroom* and *World Press* were in danger. The relaxed presenters became momentarily almost desperate as they appealed to viewers to write in and say if they found the programmes useful.

Useful! You have to live in a centre of advanced communications technology and try in any other way to find out what is happening in the world to have any notion of how useful and indispensable they are. The *New York Times* arrives late, and otherwise there is the one independent radio station and this one struggling Public Television channel, plus only a very few outlets in the majority channels. The national networked News, in its three versions, is not bad, but it cannot handle the amount and level of information that living in the United States now involves and requires. It is interesting that the networks have been in continuous trouble with the Nixon administration. If their reporting could be emasculated, and the discussion programmes phased out of Public Television, it would be a society with great power but very little real information, among the great majority of its citizens. I remember struggling to get any real facts about the French elections, the Chilean election, even the dollar crisis. Meanwhile I knew with unforgettable clarity every damned ploy there is in selling coffee or cereals or cars.

I also, to be fair, knew just about every move of the San Francisco Board of Supervisors and the extraordinary Mayor Alioto. It made me think again about regional and local news, and what is called community television. Of course, as a visitor I was less involved. But any night, on the majority channels, I could see three times as much local news as national and international news. These local news programmes are a laugh as much as anything. Four men are there in the studio: two for news, one for sport, one for weather.

It has become a convention that the weatherman is the butt. So, for example, the leading news announcer, talking very fast towards the end of the programme, after all the local news, will say: "Coming up next, Pete with the weather—his tan, I can tell you, makes a pretty clash with his tie. Then elections in France and Chile, the dollar still under attack abroad, all that and more as *News Scene* moves along." This "moves along" formula is worth a note, because it is just what doesn't happen: it's like the end of *Waiting for Godot*. *News Scene* and its like only "move along" when they are about to take a commercial break. But back, eventually, to the weatherman. He has maps and signs, but usually before he can open his mouth the business about the tie or the tan starts up, and in the little time remaining he goes so fast across the continent you can't see him for tornadoes. As it happened, this winter it was very odd weather in California, much more rain than usual, so that the closing weather caption was too often "GO DO IT (but take an umbrella)." One night one of the Petes cut loose and talked intelligently and informatively about the unusual weather. There were looks of amused amazement along the three faces behind their desk.

It wears you down. It's like the predominant style in commercials, which trill and suggest and look winsome or irritable in ways we all know, but which often have an extra line, after what one expects to be the climax, such as "That's quite right, I'll try some," or "Good idea!" I can only repeat my astonishment at the distance between all this and the people one meets. California is supposed to be fast: I found it, on the surface, unusually relaxed, even sleepy. I doubt if it's the future, but if it is, there among the jets and the military electronics there is an extraordinary, almost tactile privatisation. Under the constant external assault, so much quiet intelligence, so much sensitive gentleness; also, by the evidence of results, so much isolated despair. Hardly any of this finds a public voice. Nor, except occasionally, does the poverty, for there in wealthy California—on its own, the ninth-richest state in the world—you have only to travel on public transport to see the real poverty, not only of so many Blacks and Chicanos and some Chinese, but of poor whites, living hard. A larger than usual middle class, affluent but crowded, can seem to blot this out, until you push around, along unusual channels. These are not, needless to say, the channels of television.

I saw some good old movies on Californian TV. But as I saw what was happening in the spaces between the movies—the machine-turned police serials, the exploitative parlour games, the occasional limited success like *All in the Family* and the more responsive open-line shows, and of course some good sport—I recognised the consequences of a broadcasting system which does not finance, in guaranteed and long-term ways, any primary independent production. What was blatantly missing was original drama (though the talent is there in the little theatres, and the early days of American television drama were remarkable) and the whole body of features, documentaries, special reports, which is a central strength of British television. I came back to Britain feeling in most other ways very detached from our current local institutions and attitudes and certainly with no tendency to underrate the current decline in our own broadcasting, much of it, increasingly, following the wrong American models. But then this is the moment to recall what an intelligent Californian said as we were leaving (in these days of the "Orange County Mafia" it seems particularly appropriate): "Don't let them californicate the world."

The Listener, 7 June 1973

Part II

The "Listener" Columns:
Television Forms and Conventions

As We See Others

It didn't seem a good week to begin television reviewing. The late July programmes looked like the summary of television which I over-hear from my older Cambridge acquaintances who haven't got sets: hours of sport, Westerns, old films, repeats. I watched a fair amount, but I didn't see any new programme that deserved extensive review. *The Vanished City* (BBC-1) had looked interesting: London before the Industrial Revolution, on engravings and on film, with accom-panying 18th-century music and verse. Some of this was pleasant, but very little illuminating. The fashion for mood programmes, suck-ing in words, music and images to what is called at the conference the flow, has had its successes, but the technique cannot reasonably include the disguised thesis: here, a familiar nostalgia for the 18th century and an implication of the ugliness of modernity. It wasn't only that in the stylish filming this visual contrast wasn't made out; there was also the verse, telling some of the truth the visual images didn't catch, though read in an "impressive" poetry-reading monotone; and the delightful music, which washed over the riverside works and the fine glass towers as persuasively, in mood, as over the Georgian squares and terraces. Mood, indeed, manages all, as the commercials keep reminding us; the connections of imagination and argument require a different discipline.

That programme was late, as most such programmes are. The pull of the peak-hours is still mechanical, even in an off-peak period. Of course the categories—sport, Westerns, etc—conceal as much as they show. There is some pleasure in watching *The Virginian* to see what nice country and strong young men can do for the American way of life. What continually interests me in this series is the involun-tary revelation of the character of its reverent father-figure, Judge Garth, and the economic system he represents. So much is done for him, so many good men put at risk, that in one or two episodes I have suspected satire; the series is in any case unusual in that it shows, in some detail, what all the fighting in the West was about. But the conversion of sweat and courage into somebody else's property is too regular, too willed, too much assented to, to be anything in the end but a hymn—a contemporary hymn, for the new-time religion.

The other category, sport, is of course one of the very best things about television; I would keep my set for it alone. The only three sports I've been involved in—athletics, football, tennis—weren't much there this week. The Leicester athletics meeting was spoiled by the weather, and the commentators' appetite for qualifying times, against the conditions, made things more miserable. For a while one just snarls, "Get out of that box and try to run it yourself," and then, wisely, as with most sport on television, switches off the sound. Actually the best thing to do was to switch to ITV* and see the marvellous half-mile in the Women's Championships: the cameras got that superb second-lap kick exactly. But it was mainly show-jumping and cricket, and I didn't have time for the cricket.

Listening for a while to the show-jumping commentary, I found myself reflecting on *Panorama*. There's always a problem about show-jumping, which I have watched, though at smaller shows, for most of my life. It's presented, on BBC, with an ideology on its tail: not just the implication that the horses are one of the better types of Englishmen, but more than the usual chauvinism in commentary—"and now, for Britain . . ."—and of course the social atmosphere of monarchism, army, and the sponsoring capitalist corporations. It's a pity the horses have to carry all that; most urban democrats have taken against anything to do with horses because of the overtones—even hunting, to my surprise, is now one of the radical Home Office issues. But the jumping is good, and the interest, this week, apart from that, was to watch the social atmosphere and the results collide: a German and an American won the night I watched. I still remember my surprise, having never seen rowing till I came to Cambridge, and having picked up the impression that superiority in it had profound connections with the so-called public schools, when I watched international competition and saw the East Germans or the

*Sponsored by a Conservative government, commercial television broadcasting in Britain was started in 1955. The Independent Broadcasting Authority (IBA) does not make programmes but licenses and regulates commercial radio and television. Commercial television was given the somewhat misleading name of Independent Television (ITV).

Russian Navy. Television ought, in widening our real area of vision, to be correcting these prejudices all the time, and of course on matters more important than these passing competitions. This was what took my mind back to *Panorama*, and to Robin Day* in Prague.

BBC current affairs programmes are going through a very bad patch, even by their own internal and orthodox standards. It was absurdly unprofessional, on *24 Hours,* to have four people and a chairman trying to discuss the Public Schools report. No important and sustained argument can then possibly take place, and it's no use ringing the changes on who can say nicely: "I'm afraid we haven't got time." The report, as it happened, was barely worth discussing, but it's at this repeated, ritual moment of cut-off that one remembers the longueurs of cricket commentary, the endless amplifications of uncomplicated detail, and inspects the Corporation with a cold, alien eye.

I've been talking to Czechs these last weeks; I have political friends there; in any case the crisis is of major importance in the development of socialism. It isn't merely that I dissent from Day; that when he tells us that the Czechs are struggling for things we've already got, I tell him to keep his "we" to himself. It's the decline— or perhaps it isn't a decline, perhaps it's simply more evident now— in the standards of reporting that is suggested. There was also a *24 Hours* report from Nigeria. The starving women and children showed all that was necessary, as experience: the ugliness and brutality of famine. The few people helping them, able to get to help them, were too busy to take part in a play; the cameras were irrelevant to them, as to the distorted bodies, unless they brought, indirectly, food. The reporter has done all he can at this point, unless he or a colleague follows the trail back: to the politicians, including the London politicians; there, and there only, can the pressing questions be put. But the pressing question has become a mannerism: pushed, reporter-style, wherever and however. Didn't it depress the nurse from London that there was so little she could do? When the only relevant response was to thank her for what she was doing and get back to bang on some office doors.

---

*Robin Day. Television and radio journalist. One of the first newscasters of Independent Television News, he later moved to the BBC. Day gained a reputation for his forceful interviews of national politicians, and was knighted in 1981.

This is the point about mannerism: the detachment from consciousness. "Do you think that communism is compatible with democracy?"—the unvarying, mechanical question. At about the third reply—"yes, socialism must become more democratic"—even a slow reporter might reach from his fixed consciousness to ask why "socialism" every time and not "communism", a distinction any socialist would understand. That would be one way into the crisis as the Czechs see it. The tiny political world, with its rigid assumptions, which English commentators now represent is an abuse of television. One realises how much it is so watching the invaluable *Europa* (BBC-2), which in its very contrast of national approaches and assumptions inhabits a modern as opposed to a fake-contemporary world.

1 August 1968

Private Worlds

I had seen no television for a month, and the first critical response I have to report was a headache. It takes a few days to get back to living in rooms and watching that small lighted box. I had watched films on holiday, but in an open-air cinema where it was easy to lean back in the cloudier sequences and look at the night sky: an orbiting satellite, moving through and disturbing the shape of the Plough, was at least in another dimension from *The Four Sons of Katy Elder* in French. That too, however, had its interest. So much of the meaning of the Western is its speech convention, not simply the laconic drawl, but what it is used for: a relaxed but constant aggression; a willed inability to communicate, which establishes that 20th-century hero, locked in a damaging privacy, an unsharable destiny, which is then projected as an external, admired identity. To hear this done in French, with a certain inevitable formality, lucidity, politeness, was to realise very sharply the problems of translation, not only between languages but between forms.

It is still, I suppose, not quite the big period. The BBC keeps advertising forthcoming attractions, in a kind of desperate bombast. Perhaps somebody thought a campaign would be necessary, against the new commercial companies, but from what I've seen of those it's just a change of label, and all this Autumn Promise belongs with the advertisers: men raising or slurring or sliming their voices because they have nothing intrinsically convincing to say. We must see how it all turns out, but the constant implication that we were living just before the dawn of the Big Entertainment was not only irritating but stupid. There was enough on television this week for a festival. I watched, in a few nights, *Saint Joan, The Playboy of the Western World, The Trial,* and episodes of *Nana* and *North and South*: all interesting, and all raising critical problems of the translation between forms.

The Playboy of the Western World and *The Trial* were made for the cinema, but television would be useful if only to correct some of the idiocies of film distribution. I had not previously been able to see either, and *The Playboy* (BBC-2) had never even got a general release. I have admired Synge's play for so long that I was surprised to find the film confirming an objection to it which has been growing in my mind in recent years. What is not usually said about Synge's elaborate language is that it covers, and is seen as covering, an unmistakable poverty and despair. Siobhan McKenna, lathering the accent of Pegeen beyond the straight Irishness of the she-been, took the romantic fantasy to the point where the underlying theme inevitably appeared: not a play about a community, as it is still conventionally described, but about a disintegration, a hopelessness which the separated individual dreams and romances his way out of. That lovely hill and beach were then backcloth; the heavily populated sports on the strand an interlude for entertainment—what is called, mechanically, visual excitement. It had depended, that surface convention, on a stage; on not seeing, even briefly, the real Ireland, but rather isolating a room, in which people come and go, rehearsing their fixed attitudes: the playwright in narrow control, making a figure, a bitter disintegrated figure, of the Irish people he overheard.

It was not only the succession of nights that related the film of Synge's play to the television production of Shaw's *Saint Joan* (BBC-1). I have seen Siobhan McKenna play Joan, and now it was Janet Suzman. Too much weight is put on performance, in orthodox critical reaction. It is easier to talk about than the shape of the play, the structure of feeling, which is being actually performed. In fact, the silence beyond the television screen was very interesting here. The knockabout of the early scenes—"Polly! You impudent baggage" or "Coom, Bluebeard! Thou canst not fool me. Where be Dauphin?"—is so clearly written for the titter in the stalls, that amused, chocolate-chewing writhe of the shoulders at the sweet vulgar accents and impudences of the newly arrived outsider, that to hear nothing of this, to watch an actress trying to make drama of it, within an action, was very revealing: not of the actress but of Shaw.

Joan of Arc, in these first scenes, is the Chocolate Soldier, with a change of sex Shaw insists we must not insist upon. But what she has then to live through is defeat and pain; the superb false rhetoric of the trial; the sense of history happening to a West End character part. Once again, as in Synge, the crucial action is elsewhere; the play is reaction to it, inside a succession of rooms. Wisely, the director didn't include the battle scenes, the burning, which are the significant history; not even the real pain of the trial, which was so unforget-tably realised in the finest work made from this history, Dreyer's great film *Jeanne d'Arc*. He stayed, for better or worse, with Shaw; right through to the epilogue, which isn't always performed. There were some bad cuts in the text, but we got through to the climax: Shaw's clearest example of the structure of feeling which relates him to *The Four Sons of Katy Elder* and to Synge—the isolated self, in one or other kind of radiance, against the uncomprehending world; the point being, always, that the audience, watching this, are not the uncomprehending world but, in rows and in millions, that isolated misunderstood self. The soldier, asking what they all amount to, those great ones of the world, is interrupted, by the dramatist, at just the point when he might tell us—when he might become, that is to say, uncomfortable. When the action ended, in *The Playboy*, there was a blur, a pause, and then the lonely figure said: "I've lost him surely." When the action ended, in *Saint Joan*, there was the same blur, the same pause, and then: "How long, O Lord, how long?" For as long, actually, as we are more interested in an isolated attitude than in history; or, to put it another way, for as long as the end of the play is the receiving of saints, the sunset, the lonely look to the distance; the 20th century's social and dramatic alternative to an action in common.

Surely the real trial—Kafka's novel *The Trial*, directed for cinema by Orson Welles—should have cleared that blur. It is so crys-talline in the novel; so uncompromising in the truth about isolation. The uncomprehending world is seen as a system: the mad, accusing bureaucracy and police depend, for their hold, on the private guilt which is not talked about, which is forgotten in embraces, which destroys because it is isolated, against a destructive order. Orson

Welles took the easier half of Kafka: the corridors, the emptiness, the spaces in which men are reduced to objects. And the heart goes with that; it has been so often seen and feared. But there was then an elementary error of convention. The story of the trial is told, in the novel, from within the consciousness of the accused. This is perfectly possible in film, as in Bergman's *Wild Strawberries,* but Welles went the other way: showing it happening to him from outside, and so losing his consciousness. It was then not the fault of the actor that this dry, hard alienation came to resemble, in some scenes, a nasty misunderstanding in the daily life of a nice American boy in a rooming-house.

These are not primarily problems of relations between media, but of choices within media: choices governed by an orthodox structure of feeling. It is interesting how much flows back, given time, from an older structure, as in the adaptation of Elizabeth Gaskell's *North and South,* now being repeated on BBC-1. I find that novel as alien as Shaw, but what was interesting about the direction and playing of the adaptation was the connection, the imaginative connection, with a world in which relationships were articulate and settlements were arrived at. It is as if some part of the BBC, some part of England, turns with particular readiness to the years before 1900: with nostalgia, of course, as we shall see in *The Forsyte Saga;* but also with interest, with a connection to that history of the industrial revolution, the class war, the struggle for democracy, which is so clearly unfinished but which can be looked at, carefully and seriously, if there is a bonnet or two about. There was certainly care and feeling in this production by Hugh David, this adaptation by David Turner; and there was some fine acting by Wendy Williams, Richard Leech, Edwin Richfield, Sonia Dresdel.

Nana (BBC-1) is a different matter. The brilliant adaptation, some months ago, of Balzac's *Père Goriot* should have been followed, not by this Balzac-and-water, but by *Lost Illusions,* in which the young men who stand about intriguing in Zola, the old men who buy flesh, are not figures in a generalised spectacle but social agents, revealing their history not in a formula but in detail. As I watched these competent players I saw behind the screen Zola's head in that group portrait of the young Impressionists in the Jeu de Paume entrance: a literary naturalist among painter impressionists, and if he could have written what Renoir painted, as flesh, there would not have been this difficulty—this sense of an old party in which there are intermittent party-turns of cynicism and shock. The real history had been wholly written by Balzac, as these adaptations remind us, and we have then of course to say that we got both on the same service, on that box it seemed difficult to come back to.

12 September 1968

Shoot the Prime Minister

It is easy to make a simple case for the pleasures of television. The three programmes I most enjoyed last week were the Schubert recital which replaced *Workshop* (BBC-2), Heinz Sielmann's film of caribou, bear and beaver in the Canadian late autumn, *Wild New World* (BBC-1), and the repeat of *Black Sound, Deep Song*, the film on Lorca and Andalusia (BBC-2). Here in each case was fine professional work, on interests I already have and with resources not otherwise available to me. But of course I notice, not only that two of these were on BBC-2, which is increasingly operating as a kind of Third Programme,* but also that they all belong to an already structured world, of observation, imagination and performance, in which television functions as a superbly efficient and convenient transmitter. I think this case needs to be made from time to time: some of the least reviewed programmes are among the most valuable work we get. But I think also that this kind of selective viewing, within a known structure, falls short of the critical response which television demands: that scrutiny, of what is now characteristic in the use of the medium, which a correspondent describes as "an absolutely worthwhile commitment to the ephemeral". It is just because Schubert, Lorca and the natural history film inhabit their own still relatively secure cultural areas that the viewer turned critic must look also at what is, as yet, uncertain and undefined.

One urgent area for definition is that of realism, as it emerges in television drama, documentary and commentary. The problem was

---

*BBC-2 is the more serious of the two BBC television channels. Williams himself gave occasional radio talks for the Third Programme (the other BBC radio stations were the Home Service and the Light Programme). The Third Programme of serious talks and classical music, which later became BBC-3 Radio, never attracted more than one to two percent of radio listeners.

posed most sharply by the coincidence of two plays on political assassination, on successive evenings: *Thirty-Minute Theatre's The Chequers Manoeuvre* and the adaptation (inappropriately in *The Jazz Age* series) of Liam O'Flaherty's *The Assassin*. The *Chequers Manoeuvre* was a fraud, though perhaps intended as an irony and in any case defended by a particular convention. We saw a stylised group planning to shoot the Prime Minister on his way to Chequers, and at the last moment we had it identified as a security exercise. The irony, and no doubt the intended pleasure, was in the fact of a game—the assassination game. It was corrupt in small ways: the dramatic use of gunsights, framing a face, when nothing of the kind was intended. But its central corruption was in its tone: not only the stylised game on a screen where we have seen so many real assassinations, but the link with reality, even within the game, which showed so notably when we saw, briefly, the Prime Minister. This, at the familiar door, was a stereotype of a generation before the war: the rigid, formally dressed, consciously upper-class figure, who has in fact been replaced by a series of demotic characters, consciously acting an appearance—not caught by the camera but coming out to it, as part of a style of government. It was a real shock, to be contained only by dividing one's experience and calling one part aesthetic or play, when an all-too-recognisable contemporary prime minister appeared on the screen shortly afterwards. It often happens, in film and television, that a spurious contemporary link is forged, to give title to the world of cars and guns and clothes that so obviously holds the producer's feelings. The convention says that it is all a game anyway; but it is a game with fantasies of violence which are at once indulged and, at the crucial point, denied. Some writers and producers seem to think that by making the form a fantasy they can at once release and protect their own real fantasies.

It wasn't so much that I admired the adaptation of O'Flaherty: it was emotionally muddled, with that piling-up of motives which happened in routine art after some of the intellectual revolutions of this century—bits of social, psycho-analytic and existential concepts, thrown after an action like cries in the wind. Yet it had a certain power, in that it faced a place and a people: not the dissociated game, but at least that identifiable world in which men move to violence, and also to despair and remorse. There was another contrast on Thursday, when *The Avengers* (ITV) was followed by *Softly, Softly* (BBC-1). *The Avengers* is all game, though lately it has got to look more and more like a petrol commercial, with sexual potency and assault played, through cold minds, in images of cars and guillotines. It is probably worth noticing that the British upper-class uniform of bowler hat and umbrella contains, in this successful fantasy, a steel helmet and a swordstick. There is obviously a lot of this about, in feeling if not in machinery, to judge by some of the new tones in English politics. But the thing to watch was the contrast in style with the police—who says the real police?—in *Softly, Softly*. Here is the wholly demotic style, and there are no swordsticks to alert one to the dramatic game. Alan Plater's episode, *See the Rabbit*, was one of the most successful: looking at what happens to a constable who starts a private punch-up. It would not work, in the way it now does, without the awareness of these men as friends. Dramatically this is done by a concentration of ordinariness, in accents, beer,the irritation and fatigue of routine. Ordinariness is now so finely acted that acting itself comes in question. The almost irresistible suggestion, of these ordinary members of the crime squad, is that their way of looking at the world is the only available honest way. It is extremely interesting that kinds of dialogue and acted behaviour, historically connected with a naturalism that insists on exploring contemporary reality, should have been mainly used, in television, as an approach to the world which has doctors and police as intermediaries. Some part of this is the problem of the middle-class writer, whose approach is that of an observer, a specialised worker. The capacity to write of ordinary life from a position wholly inside its own normal world is still obviously rare. I find I am glad to see our own streets and houses, to hear some of our own voices, but of course I watch the feeling that is mediated through this, and on the whole it is the helplessness, the foolishness, of ordinary people; the irresolvable muddle of our life as a society; and within this a resigned, disillusioned, stale but still rigid acceptance of the routines of duty: what has to be, if you are a reasonable and decent man.

Documentary and commentary seem a different matter. All I have to say, there, is that nobody would believe there are 56 million people in Britain: we see and hear so few of them. I switched from *Panorama* to a fine *World in Action* (ITV) programme on workers' control in the steel industry, in which a bricklayer's mate showed, against the odds, more capacity for impromptu political argument than any of the regular professionals. *Panorama* improved, later, with a useful documentary on West Cumberland, but the prestige, still, seems to be in getting onto the screen men who we know, because we have heard them so often, will say nothing but say it purposively and with an official presence. I tried to watch the Labour Party conference, but in the parts I saw it was "From Blackpool—the Harold Wilson Show, with guest stars George Brown and Barbara Castle". Following the example of David Frost, there was some audience participation. It may not have felt like that in the hall, but was that where the real operation took place anyway? Certainly no writer of realism could have produced so artificial a script, and if he'd been tempted to turn it, following the other convention, into a game, he'd have found the manipulation slow, every style-punch signalled, and every decision undecided. That it had notionally to do with how the rest of us are living might have seemed, though, in the end, an effective irony.

10 October 1968

The Miner and the City

Two days separated *Death of a Miner* and *Towards Tomorrow: Super City?* (both BBC-1). The titles indicated a past and a future, but the real bearings of both were the present. The strength of *Death of a Miner* was the talk of Jack and Emma Elliot, and of their family. It isn't often, on television, that we get working-class men and women talking as subjects, about the shapes of their lives, rather than as objects in a temporary dispute or a street interview. But it is then significant that we heard them when Jack Elliot had died, and when the pit in which he had worked was closing. This, I suppose, is what guided it to Sunday, where for an early-evening interval the religious programmes come and a detached reverence can be assumed. Yet there was nothing detached in what the Elliots had to say: this was the human reality of a continuing social experience which may be acceptable only on Sundays and about the past, but which is in fact weekday and contemporary: what is now happening to many hundreds of thousands of men. The worst letter anyone ever wrote to me was when I had published *Border Country* and, as an attempted compliment, Harry Price the signalman—strong, respected, dead—was held up as an example to the railwaymen who now made the correspondent late for the office. It is a familiar orthodox pattern: dead workers, like dead radicals, can be seen as human beings; alive they are only instrumental and inconvenient. Philip Donnellan, who made *Death of a Miner,* did a very fine job, but it was others who put the frame round it, and the critic's job is to break it.

What the Elliots had to say about the quality of living close together in a crowded mining village would have been worth hearing in *Super-City?* I was deeply interested in this programme, but it attempted too little. Some of the film belonged in the detached atmosphere of *Tomorrow's World,* where devices and techniques can be looked at in themselves. The mouse-city experiment in Washington could, I suppose, have been put into almost any programme, and the two-mile-high city inspired by the termites might go nicely with it in a programme about animal analogies in current social thinking: *The Herd, the Swinish Multitude and After.* But these things were mixed up with some interesting research on the human scale: the size of the self in small rooms and large; and with some intelligent talk by Lewis Mumford about the crisis of the modern conurbation. There is in fact a lot of current English research on the city which the producer hadn't got on to, and it is clear, looking back, that this should have been one of a series of programmes, with some serious attempt to face social planning as more than an architectural and behavioural technique. What worries me most is the alternation, in social television, between a fine old past and a gimmicky future. A failure of respect for people is at the root of both attitudes, which is why I wanted to hear Jack Elliot or someone like him, who has struggled for a future against the brutal ugliness of the past, coming in with first right to speak about the models into which it is now proposed we should be directed.

The right to speak on television has now been nationally discussed: or what we call a national discussion, when a Minister makes a speech and other people talk about the Minister. The only thing to do, as the nine-day Talking-Point fades, is to go on collecting the ideas and the evidence. ITV deserves credit for *Round House*—or at any rate Ian Mackenzie and Helen Standage deserve credit; we must see how long the experiment lasts. It's not the ideal shape for a free-discussion programme, especially with the lecterns, but it was interesting to hear a few people talking on their own account and being interrupted. *World in Action,* again ITV, had a good programme in which the LSE students spoke in their own terms, in the course of their occupation, as against the usual filtering through an interviewer. It still seems very difficult to get this point across, at the level of policy. Many relationships are possible, in the presentation of talk, but what is most stultifying is the all-purpose presenter, through whom all men and all issues flow, and who in the end is a substitute for men and issues. There are too many of these presenters to list, in current affairs and sports programmes, but it would also be unkind to list them as individuals; it is the *function* that needs to be criticised. I come back to the point that we see too few faces, hear too few voices, and that these faces and voices are offered as television dealing with life. It is then interesting to see which bits of life escape them. One of the most consistently serious and interesting magazine programmes is *Farming* (BBC-1).

It escapes the treatment which flattens so many other comparable interests because, I suppose, it is regarded as specialised (though it is put on at a quite general time: Sunday for the Country and other reverent detachments) and in any case metropolitan interviewers would be frightened of it. Last week's programme about farming steep land was a model of interest and intelligence, with the regular interviewers, farmers themselves, talking to other farmers and letting the camera see the ground. Where professionals and presentation are really needed, this is surely the right way to do it. The point would then be that, serious and pleasant as these men are, we would not want to see them, over the next seven days, looking over their cues at Vietnam, the universities, an air-crash, a strike, Rhodesia, car-sales, a prison escape, cheese imports, a philosopher, Czechoslovakia, suicides.

Gentlemen, we note finally, can talk straight to camera: not always, we also note, with as much appeal though as little technique as Sir John Rothenstein, in *Collection and Recollection* (BBC-2). It is probably still not believed in offices, but a man talking and showing us his work is among the best television there is.

7 November 1968

A Moral Rejection

In any work, the structure of feeling is decisive. The greatness of Tolstoy's *Resurrection* is that one of the profound transitional moments, in modern feeling and relationship, is brought alive in a meeting between two people: a meeting that extends to an action. In immediate terms, it is a meeting between a prince and the working-class girl he has seduced. His offer of money, when she was a ward and had taken his desire as love, is the first step in a reduction of her life to money relationships: as the prostitute who is accused of killing and stealing from a client. That social process is very sharply seen, but it is only the condition for a much harder insight: something Tolstoy could not resolve but incomparably dramatises.

In the Christian tradition, and in that liberal ethic which derives from it, a great wrong must provoke an offer of atonement: of help and restitution, to the object of that wrong; of confession, self-humiliation, self-sacrifice, by its guilty agent. That seems to have been Tolstoy's conscious purpose; it is what provokes the easy comment on his moralising. But what Tolstoy does is to bring that movement, an offered atonement, into collision with the very different morality of the insulted and injured: a morality that comes through, in all older terms, as indifference, hardness, contempt.

What Maslova sees, as Dmitri tries to make his atonement, is yet another demand on her. She is to be an object in his spiritual as once in his physical life. Perhaps we shall go on looking at his crisis of conscience: that drama of the self which preoccupies orthodox thinking and art. But what is really there to be looked at is that harder knowledge of actual relationships which is not, on the surface, moral at all: Maslova, drunk, calculating, indifferent; her only moral action is to spit in his face.

It is a moment which in and through its convincing personal immediacy is in its way historical: that refusal to be an object, of any kind of exploitation, which is not dignified, not accessible, but in its own hard confidence makes its own different world. It is only a girl in prison, spitting in the face of her guilty benefactor, but it is the moment in which the morality of revolution is opposed to the morality of conscience and charity.

The whole scene was brilliantly played by Bridget Turner and Alan Dobie in the serial adaptation by Alexander Baron, directed by David Giles, on BBC-2. While it lasted it made everything we normally see on the screen pale, tentative, confused. Among other things it made the conventional argument about a verbal or visual medium irrelevant. The words commanded the scene, but at the same time the physical girl made the point about strength in helplessness, vitality in degradation, feeling in indifference. The drawn, anxious formality of the man and his offer was the exact physical realisation of the written movement. Indeed I wondered, watching it, if some moment had been reached, in ourselves, when that substance, at last, could be made physically actual. Only at a distance perhaps. Only in a classic serial. The difficulties, when we come closer, seem very formidable. But it is again a question of the structure of feeling. David Mercer, in *On the Eve of Publication* (BBC-1), seemed concerned, consciously, with a comparable dramatisation of history and conscience. His hero, a dying writer, raged at his impotence, but this was a crisis of isolation and breakdown in which both persons and history were flickering obsessional objects. The centre of interest was in the account, not the action: the liberal reckoning with the self, now bitter and disgusted, with reality unattainable except as images of a private process. The writer was supposed to have been a Marxist: that word which is thrown about now in quite stultifying ways. But neither writer, neither hero nor dramatist, was thinking or feeling in these terms. A structure of feeling of the past 15 years in Britain came through with unusual clarity: that hostile demand for response in women which lies in the same bed as an indifferent using and leaving of persons and bodies; that rough, cursing monologue, overriding precision as it overrides what others might say; that howl for attention to the isolated body's hairs and juices which converts the cries of history—the banners, the barricades, the revolutionary crowd, the name of Che— to its own angry echoes.

I have watched this develop from *Look Back in Anger* to *On the Eve of Publication*: acquiring and refining its technical facilities; extending its power—for it is an authentic structure—to connect and to confuse. I think very much depends on our power to break it down, for it is the running orthodoxy behind the bland, glossy surface of a commercial culture which, connecting with nothing substantial, deceives nobody for long. This apparent dissent is, hopefully, the last kick of liberalism: a bitter, confused, phantasmagoric attempt to change the world in the mind rather than in social action and relation. The measure of its despair is that this is now an old man, looking to the young to redeem his process. I hope that they will have the nerve to spit in his face.

Or put it another way: Gulley Jimson rode again, not on Art but on History. That comic edge, which was almost complete in Joyce Cary's novel, was the only real vitality of the play. Yet commercial producers (and actors, obviously) love angry, incoherent old men: an image for everybody, an image that can be patronised, of muddle, displacement and restless success. An older image also popped up this week: the admired, manipulating, rich bitch mother: called Mrs Kent-Cumberland in the dramatisation of Evelyn Waugh's *Winner takes all* (BBC-2). It was something to hear Malcolm Muggeridge's narration in its proper medium: fizz, as they used to say in "the jazz age", with just a dash of bitters. For the point about Mrs Kent-Cumberland is that art exposes her as a way of admiring her: a rich, manipulating, heartless world, which we have no illusions about—oh dear no!—but which we look at sad and wise and amused and resigned. *Basta!*

5 December 1968

A New Way of Seeing

I remember one view of the Earth from 90,000 miles out: the north and west in ragged shadow; the bright Caribbean; the atlas shapes of the Americas; a high cone of storm cloud in the far South Atlantic. I glanced from its memory to the spinning globe of BBC-1 presentation: light, untextured, slightly oiled. It was necessary to remember that both were television. The old art-and-reality contrasts seemed particularly useless in a week like that. If the medium is the message, the massage, the messuage, or whatever the latest slogan may be, it is still surprisingly plural. What we see is what we are, but to be moved, abruptly, to a quite different viewpoint was a technical achievement with some of the qualities of major art: a brief transcendence, in the power of a new way of seeing.

The general character of the week underlined this emphasis. Past that light spinning globe, past the smooth light voice of the BBC-2 linkman, past the hazy beers and the belching detergent of ITA, there was a general rattling of cans. I got ten minutes into *Frost over Christmas* (BBC-1) before I remembered seeing it last year. Much the same thing happened, literally or substantially, all over the week. It's fair enough, I suppose. On Christmas Eve I put a manuscript away and cleared my post; I didn't want anyone else to be working either. Alan Plater had anticipated this feeling in an episode of *Softly, Softly*: a contrast of the lonely duty policeman and the rich Christmas hotel guests. But it's more than that. Writers are using these police and doctor series to touch on feelings which, in a less prejudiced system, could be directly explored. We should be past the stage, in television drama, where social implication, or social comment, are made to make do, in the gaps of another set of interests. It only seems some way on when, in a season of nostalgia and commonplaces, we are reminded of what the West End used to look like in 1951. At the *Play of the Month*—N.C. Hunter's *The Waters of the Moon* (BBC-1)—I have to confess I laughed from the heart: at what the English middle-class theatre made of Chekhov; that self-conscious icing of half-cock relationships, in an insular world in which a very comfortable hotel on Dartmoor could be looked down on while a hotel in Montreux, of all places, indicated the rich fulfilments beyond. It used to be called acting, even the magic of theatre; it needed that kind of self-deceiving assent.

There are laughs of so many kinds. Those induced don't usually last. To the comedians I like I find I go more than half-way. I find myself sitting with a rictus of amused incredulity and surprise, like a man at a bar watching one of the regulars' acts. It breaks to pleasure often enough: at Marty Feldman's almighty and merciful god wanting to be carried home from the bus-stop; at Ronnie Barker's official spokesman doing a regional reorganisation of Christmas; at Henry McGee as an arts interviewer to Benny Hill's Godard. Harry Worth this autumn has been reduced to too rigid a formula: situation comedy needs more than a list of standard situations—making a will, wanting to get married, visiting the dentist; and the muddle has lost most of its genuine surprise as the despairing reaction of those he encounters comes early and prearranged.

There is, of course, so much comedy that we can all feel the strain. The rictus begins to ache, as the old cogs engage. And then nothing is funnier than to go on sitting there, complaining we aren't amused. All I've noticed, recently, is how little *television* comedy there has been, as distinct from transmission of other kinds. I've seen bits of everything in the last seven days, from the old bottom-burning with a pantomime iron to elaborate parodies of almost every kind of current film and television show. It all comes across much as it would anywhere else: people doing a skilled job, keeping organised entertainment going.

Rowan and Martin's Laugh-In (BBC-2) has only one merit. The two principals, if in different ways, are among the least funny and least engaging performers I have ever seen; many of the local American jokes are incomprehensible; but the show has used cutting and close-up, and, above all, an extraordinary speed, to make new comic effects, as well as transforming the repeat spot and the slogan flash of advertising until their very emptiness is funny. Only Marty, again, has used a comparably inventive mobility: his golf-round from lorry and train and down a bathroom pipe was very much better than the usual comic outside broadcast romp; and the stylised footwork in the portrait of the football hero Danny (was it?) Gruntfuttock had the same quality. Print, of course, makes it look ridiculous in quite other ways.

On Friday, after the splashdown, a good idea was almost wasted in *Bird's Eye View of Great Britain* (BBC-2). The old-literary commentary and the bumper sound effects were overridden, fortunately, by the beauty and strangeness of the land seen from the air. What came nearer to spoiling it was the rush towards the end: south of the Pennines and east of Wales is a large country, and the need to look, to seem to be looking for oneself from an unexpected new viewpoint, was chipped away by wrong timing: the strength of the view from the helicopter crammed down to a coach tour. Yet what could be seen, earlier, was so fine and so impressive that I felt like writing to ask for a series of helicopter programmes, taking each region as it came. It would be less expensive and less dangerous, anyway, than a repeat performance of that unforgettable view of the hanging and shadowed Earth.

2 January 1969

Persuasion

It has been interesting watching television on the subject of *The Persuaders* (BBC-1). Not only because of the structural irony: calculated programmes, in a calculating medium, examining the calculations of others. But also because so much can be done, given television resources, to transmit one kind of critical analysis. The three programmes so far, on women's magazines, petrol advertising and charity appeals, have varied considerably. The programme on the magazines, like some earlier attempts in an educational series, was limited by its insider emphasis. Editors explained what they were trying to do, and there was a brief critical comment from a woman's page journalist on a newspaper. But there was no sharp questioning from outside the system, about the way a set of "women's interests" is arrived at—where the exclusions are what matter—or about the decisive relations between the projected way of life and the supporting advertising.

Curiously, a similar limitation in the petrol programme seemed much less restricting. The point that, grade for grade, most petrols are the same, so that the function of advertising is to create spurious differences, was in effect conceded, and agents were shown discussing how this was best done: an effective unconscious exposure, which a later argument confirmed. But then this cuts both ways. The charity appeals raise very different questions, and the effectiveness of particular methods and styles is, or ought to be, subsidiary. No discussion of persuasion, which is of course universal, can get very far unless we ask what the persuasion is for. The slipping away from questions of social motive, and the slipping back to isolated questions of method, show a limitation of consciousness, a moral nervousness.

Probably some of this is by now built-in. In the programme on magazines the question was directly put: Would you pay more for your magazine to do away with the advertising? The answer was a predictable no. It might well have seemed too difficult to ask women who don't buy the magazines whether they like subsidising their neighbours' reading through the advertising costs built into other prices. But there was an overbearing confidence in the way Michelmore* asked the simplifying question that somehow didn't carry over, in form or content, to the later programme. Should petrol prices be reduced, immediately, by x pence—the cost of the advertising—per gallon? It was the way that question didn't get asked, in a sharp, simplifying, pocket-hitting form, that reminded one of the methods of persuasion.

Back in the Forties, when I started teaching communications in adult classes, I read somewhere about an American machine called (if I remember rightly) the Lazarsfeld-Stanton Programme Analyser. A selected sample audience watched a trial run of a programme, with buttons in their hands, pressing when they were liking or disliking it. This fed into a chart which showed high and low points of appeal,

---

*Clifford Michelmore. TV broadcaster and producer.

and the producer, presumably, could get back to work. I wonder about the evolution from that to the selected sample audience in *The Persuaders* and *Talkback,* pressing buttons for yes and no, or making simple choices from lists, as an indication of public opinion. It's surely better to know than not to know, even in so mechanical a procedure, but if we watch the form of the questions, and the questions not asked, the choices not given, we gain some insight, also, into the workings of another kind of mind: the man inside an organisation who wants simple statistical material, as an indication of basic opinion, rather than public argument, which would be reciprocal and would often involve challenging the framework of the inquiry. I find myself watching, not the sharply articulating questioner, and not always what comes up on the dials, but the glimpses of faces, of hands feeling for the buttons. Of course, unlike the button pressing we see in animal learning experiments, there are no rewards, no banana capsules. But that is not at all the reason for the sense of an induced passivity: people lined up in rows, being instructed and required to react. And I am afraid this is what some mean by increased social participation, made possible by advances in technology.

I watched last week a very interesting film of a journey towards the source of the Orinoco: *River of Death* in the admirable *World About Us* series (BBC-2). There was a curious naivety, though, in the frank description of how destructive, physically and socially, the culture-contacts with these remote peoples could be, and then the failure to relate this to the persistence of the journey, with all its physical dangers, and to the really disturbing persistence of the missionaries. In mood and place the film was like Conrad's *Heart of Darkness,* but with only the questioning, not the answering, conscience.

30 January 1969

To the Last Word: on "The Possessed"

The trailer for the television adaptation of Dostoevsky's *The Possessed* went out of its way to relate its story to the demonstrations in Grosvenor Square. We saw the adapter looking self-conscious on the empty steps of the American Embassy, and the clips of the fighting, which seem to turn up now about once a week in a wide variety of programmes. Some people, of course, will take any association of images offered to them in this sensitive area. If television was run by men under 30, I've no doubt we should keep seeing an award-winning feature: *Respectable Violence—The Problem of Our Middle-Aged Generation,* with clips from Harold Wilson in Berlin. *The Avengers, The Saturday Thriller,* Lyndon Johnson in Vietnam, *High Chaparral, Callan,* Brezhnev in Czechoslovakia, *Maigret, The Inside Man.* For where reason, fact and discrimination are now urgently necessary, we are sodden with montage. What was originally a creative technique to express newly perceived relationships has become a manipulative evasion of all substantial connections. Nothing flows, nowadays, so well as an Oxo commercial, a genteel art film, an elderly commentator's reminiscences of history. In this kind of work, where form is everything, we see dissolves of sunlit woods and revolutionary crowds and waves breaking and mouths opening and rockets and streaming hair. At any time in a generation in which so much art or pseudo-art is produced, the production habits of a majority of professionals compose a structure of associations, images, tones, which sets limits to actual insights and perceptions, yet ensures, in the programmes that follow each other so closely, a certain confidence of address. The sheer bloody nerve of that trailer for *The Possessed* was not, as the people concerned might like to think, intellectual or creative daring. It was a busy producer's unsurpassable confidence in the currently available clichés.

People who hadn't read Dostoevsky's novel must have been waiting, through the first three episodes, for the action to start. A hundred years ago a scripture teacher and external university student, Nechaev, left Petersburg for Geneva to join Bakunin. On his return in the autumn he murdered, with four others, a Moscow student, Ivanov, who had been a member of their group. The techniques of assassination and terrorism, which Nechaev at once propagated and perverted, were severely criticised, and eventually rejected, by the growing revolutionary movement. Dostoevsky wrote his novel to argue (the emphasis is right—he spoke of the danger of its becoming a tract) that liberalism, religious doubt and revolution were parts of the same Western heresy that was destroying the submissiveness, physical, spiritual and political, of the Russian people to its land and its absolute rulers. "What I am writing now is a tendentious thing. I feel like saying everything as passionately as possible. I shall say everything to the last word."

But then it is obviously this passion, this action to the last word, that is missing from the BBC-2 serial. It is interesting, quiet, domestic; its ideas angular and idiosyncratic rather than passionate and common. I think it is not only the reappearance of that excellent actor David Collings, the idle young man who incited a murder for amusement in the serial of Aldous Huxley's *Point Counter Point,* that suggests what has happened. In Dostoevsky there is little serious exposition of the ideas of the revolutionary anarchists, and much that is there is tendentious. But for him, always, belief constituted a man, and the rest was incidental. Almost all English versions of Russian literature reverse this proposition: the precise difference, and distance, between Dostoevsky and Huxley.

That is the point about the suggestions of the trailer. To observe the behaviour, and put the beliefs aside in an indifferent margin, over the immense historical distance of those 100 years, is to limit the capacity to think and feel. This is all the worse in that there are certainly times, in the frustration of a revolutionary movement, when major ideas and causes release irrelevant as well as relevant disturbance: certain kinds of destruction, cruelty, perversion, betrayal. I hold my breath, reading Dostoevsky, when I see how closely he understood, and indeed lived, just this. There would be valid as well as conventional connections, if the central passion could be grasped. I wrote a television play, *The Volunteer,* about a man who betrayed such a movement from inside and while believing in it. I don't know whether I succeeded; the time was in any case not ripe.

Europa had for its 100th edition French, Dutch and Russian commentators reviewing recent history with film-clips. At the end of M. de la Vigerie's piece I thought the Prague Spring had at last reached the BBC. The young were marching on the professional politicians: bored, half-empty parliamentary benches; old statesman-actor faces; misery. The negative images get through very powerfully. But the substance of action is more difficult to communicate. Valentin Zorin gave a strong, orthodox Soviet view—20 million Russians killed by Fascism: it must not happen again. But a two-minute extract, later in the week, from Granada's *Cities at War,* on the siege of Leningrad, made so much more sense, in physical fact, of what had become an abstraction in a political argument, that I come to understand my preference for reporters and historians, my aversion from presenters.

The Granada excerpt was on BBC because it had won a Guild award. I read such stuff in the papers now, about what goes on at policy level (how many floors up?) in the BBC, that I'm just amazed and confused. But I hope somebody has noticed—and banged the odd desk—that though BBC programmes, justly enough, got most of the awards, there was an equally just preference, in news and current affairs, for ITV. That irony needs writing up somewhere. The BBC's strengths, the awards made it appear, were in being zany, whimsical, outdoor and artistic: ITV's in being informative. Given the degree of selection, and of course of fashion mixed up with it, it isn't at all the whole truth. But I have once or twice thought of starting this television review with "Since the BBC went commercial . . .", and my sentiments, really, are those of the group of producers and directors who have a letter in this week's *Radio Times*: an admirable statement, against what they call "the quietists".

20 February 1969

Personal Relief Time

Critical theory, not so long ago, used to assume a calm, leisured, detached man: his finger perhaps on lip or temple, his eyes unfocused, his periods already rolling into his meditative and allusive features. It was always a doubtful theory: art jumps us more than that. And though the critic must always reason, there is something preternatural about that still figure, secure in his property as a consumer of other men's work. The responses that now connect are active and everyday: a life, not a profession. The old posture went through its last phases, justly, as advertising pictures of the book-lover, but there may somewhere still, I suppose, be people who settle down like that to television: the end of the day, the armchair, the lapse of personality. But whatever else is happening, as that posture is assumed, it is unlikely to be criticism. The flow of programmes is too miscellaneous, too insistent, to leave us in any doubt about what is happening behind that composed brow.

There are weeks when it isn't the programmes but all the other things that are happening that really determine one's response. The last week of a university term, in particular, is no time to watch television seriously. Almost all the images have intrusive and intractable competitors. We often use the cliché of the tired businessman to define the low response (I doubt it) that sustains leg-shows. But though the pressures of the system are turning teachers, at least temporarily, into businessmen, they don't at all, I find, have this secondary effect. Television's shows for the tired are too weak and tasteless to take any significant amount of attention away from the always unfinished business. In the way of direct sensation, only the fight between Cooper* and Tomasoni really got through, but then that was exceptional by most standards. It was very strange, watching Cooper, that taut plain man, the easiest heavyweight ever to underestimate, at a physical limit after what seemed low punches (though in spite of the commentary we couldn't really see), suddenly finding his strength and control, and the other body falling across him. It is usually a sad, desperate business, but, crude as this fight was, the final moments were simple and brave.

I watched Bernard Braden in *Cage me a Leacock* (BBC-2) by chance. It was surprising and delightful. I can never read Leacock for long: the remorseless contrivance of most self-conscious humour is depressing. But Braden can do better roles than the benevolent urchin—bringing low-pressure and marginal social inquiry—of *Braden's Week*. The ironies of the visit to provincial London were deeper and more intelligent than most writing that now gets through to the screen.

Another Canadian, this time in an involuntary performance, provoked quite different responses. Robert McKenzie, in *24 Hours,* was interviewing shop stewards from Ford's. It is seven years now since I wrote in *Second Generation* a fictional chapter on television treatment of a car strike. I have looked it up, several times, this week to compare notes, and the sense of a play—of news as a play—was fully confirmed, though most of the details were different. News and opinion are arranged as it were dramatically. The representative spokesmen are all there but in a framework and with a plot-line which seeks to direct our response. But then, as it becomes a play, we have the resources of dramatic criticism. What I saw, in the McKenzie interview, was not the isolable facts but the deciding relationships. Here was the calm academic, down to question the stewards people are calling wildcats. But the scene went wrong, with a master's touch. Not only were the stewards grave and wordy men, their

---

*Henry Cooper. Popular English boxer who defeated Italian champion Piero Tomasoni in defence of his European title which he had held since 1959.

academic questioner a clock-watcher, a rusher, a very practitioner in loose ends. But also the bits of reality to which the scene ironically referred came through and were neglected, as the stewards talked. Nineteen minutes (was it?) of "Personal Relief Time," in an eight-hour shift. It wasn't the ratio, it was the idea, that few dramatists could have conceived. Personal Relief Time: a mentality was coming through, a mentality profoundly inhuman and mechanical. Personal Relief Time: against a background quickly sketched and offered (but only to be ignored) of the speed of the assembly lines, the heat of the foundry. Steady, patient, informative talk, against scraps of ideology, debating points, hammers of public-opinion polls. The dramatic situation could hardly have been clearer: the roles going wrong, the reality appearing involuntarily. Personal Relief Time: all the euphemism, the meanness, the subordination of men to a system; all the actual causes, behind the routine talk about constitutions and exports; human politics appearing, unlooked-for, past the edgy, dom-inative manner of the public interview.

The third programme in the series on *Civilisation* (BBC-2) seemed to me very much better than the first two. I like picture post-cards, and this collection, aided by some camera movement, was delightful. The commentary, also, was less bizarre than hitherto, though at the same time no more authoritative. The observations on detail are often convincing; the historical generalisations neither here nor there, since in that old dinner-table style they keep slipping away into mannerism. But where I had been roused to argument, talking back at the screen, in the first two programmes, I now found myself letting the decorated pages turn. It is of course fantastic that the gen-eral title, even with the qualification of a "personal view", should enact so plainly not only a Europocentrism but that particular selec-tive tradition which combines versions of the Classical period and medievalism into a 20th-century nostalgia. The structure of feeling is very open and familiar, but since the style is informal it keeps slip-ping away while there is so much worth looking at. In the end I suppose it is like that superbly furnished *Forsyte Saga*: a long last gathering-up, by sad and polished minds, of an Edwardian world-view; an enacting of pieties learned very young and very hard, and now with all the emphasis of a public corporation. The finger to the lip or temple? I remember Personal Relief Time.

20 March 1969

A Noble Past

Television's intense propaganda of a noble past, as a way of rejecting our own world, cannot be planned. It comes up too blithe and naive, like Mr Betjeman* in a balloon. As we all have reason to know, it was actually a helicopter (*Bird's-Eye View,* BBC-2): some of the approaches and angles would simply have burst a balloon. But the tone was that: floating and gaseous. *The Englishman's Home,* the first programme in this series, was almost too precisely the cultural pattern, the ideology, that I have so often attacked. Apart from a few primitive circles in Anglesey, the only "Englishmen's" homes before the late 19th century were the mansions and terraces of the aristocracy. Seen in isolation, from where the rest of us were then living, they were made the basis for the simplest version of 20th-century decline. In Peacehaven, even, people could still plant what flowers they liked in their gardens (but not in the ranch-style houses in Kent?). Our contemporary world was the tower-block: reasonably criticised, on social grounds, but with a revealing change of criterion: visually—and this had been the overt recommendation of the mansions—they have their own nobility. And this is the key to the pattern: the past is all art and buildings; the present all people and confusion. What is really astonishing, and would provoke anger against a more substantial target, is that all this is done from a mid-20th-century machine through mid-20th-century electronic equipment. I suppose it is to maintain this disjunction between the medium and the message (which has, incidentally, a decisive theoretical relevance) that we have mandarins and governors.

But still it is not planned. The decisive tones have been learned elsewhere, and come naturally and are liked, by a still very homogeneous group. Another example of the disjunction was the printed sentence in a recent *Radio Times,* advertising (among the instant coffee and the lawn food) the sixth programme of *Civilisation:* "Still, on balance, I suppose that printing has done more good than harm." The trick is turned by the rhythm: the charm of naive paradox, of the Edwardian daring thought, of reaction propagated at the very centre of a busy communications industry, could be achieved in no other way.

*Sir John Betjeman (1906-1984). Poet and writer on architecture and the countryside. Known for his nostalgia for the recent past.

There is of course, here, another kind of disjunction. Programmes obviously conceived for mainly visual reasons—like *Bird's-Eye View* or *Civilisation*—seem still, in some old habit, to require the sponsorship of commentary. When the first helicopter programme was put out at the turn of the year, I said here that I found it so interesting visually that I hoped we should get a series. It is coming, apparently, but so far with characteristically older ways of seeing attached by voice. So much that is exciting and delightful is now filmed that the persistence of commentary must be ideological. I wish I could not remember that terrible voice that accompanies and disrupts the replays of silent-film comedy. In most sport (Maskell on tennis is an exception) brief visual identifications —now used, ironically, mainly in discussion programmes—would be simpler and purer. The same, I would say, with the views from the helicopters: a few place-name titles; a briefly superimposed map. The alternative pattern, of the marginal talk, reminds me so closely of the routine intervention of the interviewer (between source and viewer) that it is probably part of some very deep structure—some version of necessary human relationships. If it is indeed this, I can say only that I find it archaic and wish some means could be found (the problem will be social not artistic) to explore beyond it.

The more difficult case is where things positively need to be said and shown. I have tried to work on this in drama, in theory and practice. I found, when working with a director on a television play in Wales, that though I had written an action that was to be seen and heard, the camera produced, even under the most sympathetic direction, images that were other and strange, and that could not, within the convention, be rendered back to the originating words. At what stage—not in marginal commentary but in a single word-and-image action—should the words be decided? Some professionals are very skilful in talking at and over material already filmed; but that is basically hack work. When a man chooses his visual material from a written outline, what kind of creation, what kind of accommodation, occurs when he sees the actual film, which is always different? There must be an extraordinary amount of experience of this problem inside television, but it simply doesn't get used.

The problem came again to my mind at the end of the seventh programme in *Civilisation* (BBC-2). My initial response to the series has been confirmed as it continues. Though in the first few minutes of each new programme I think I was too harsh, it never takes long for something to happen, like the Shakespeare episode, which drives me back. This is nothing to do with popularisation as such: but with what is being popularised (the Shakespeare piece, for example, was an expensively dressed schoolboy's error, significant because it carried the common underlying cultural lesson, which is of our own century and not of those others). The particular problem was disjunction. Not just the "hellish traffic" around the "ancient church": traffic to which the team, the cameras, the cables were contributing, but of course out of image. It was at the end: a sentence written, presumably, in some small and distant apartment, but now spoken, with some satisfaction, as the camera drew back from the face and receded—endlessly, it seemed—down a great Roman saloon. "I wonder," the voice said, "if a single thought that has helped forward the human spirit has ever been conceived or written down in an enormous room." The immediate disjunction was almost too embarrassing to notice. What mattered was the evident physical delight in the enormous size of that ceiling: the swell of a climax, to which the thought, the reservation, was no more than a grace-note or a velleity. When television does that, it needs criticism, not commentary.

17 April 1969

Combined Operation

It looked like a dance: the women in white, moving in repeated half-circles, lifting their loose dresses until they swayed like sails. It was a few peasant women in East Africa trying desperately to drive away a huge swarm of locusts which was setting on their crops. If they didn't succeed, or weren't helped, many of their families would starve within the year.

Some help was coming, from a little control room, from a few light planes. And then within a minute we were in another control room, at the top of the Post Office Tower. With a sense of urgency, from this other operations room, we were taken to New York where a chimpanzee was "giving a press conference". We had seen the animal before: sponsored by a tea company and with a jacket saying *Daily Mail* on its chest. The press conference was a group of jostling reporters and cameramen shouting "Hi, Tina," and similar encouragements. The chimpanzee, so far as I saw, simply moped and mowed. It didn't matter, perhaps. The name of the product got into the camera anyway. I remembered Wordsworth's image, in *The Prelude*, of the blind beggar in the crowded London street, who

> with upright face
> Stood propp'd against a Wall, upon his Chest
> Wearing a written paper, to explain
> The story of the Man, and who he was.
> My mind did at this spectacle turn round
> As with the might of waters, and it seem'd
> To me that in this Label was a type,
> Or emblem...

For Wordsworth, "of the utmost that we know, both of ourselves and of the universe". Maybe, but the beggar had put on his own label. The press conference was another and deeper kind of alienation. Remembering that field in East Africa, I remembered Wordsworth's final comment:

> I look'd
> As if admonish'd from another world.

What had produced this conjunction? It was ordinary BBC-2 planning: a repeat of *The Years of the Locust* followed by a "progress report" of the Transatlantic Air Race. The *Horizon* film was television at its best: serious, practical, mobile—a detailed showing of the return of the locust plague, out of the Arabian desert into a belt across Africa. The people fighting the locusts had the everyday commitment and comradeship of a clear and uncomplicated social purpose. I remember the Eritrean, a former fighter-pilot, flying his light plane through the swarm that was bursting on his windscreen like machine-gun fire: his calm eyes and voice, his hands on the simple controls. There was a very similar pilot, an Irishman on Aer Lingus somewhere over the Atlantic, being interviewed about the Air Race. It took him several seconds of embarrassed decency to bring out the word "stunt". He didn't want to be offensive; he just knew the difference between that and Alcock and Brown.* It isn't often we get so complete and transparent a festival of the society so many

---

*John Alcock and Arthur Brown flew an airplane for Vickers Aircraft across the Atlantic Ocean in 1919 for a £10,000 prize offered by the London *Daily Mail*.

powerful interests are trying to establish. What was most remarkable was the combined operation: between the BBC and the *Daily Mail*; between business firms and the Air Force and the Navy. This is all critically different from commercial breaks. True, the definition says "natural breaks" while in fact most of them are artificial, inside plays and news programmes. But that is a primitive form. The next stage is planned integration: a manufactured news event, given a spurious urgency by reports from a television operations-room, advertising not only a newspaper and assorted companies but military planes and arms exports. The combined operation is then in turn reported, outside itself, as news.

The transparency is crucial. No insight is needed to see what is happening. When such corporations combine, they don't need to hide. Tuesday's early-evening news bulletin could report, after one crossing, that the makers "hope to cash in on its unique performance and boost export sales". The language of a public corporation now comes straight from the popular business columns. And room was found, in a short bulletin on the present condition of the world, for the chimpanzee again, with the comment that as far as the animal was concerned, "it could have been another TV commercial." And that's it, I suppose: what passes for sophistication: placing it, certainly, but as an accepted and normal event.

They were so short of resources, fighting the locusts. They were poor people in poor countries. It is, then, not only that the Air Race was a conspicuous waste of resources; in television terms, it was a waste and a diversion of attention. But of course not just to a game. "A good plane with a lot of commonality," as a Labour Minister recently described a "multi-role combat aircraft". "A real winner." "Boosting export sales" to do what? "Hoping to cash in" on what? It isn't often an evening's television dramatises, so visibly, the conflicts and contradictions of a politically intolerable world.

Europa (BBC-2) made a significant contribution in the same area. It showed a West German film analysing military advertising in various countries. Four million pounds a year in Britain on recruiting commercials: a figure to bear in mind as an index for social service cuts. It was a fine insight into the different ways in which militarism, East and West, sells itself.

After these, after all these, Dürrenmatt's *Conversation at Night* (*Thirty-Minute Theatre*, BBC-2). This encounter between a freedom writer and his state executioner seemed curiously abstract. I sensed a disjunction between text and actors. What freedom could that wraith have written about? And the philosophical executioner, drawing attention to his idiosyncrasy, recommending humility as victory? Sad, empty, resigned: that neutral post-war humanism, with the knife on stage: sophistication, dwindling down, above empty streets. Only one line stuck in my mind, connecting to our own and different world: "I'm delighted to hear that education is becoming a danger once again."

15 May 1969

Based on Reality

"Demands?" said the First Lady, with a kindly but deprecating smile.

"Well, suggestions," said the student.

"That's better," said the First Lady.

The demands were for local radio. A group of technical college students, on a radio course, reacted to the council's unwillingness to set up a local station by starting one of their own, in an abandoned railway waiting-room and then in the tower of the Town Hall. Negotiating with Sarah Danby (BBC-1), they wanted no victimisation, a committee of inquiry, and the employment of local talent. The councillors laughed, in spite of themselves, when they found where the station was. Fade.

It was quite a week in which to have that little action. I had been thinking of the BBC's statement about the changes in radio now being discussed. It would be presenting its own ideas, "based on reality". But when I hear that phrase, from any office, I expect the worst. "Reality", after all, is controversial and difficult. The ordinary translation, from Newspeak, is "expediency" or "convenience". For what is called reality, in political and administrative arguments, is almost invariably arranged: a selection of certain priorities, and a rejection of others. Political rhetoric, in describing its own set of values as reality, deceives only itself.

The First Lady, by contrast, was innocent and pastoral. "Based on reality"? It was certainly local, ordinary, friendly. I wish I had its confidence about councillors. In other places than Furness, they have called in the police and dogs. But though to a stranger, at least, its lovable strings were showing, it offered a version of spirit and decision which was welcome, and especially this week. For one thing, the councillors had been elected. I have been trying all week to compose the right kind of note to the Governors of the BBC, reminding them, politely, that they are appointed figures; that if they try to trace their legitimacy, or that of their senior advisers, from any specific act of public choice they may find it harder than Mrs Danby; and that a conscientious person, in a situation like this affecting a national institution, would naturally remind himself, before casting any vote and quite apart from the bonhomie of committees, that he is only one among 55 million.

"Demands?"

"Well, suggestions."

"That's better," said the Governor.

But composition was interrupted by the Rt Hon. Anthony Wedgwood Benn MP, on *Machines and People (Horizon,* BBC-2). I don't propose to go over my past disputes with Mr Benn; they were, as it happens, about local radio. But his interesting talk, illustrated with great visual facility, brought me back to "reality." It has been clear for some time that a 19th-century variant of determinism has been the defining characteristic of our orthodox progressive politicians. It was sad to watch a mind attuned to every aspect of modern life except its social thought. There, among the computers and the communications satellites, was the old steam-age assumption that technology determines social relations, and that it was all in the mind—whether we saw the size of this challenge or not. It would even have been funny, if the speaker had not been a Minister, to hear international companies described in this technical way, with no reference to their actual social and economic purposes, or to the social, economic and international relations, which, through the unmentioned factor of capital, enable them to operate as they do. "Its own ideas, based on reality." It needs great patience, now, to keep saying, politely, that the use of technology, or the use of resources, is a human decision; that what is called "reality", indicating certain choices and excluding others, is in all social circumstances an act of will, subject to challenge; and that the only relevant question, when such issues are at stake, is about who, in this way, set the reality up.

In broadcasting, now, this question is very urgent. When we saw the Czech broadcasters, last year, suppressed by open political and military intervention, or the French broadcasters, also last year, dismissed by an authoritarian government, we knew how to react, because that model has been learned. In fact we supported the Czechs more than the French, and neither enough; but at least the model was simple. In societies like our own, the methods of intervention are different. The invading forces, we might say, are accountants (only, like soldiers, doing the job they have been asked to do). Accountants' reality, like soldiers' reality, has a limited but powerful reference to the reality of communications. Amateurs, watching from a distance or on boards and committees, can easily adjust to the definitions thus imposed. Producers, writers, performers know only one thing: that you can't make programmes with a financial and administrative structure, any more than you can dig coal with bayonets. When "reality" is defined by financial and administrative convenience, instead of by the only practical need, which is creation and communication, we get streamlined accounting and managerial systems but, in the end, bad programmes. It is a more subtle invasion, and we have not learned our reactions to it; but it is now happening everywhere and there has never been more need to fight.

Take an example which is at a distance from our own uncertainties. I spent some time recently with Radio Telefis Eireann, in Dublin, doing a few programmes and some seminars with producers. I enjoyed it very much, and still think Dublin the only place in the world where I would be asked to give a seminar in the Light Entertainment Department. I met so many creative and committed people, trying desperately, under the obvious difficulties of scale, to make Irish broadcasting. Their anniversary programme, *Insurrection,* was one of the finest television works made anywhere in Europe (we saw it on BBC in an abridged version). Now, in the last two weeks, some of the very best of these people are resigning, after a dispute with the authority about just these issues, and specifically about the effects on programmes of managerial, accounting and commercial pressures. I think they need the urgent support of all their British colleagues, just as the Czechs and French did. Not only as a matter of professional conscience, but because their difficulties, in a smal country within an Anglo-American sphere of influence that exerts its technical and financial "realities" in very open and pressing ways, are structurally very similar to our own problems about the regions and about the self-governing conditions which are necessary if original and creative work—all the way from news and entertainment to plays and music—is to go on being done.

It was with all this in mind that I watched John Berger's programme on the Soviet sculptor, Neisvestny, who has to keep his work in a disused shop because of official disapproval ("reality" is against him again). The programme (*An Artist from Moscow,* BBC-1) followed Robert Conquest on Revolution —a partisan view, from the right. Berger was very convincing, but I was never sure what was really coming through: Neisvestny's drawings, seen in virtual montage; Berger's interpretation, in itself creative but sometimes, I thought, a bit different from the drawings; or the sequences of Russian faces and war scenes, very powerful in themselves. I would like to see it again, while our own invasion is happening. Another relevant contribution was Barry Bermange's *Invasion (Thirty-Minute Theatre,* BBC-2). Here the talk was of art and theatre, of commodities, and of the intricacies of the self, and one by one the dinner guests saw on the television screen what was really happening in Vietnam, and became its mutilated victims while the talk of the others flowed on. It was a convincing image of how things happen at what seems a safe distance; the only guest left, in the end, had her back to the screen, though the invasion had come through and destroyed the room. What was most brilliantly acted was the moment of attention being caught: the almost casual glance, at what has become familiar, one of the "realities," and then the involuntary connection, the steadily more attentive and hardening look, past the protections of routine, and then the final outrage. They were all victims, of course. Perhaps that is how it will be. We shall sit around, self-enclosed, till it happens. Maybe not, though, to judge from my post.

"Suggestions?"
"Well, demands."
"That's better."

12 June 1969

Watching from Elsewhere

Two English festivals last week—the Investiture and the tennis. But the weather was so good I saw very little of either. Wimbledon, in ordinary circumstances, is certainly worth watching, since the scale of the court fits television so exactly and the repetitions and predictable crises of the game make an almost compulsive rhythm. Almost. I watched parts of Gonzales-Pasarell and Laver-Newcome, but in the evenings, in edited versions, already knowing who had won. Caernarvon, on the other hand, I had quite forgotten, until the shops in Abergavenny began to close early, led by an international supermarket. By the time I got back, anxious to learn how to build a dry-stone wall, I had forgotten it again. And that's how it had better stay. In offices and places where men calculate, a planned public relations operation is known to have two effects: direct, in manipulating opinion and sentiment; indirect, in forcing critics to react to it. Fearless exposures, satirical comments, earnest protests: these are all grist to the mill. The thing to do, when the operation starts to buzz, is go away and get on with one's own life.

That raises, though, a more general point about television. It's always said that the summer programmes are the light time, since the planners know many people are in the garden or on holiday. But is that the only explanation for one's sense, recently, of almost unbelievable banality? In teaching communications I've always taken the view that I'm the first to be influenced, even hooked. I used to begin a class by asking if anyone present had ever been influenced by advertising, and when I got the general negative I said that I had been, many times, and that was what I was there to talk about. In those days, in the Fifties, I could never get anyone to talk about the influence of television on themselves. The only way a discussion could be started was to mention its influence on children, and then, an hour or so later, we could work round to being honest. Perhaps it's the same thing now. I know I've come in from something interesting outside and looked at that blue screen as if I'd never seen it before. The connections of habit were broken, and a chair in front of it was very far from the most attractive place. Do we then project the banality onto the summer programme-planners, or should we trace part of it back to ourselves?

There have been things so bad recently, yet so characteristic, that the struggle over whether to mention them is acute. But what sort of life can we be living if we are prepared to sit down and watch a quiz show between "the William Rushton trio" and "the team of the Rt Hon. Quintin Hogg MP"? I came across it, flicking the channels, and I felt a lurch back to a period which I thought was ended, but which I am now afraid is the predictable pattern of the Seventies. I was at a sufficient distance from the world I know, in Cambridge and London, to get an alternative sense of the effects of this degutted, personality-mongering service that now has the weight of authority behind it.

Ordinarily I meet, regularly enough, the people who make and appear in programmes, and share that particular sense—that stale but knowledgeable air of the corridors—of a mixed output. We know, that is to say, what goes on; like some of it; admire a little; for the rest have eloquent shrugs or curses in the bar. But when you watch it all from quite elsewhere, another element is identifiable in that air of the corridors: the sharp smell of complicity. It takes distance, perspective, to see the whole service as a general operation; to pick up the sense of those beaming and flickering luminaries not as old so-and-so doing his act but as authorities, packaged authorities: a more effective, more penetrating power than any of the visible mummery of the state. Seen from that distance, the planned sequences, the insinuations, the powerful directions of attention, produced a cold anger: something very different from that more acceptable commodity, informed criticism. And it was then no surprise at all to go from the flexible photography and rigid little attitudes of Sir Con O'Neill's *One Pair of Eyes* (he was looking for Working Men to tell them to work harder for British Influence Abroad) to the apparently alternative world of *Release,* in which, in a sharp fast way, New York Pop Art ("depriving objects of their functions") was shown as "Young, Witty, Sexy, Glamorous and Big Business". It would have seemed improbable, ten years ago, that those two worlds could cohabit, but that is now the pattern of the settlement: old orders and young pseudo-freedoms. It is necessary to say, flatly, that one doesn't like the look of it.

Degutted and personality-mongering. The phrase recurred when I saw the cover of *The Open Secret,* in which the first operation is shown in process, and which anyway deserves a public welcome. It is the first publication of the Free Communications Group—an organisation of people working in television, newspapers and films who want to change the system in which they now serve. The scoop of the first issue is the publication of London Weekend Television's submission to the ITA for a licence, alongside a detailed account of how it has been working out in practice. The stress and force of this initiative are encouraging.

A final word, perhaps, about *A Night with Mrs Da Tanka,* William Trevor's *Wednesday Play* repeated last week. It was very well done, with a brilliant performance by Jean Kent and with convincing support from the stiff, weak impotence of Geoffrey Bayldon's civil servant, Mr Mileson. John Gorrie's direction was clear and powerful. But the play seemed to me sad, in the wrong way. Certainly the vitality of Mrs Da Tanka wouldn't last the night, although, as a challenge to the genteel rituals of the hotel and Mileson's fantasy of his lost girl, it made a necessary impression. What I rejected, in the end, was that stance of the middle-class artist, who is content to watch from a corner (perhaps with Henry James's ghost beside him) and simply record the weaknesses of his fellow creatures. Of course this communicates, in a world of watchers: of reserved individuals, who never put themselves at stake but who watch, with what is left of insight and intelligence, the errors, the oddities, of others. It is wretched, I cannot help feeling, to leave people standing there, lonely and hopeless, and imagine some aesthetic pleasure, some psychological perception: purely gratuitous style. It's the way they're dropped, at the end, these people we've felt struggling to live and find meanings, that continues to shock me. That over, and a night with Mrs Whoever tomorrow—whoever happens to book in and can be watched from the corner of this perpetual hotel. One day, perhaps, we shall acknowledge connections, as something other than fellow-guests of the establishment; meet not as objects but as ourselves without the protections—the prized protections—of this orthodox, disconnecting art.

10 July 1969

Crimes and Crimes

I want to write about what might be called the criminal elements in respectable entertainment. I don't intend, though, to get diverted into violence on television, as that problem is usually formulated. Violence offered as entertainment preceded television by so long that I suspect the formula as one of the usual covert attacks on any active popular culture. Especially when the formula appears as sex-and-violence on television, by which time it is clear that the campaigners, if they were serious, would be having a go at something rather bigger than the box. What mainly interests me is the reservation that is made for respectable violence. And I don't only mean wars, which seem somehow not to bring many angry letters: mutilation and debauchery have often had those proportions for one particular kind of conscience. I mean the sort that is described in conversation as a good crime; the sort of thing that turned Penguins green; that appears in the papers as "Crimeshelf" or "Crimes of the

Month"; that comes through in television as *Detective—a crime series*.

The detective story is an odd cultural phenomenon in itself. As a popular form it dates from that critical period of transition in the 1890s, which literary historians see as the emergence of Modernism but which cultural historians are bound to see as the stabilisation of modern middle-class forms. Between about 1920 and the mid-1950s the detective story was the complete embodiment of that narrow but effective imagination: a kind of practically engineered ethics between fixed social characters and responses. More variable than crosswords but safely less variable than literature, it reached a kind of technical maturity which, when one looks back on it, had enclosed and stabilised certain attitudes to crime. It was never really the question of who done it, since hardly any real persons were present and a case could usually be made, as in intelligence testing, for any of the possible solutions. The effective and covert interest was in how it was done: a repertory of methods of killing which had been made to consort, very comfortably, with afternoon tea, residential villages, cricket and a classical education.

It is then interesting how that particular style came to fail on television. Maigret got by on a kind of visitors' French, although some of the savagery of Simenon was just marginally there. Sherlock Holmes looked ridiculous when the successful literary tricks of the *Strand* short story had to be seen as real tobacco-slippers, bullet pocks and cockiness. Of what are called the later classics, hardly anything has really succeeded: the *Detective* series, with its playful knives, railway tickets and chalk marks for the body, has on the whole been dismal. Meanwhile the young had started reading science fiction, for even more amazing versions of how it was done.

Television, we can say, pulled crime fiction back to naturalism. This is often the source of the complaint about violence. When I remember the coarse horrors of the fiction of Dorothy Sayers, I am astonished that anybody can now complain about nastiness: except on just this assumption, that the old style, while it lasted, had sealed off and even embalmed what it was in the habit of calling a nice corpse. There was one successful translation: the very enjoyable *Cluff* series, but that was mainly the moors and the dog.

So what, in the new style, have we got instead? *Z Cars* and *Softly, Softly*: a different, more practical class of crime, though as series mainly successful, I think, because they are among the very few that have tried to convey some of the stale but tense atmosphere of everyday work. It's a bit of social history in itself that the eccentric gentleman-detective, giving the lower-class police a few tips, has vanished to a period habit, along with the middle-class ladies who used, we are told, before setting out on a journey, to have a few instructive words with the engine-driver. But then that, suddenly, was the interest of *The Expert*: a scientist now, of course, with a sort of lab, though, week by week, expert in so many kinds of science that we recognise him as, at best, a nephew of Sherlock Holmes. With a doctor wife, a West Indian assistant: Sixties tailoring.

Leave them long enough, they used to say in the crime stories, and they'll make their mistake. In *The Expert* it was a very sad one. Here had been these little technical puzzles, nicely solved with a brisk intelligence by Marius Goring, no less, and a helpful, tired, equal inspector. Then the series reached that point which seems to be one of the laws of popular television: the characters who have been palpable devices to explore something that is more interesting than themselves suddenly become the levers of the series. Crime, or whatever, is instrumental to them. It happened to *Dr Finlay's Casebook*, which has looked from the viewing end, in its latter stages, like ideas on the back of an envelope: personal crises, in roughly computed order, for Cameron, Janet, Finlay, who begin to look like father, mother, son, while the original point—the other lives to which a doctor has entry—slipped away forgotten. It happened to *The Expert* when the gruff, brave, stiff-lipped man, so clever with his instruments, was threatened in order to stop him giving evidence, and this rated two episodes. At the end of the first his wife was stabbed. I had to drive ten miles to fetch three nephews, who were temporarily stranded without a set, to see the next thrilling instalment. And with outrageous bluff, or what in professional circles is known as serial character's luck, it wasn't her at all, but a woman very like her in the same coat, and she was very sad about it and so was the expert, who still at the end marched purposefully into the court.

Not dead, then; only something quite like it. ITV had a genteel bloody series called *The Fellows*, which seems to have taken itself off, and a more stylish old puzzle series, played for laughs, in *The Mind of J. G. Reeder*. As a form I wouldn't give most of it another three months, but there must be miles of cans of *Ironside*, *Wojeck* and other packaged transatlantic crime. Simply, when the next morality debate starts, I shall repeat the question: what, in this culture, makes the twice-nightly murder, the carefully rehearsed crime, such solid, respectable, middle-aged entertainment? Or solve the puzzle of why we are told it is the puzzle that matters, through all that arranged and prescribed blood.

21 August 1969

Death Wish in Venice

There was this man going across from Venice to Mestre and Marghera and he said Venice was the past, sinking into the sea, and Mestre and Marghera were going to take over in the future, and then he said: "I thank God I shall be dead before it comes to pass."

Seeing places through people is now an ordinary television experience: *Whicker's World, Cameron Country,* Clark's *Civilisation.* In this case, *Venice—the Vanishing Lady* (BBC-2), all the problems of the convention seemed to come up at once. E.S. Turner mentioned this programme last week, but it's worth returning to. It depends so much, of course, on who is showing you round. But if it's your only chance of seeing the place, you don't at first care much about the personality of the guide. Then you begin to notice how the place becomes a background, with the guide walking through it. "Right, James, now," and there he is in long-shot walking beside the lagoon.

I remember myself that I saw Mestre and Marghera first, by the normal route. The traffic and the oil-tanks weren't a visual experience or a portent of the future: they were what I brought with me— literally how I had come. And since I had come to see Venice I went on through and was glad, and there weren't only the churches and the palaces and the paintings and the gondolas but people reading their papers on the waterbuses on the way to work —"next stop Rialto"—and in the shops and offices, the political posters on the walls, a familiar, interesting, locally beautiful city.

Mood washed over that, James Cameron's mood. He is a travelled and civilised man, humane and reflective, but now he had the mood of this culture which the BBC selects so regularly: the sad vanishing past, the muddled and hateful present. There must be a whole group of Englishmen, in the BBC and elsewhere, who have got so used to seeing the world in this way that they think it's the camera or the sentences doing it: the medium itself having this kind of water-colour soul. I only wish I'd had a camera when three Italian girl students said they would show me the most beautiful sight in Naples and we drove up, very like a documentary film, to the viewpoint ahead and there, shown very proudly, spreading over the valley below us, was the new steel works. But of course in Features they'd have a word for that: barbarians. The girls were intelligent and articulate and they valued their city: the steel works was what would give the people of Naples a chance to live better, to get beyond the slums. It is a way of seeing the world that is hardly ever offered on television: a way to live, I'd say; a way of wanting the future. But I doubt if we shall get it, for some years ahead. That other bitter, world-weary indifferent nostalgia seems almost an act of policy.

Indifferent? Is that fair? Wasn't Venice being mourned? Yes, in an indifferent way. In a few day's papers in Venice I read not only the details of how the city is sinking but the alternative plans for saving it, full of serious technical and financial calculations. But while one man was being interviewed and was explaining the regional concept within which Venice could be saved, Cameron stood looking sad and sceptical, and the engineers, the plans, didn't appear at all. This is what I mean by a structure of feeling. The selection is so deep that is comes to appear natural. It isn't conscious propaganda— Cameron is an obviously honest man—but it has the effect of disheartening people, and of presenting false choices. Mestre and Marghera, after all, are not really the future but a chaotic capitalist present, which some of us, looking around on our own, would have the guts to fight.

On the other hand, later that evening, the experimental theatre group Freehold in *Free for All*. The company were first children quarrelling and enjoying their game, then bored in school and con-fused at work, and then old and sad until they started touching each other, caressing gently until a song started and then everybody was singing. Discuss. It was a good idea to have Michael Kustow* and some others arguing about the performance and about the meaning. *Alternatives* the piece was called: an interesting combination of very simple, even naive physical movements and a kind of advanced, even sophisticated consciousness: a theatre-style appropriate to a group that seemed at once experimental and self-absorbed. Somebody said,

---

*Michael Kustow. Theatre producer. Director of Institute of Contemporary Arts from 1967-70.

of course, that this was revolution, and the point about that word is that it now includes everything, however private, that is unofficial and done for oneself. Kustow said, reasonably, that revolution would include anger against those who had organised the boredom and confusion. But the other meaning is valid, within a pervasive culture: a way of seeing others differently, of relating differently. In hundreds of places, now, there is this kind of simple and committed sense of starting again, but then at once showing it to people: showing one's own hands moving, as if, wonderfully it had never happened before. And then someone will say in the discussion that people have moved their hands before and someone else will say that moving your hands is nice, and there'll be a few quick names and abstractions before the performance starts up again. Certainly it's like looking in on a people without history: early Christians or late Romantics, playing a game, a new life, quite shut off from the world; finding meaning only in each other and in what is felt through each other. An enclave, certainly, in a rich world: a group of anti-Forsytes, as Lawrence called it, conditioned, even overawed, by the world they are rejecting. But then the experimental play of children, or of young actors as children, is at a good and necessary distance from that other sad, endless retrospect.

What about life in between? Between the sad essayist and the playgroup? This is a space normally occupied, so far as art is concerned, by novelists and dramatists. But the only one on television just now is Dickens, with *Dombey and Son* (BBC-1). It is very good to see the Dickens repertory being extended. The shift of critical opinion which has made *Dombey, Little Dorrit, Great Expectations* and *Our Mutual Friend* the major novels is now at last coming through. The episodes seem, as always, too short, but though somebody has been reading about the symbolism of the sea, the main action of the novel is there. Dombey giving Mrs Toodles the name of Richards as he hires her milk for the survival of his son and future partner is one of those absolute actions in which the process of a society is dramatised. And when Miss Tox explains how Polly will improve herself as a servant—"you wouldn't know her"—her husband replies: "I'd know her anyhow and anywheres." It is a simplicity and an anger that has moved out into the world and shown it again in a popular art: an energy and an intelligence that are suddenly moving, alert and engaged. It seems to me that we need this, and not only in classic serials. But the quality of art, as Ruskin observed and indeed learned in Venice, relates to the quality of a wider national life. I see many years of work and struggle before we can be thankful we are alive because life and art point in the same direction—beyond Mestre and Marghera.

4 September 1969

Science, Art and Human Interest

How can it be said, without misunderstanding, that science is becoming an art-form? Some years ago there was a television programme on viruses, and I have a very clear memory of the intricate models, beautifully made and lighted, with which the studio was hung. To say that this is all I remember wouldn't be quite right, but still these intricate mobiles achieved a kind of autonomy, and what I know about viruses is mainly from elsewhere. When I discuss popularisation of the arts—productions and discussions of drama, for example—I am soon told that as a professional I am looking with the wrong eyes: these programmes are not for me but for the general viewer. In science I am a general viewer. I was at a grammar school which taught no biology, only some physics and chemistry. Now I have two sons reading science and their books are around the house. I read some texts, some periodicals, and enjoy some chances of discussion. But professional science—the detailed everyday work of experiment and inquiry—is as far from me, except for occasional eavesdropping, as the detailed everyday work of professional writing is from those who see only its products. I reflect then on what seems a substantial difference: most writing (almost all that interests me) is for the general reader or viewer; it is a cultural and communal form in that sense. Most science, as I understand it, is undertaken with an intention very similar to that indicated by the strictest aesthetic theories: as a process justified in itself, quite apart from its potential audience. The only real and qualified audience, I am often told, is other professionals; or if this is not so, as a matter of principle, in practice the reaction to popularisation reminds me of the stricter literary coteries: not an argument but an attitude seals that world off.

In spite of all this, though, a lot of popularisation of science is done, and of course regularly on television. It is easy enough to see two basic kinds: explicit education and the general interest programme. Last week, for example, "for schools and colleges": *Discovering Science* ("Air and Breathing"), *Science All Around* ("Five Senses"), *Science Session* ("Picture in the Camera"), *Science Extra: Biology* ("A Place to Live"), all on BBC; *Experiment* ("Isotherms for Carbon Dioxide"), *The World Around Us* ("History in the Rocks"), *And the Living of It* ("What kind of animal is man?"), on ITV. Whenever I've watched these, or the Sunday-morning adult series, like the current ITV *Your Living Body*, I've almost always learned something, and the idea that the viewer should learn has been quite conscious in the presentation. It isn't here, for all the occasional felicities of presentation, that science has suggested itself as an artform. But this question, and related questions, arose quite sharply as I watched "A True Madness" in *Horizon* (BBC-2), *Tomorrow's World* (BBC-1) and *The Human Zoo* (BBC-1). There were critical differences between these, but in all of them science had entered a cultural and communal world, and was a material like politics or sport to be processed and presented.

What then happens? The Moondust item on *Tomorrow's World* was a case in itself. The containers didn't come screaming in on a motor-cycle escort but the producer was playing that breathless game. The helmeted security men were presumably necessary, but moved in on cue, in the last shot, to make a spectacular pattern: the silhouettes of helmets, the tables of containers, the row of scientists with their respectable public-appearance shirtfronts, and through it all Raymond Baxter, talking more than any of the others. There were some television-microscope shots of the "dust", which someone said wasn't properly dust, and some discussion of glass marbles and diamonds and a few other brief indications of research lines ("it will take some months or years to determine"). But two things were fairly obvious: that for all we were really told, the material could have been picked up in the Television Centre* forecourt; and that the scientists had put themselves in a communication situation which no creative worker should ever allow, though the television institutions continually offer it: being there as material, to speak when spoken to, within rigid limits and through an intermediary. I felt sorry for that row of men in their collars and ties, showing their boxes to order.

---

*The start of operations at the Television Centre at Wood Lane in 1960 was a clear sign of the new priority within the BBC for television over radio.

I suppose it was partly a naive good will, or an acceptance of the publicity which has enclosed the whole project. But of course it was neither science nor art: rather a news item, blown up and overcrowded. "A True Madness" was very different, but more disturbing. Again television inserted its intermediary: Christopher Chataway. He did not appear as a questioner—this, though doubtful, as in all magazines and documentaries, can be defended—but as a presenter, though impersonal. Yet if he had been a person, there would have been every question to ask. The same voice, I mean, doing a cool professional narration, can't say such radically different things without destroying the form. Where, as with schizophrenia, there are radically contending and sometimes mutually hostile schools, the cool BBC interest-voice is a distraction or even a delusion. Certainly several of the original workers spoke for themselves, but the form of the programme, as so often now in the dramatic documentary, was primarily imaginative. The stance was not of teaching and learning, nor of exchanging evidence and opinions. It was a stance resembling art: presenting an experience with images and voices. And if we say, as I think we have to, that the result was neither art nor science, can we say it is something else, like the hybrid documentary itself: an imaginative programme informed by science; a scientific subject imaginatively presented? But the peaks of conflicting theories were too angular for the first; the flow of images and voices too disordered for the second. We fall back, I suppose, on saying "interest programme", and the interest, often real, was given by the subject. Yet for all the sincerity and incidental professional skill, this is, I think, a corrupt form: too anxious about its audience and its subject, resolving its contradictions by episodes and montage, getting by on our unsatisfied need to know.

This was in a different class, though (as *Horizon* so regularly is), from *The Human Zoo*. I remember Desmond Morris as the informed presenter, often the informed questioner, on more open *Horizons*. But the stance had altered: successful author being interviewed; on his way to being what one can call McLuhanised. There was a sequence worthy of Beachcomber on the *Naked Ape* illustrations in the *Sunday Mirror*: nude with chickens etc, and a stiffly respectable but "come on" sort of editor. Morris tried to talk seriously though at random, and Fyfe Robertson asked his roving questions, but at any moment there'd be a traffic-jam, feet, a Nuremberg rally, copulating baboons, Mao Tse-tung, skyscrapers, an artificial New Guinea penis, water cannons (no Test Match, no space-walk?). I understand there are moments when computers need to be purged before they will work again. This was a comparable moment for the documentary, the interview, television human interest and science. But then who will administer the purge? Who's left, past the interest-groups, with the clarity and the guts?

2 October 1969

Pitmen and Pilgrims

The President of the Immortals used his left hand, for a change, in the coincidence of a miners' strike with the television adaptation of *Close the coalhouse door*. Beyond that, of course, his powers are limited; the issues are between people. When Lawrence wrote *Touch and Go*, the last but not the best of his plays about colliers and their families, Katherine Mansfield objected that it was "*black* with miners". Last week, in public, another woman objected to the title-song of *Close the coalhouse door*: if there was blood inside, bones inside, bairns inside, where was there room for the coal? Order up, dear, they'll soon be back at work. A pleasant announcer will tell us the good news that the pits are no longer "idle".

Of course Alan Plater's play, from a story by Sid Chaplin, was vulnerable. There was a difficult problem of convention in running together a front-room family party, in which mining life was remembered and continued, and an open theatrical presentation of the struggle and farce of mining history. My own preference, in writing of working-class life, is for realism, because in a culture like this the hardest and most necessary task is to see people in their own terms, in a complex of working and relating, rather than as the symbolic or abstract figures for which the dominant consciousness is already prepared. Political people often tell me that this is to miss the fun, the vitality, the exuberant popular tradition of working-class life, and perhaps this is true: one kind of miss has to be balanced against another. But I was interested that, watching the play with a Durham miner, I found him objecting to what he called the comedy. And this was particularly difficult, since the play as written and performed seemed to me very much stronger in its open theatricality than in its passages of substantial realism.

The tension between the two brothers, miner and student, was only instrumentally there, and the girl swinging between them was like a commercial. The run to the pithead, after an accident—a scene often and movingly and rightly done, in the mining films and novels—was again incidental since a different tone was settled to override it. On the other hand, the two kinds of presented performance—the historical role-playing, and the songs—seemed to me wonderfully successful. The darker tones of danger and struggle were consistently powerful: this was the story that really had to be told. And much of the 20th-century farce was excellent—especially, I thought, the Sankey Commission and the MacDonald and Baldwin episodes. The alphabet song deserves to pass into the depleted repertory of political choruses, and the same might be said, I suppose, of the catchy "As soon as this pub closes", though there the problem of environment needs thinking about: the song can be used to relieve the tensions of men actually struggling in politics—a shared laugh at one's own expense—or, on television or as a cabaret turn, it can be used to mock an inadequacy which is still more adequate than most who would join in the laugh.

These problems of form and tone stay in the mind. But what most generally needs to be said is that the play showed us how rich are the resources that are now ordinarily neglected, in drama and more generally in television. Theoretically writers can go where they like, find their material where they like, explore and learn. But a cultural block seems to operate: some of it inside the institutions, which are still capable of saying things like "*black* with miners"; much of it, I think, inside writers' heads, full of post-existential and post-erotic debris, filling in working life, if at all, in a negative identification with restlessness, frustration, exposure. The push to a wider reality has been mainly made, on television, in the *Wednesday Plays,* and it is a sign of the times that *Close the coalhouse door* seemed, in that way, out of period, in the autumn of 1969: a vigorous exception to the general Safety First.

I happened to be in Television Centre last week and to see, in colour, the trailer for *The Canterbury Tales.* Back home, watching the first part in black and white, I realised not so much what I was missing—though elements of the colour were delightful—as what anyone from outside might now miss about current television policy. The technical development, fairly clearly, is in a determining stage, and there are some obvious stock responses to what is and might be colourful. Spectacle and sport—we all know about them. And then what else is colourful? Well, of course, the past. All the same I had looked forward to *The Canterbury Tales,* and perhaps the Miller's and Reeve's Tales, tonight, are what the excitement was about. I find Coghill harder to listen to than Chaucer, but most of that is pure luck. What struck me about the adaptation of the Prologue and the Knight's Tale was a sense of infinitely receding boxes: two directors on two adapters on bits of the description and on Chaucer adapting Boccaccio. Probably the tale couldn't be helped: its conventions require sophistication of a particular kind, and the choreographed tournament and the columnar grove attempted visual equivalents. Even there, the first fight between Palamon and Arcite was pulled in the other direction: the armour was left out, on a kind of unity-of-time consideration, and there was talk of spears when they were circling in daggers and shirts. Only a very polished control can sustain that narrative tone.

The case of the Prologue was simpler. Here is a superb descriptive introduction and characterisation which was simply chopped to pieces (bits of it will presumably reappear as the other tellers come forward). I can see the argument that the detailed characterisation would be static, but the visual progress of the pilgrimage was already assured, and the descriptive variety, the internal world-making and group-making, of Chaucer's actual Prologue seem to me exciting enough to prompt some creative risk. After all, it wasn't a choice between that and the colour photography: it could have been both.

A final note on a programme I don't suppose many people will have seen: the series on *Teaching Adults* (BBC-2). I watched this out of a kind of nostalgia, and to see if adult education had changed much since I left it. I was that relaxed and receptive, and then what must appear to be my King Charles's head came out and forced my attention. There was a man taking a drama class, working hard at it, a little abrupt but deeply involved. But this was only the occasion for a discussion about supervision and control, and we saw the Head of the Institute putting the teacher right about a few things, and in the studio an Inspector and another Principal, prompted by an Introducer, commenting on the Head commenting on the teacher and the class. They oozed man-management wisdom at each other in ways that made me remember one of the reasons for getting out. They told us how tactful the Head was, how well he did it, when he was advising the teacher, and I had something approaching a vision of a vast Mutual Admiration Society, of Heads and Controllers and Inspectors

and Principals and Managers, gathered in somewhere like a
Panorama studio, with a screen in front of them on which those of
us who actually live and teach and work and write and argue were
converted to material for an exercise in management.

30 October 1969

Most Doctors Recommend

Would it make a series? It is understandable that broadcasting planners now ask this so regularly. A series is more than a convenience,
filling what are now characteristically called slots. It is also a sort of
late version of character training: encouraging regular habits in the
viewers; directing them into the right channels at certain decisive
moments in their evening lives. Practically all that is now left of any
public broadcasting policy, outside certain traditionally reserved
areas, is that kind of market thinking: commercial calculations, done
quite openly in public, and backed up by the general-purpose show-
business language which is now normal in *Radio Times*. I think I can
remember, for example, when a new serial like *The Doctors* (BBC-1)
would have been introduced by its subject, but now, apart from a
few quick sentences, the publicity goes to the heart of the matter:
"Geoffrey Nicholson asked the principal actors how they felt about
their futures as household names. . . . Now, in colour, meet your new
doctors." "Most doctors recommend," as they used to say in the old
advertising.

Meanwhile the producer is willing to inform us that "the single
most important element in the success of a series is that the characters should be likable," and that he chose good-looking actors
because "the kitchen-sink era is over and the romantic era is on its
way in." I was still reflecting on this bit of history and prophecy,
which is the sort of thing that gets said going up and down in lifts,
when, within a few minutes of the start of the series, I found myself
looking at a basement slum flat, all cots and kettles and a sick bed,
and a brisk young doctor doing her rounds putting almost every item
to rights. However, there's a sociologist who has at last had a frank
talk with his wife, and one of the doctor's partners has a jealous and
ambitious wife and the other a difficult daughter and intimations of
mortality. The *romantic* era? It doesn't seem to matter what the

directives indicate. What gets written is what the writers are thinking about: the rushed and anxious lives of professionals; the connections to any wider life made by the conventionally mediating figures of doctors and policemen; other people as sickness or crime.

I have been thinking for some time about television serial fiction, and about the relation to the magazine serial fiction which in the mid-19th century was a critical feature in the extension of the novel-reading public. In the way of commercial calculation there is nothing our own planners could have taught those Early Victorian entrepreneurs. Nor could anybody honestly say that the standards of the fiction itself have declined. From the concentration of audiences it is if anything the other way. But what I have gone on asking myself is whether out of those routines, through and in spite of the external calculations, something valuable might come—as, on the whole, it did with the serial novel.

The most encouraging example I know (though unfortunately only from scripts) is Irish Television's *The Riordans*. And what can be learnt from this, as in a different way from *Coronation Street*, is that in this necessarily popular form the social basis of the fiction must be popular: a life seen and experienced from inside, rather than by professional visitors. And given the current formalism and detachment of the metropolis, this would mean, in Britain, a programme genuinely produced in a region. But we see, at once, the institutional barriers: it would not fit automatically into a national network, and it would be unlikely to be commissioned by a centralised authority. The real pressure for serials will then go on throwing up formulas like *The Doctors,* and the ordinary limits of magazine fiction are unlikely to be surpassed.

Could they ever be surpassed? Isn't the sensibility of popular fiction inevitably limited? I think it's the other way round. We usually think of sensationalism as series like *Star Trek,* or—to come to current British productions—like *Counterstrike* or the appalling *Special Project Air* (BBC-1) or *Special Branch* (ITV). Certainly the nastiness of some of these needs notice, and as it happens the science fiction usually belongs in the virtuous world of melodrama (and is occasionally genuinely exploratory), while the spy and police stories take on an increasingly explicit character as crude contemporary political propaganda. But sensationalism in its deepest sense—the isolation of an experience from its context, and then its dramatic exploitation—is to be found more often in what looks, at first sight, like more serious art. In its determined preference for the transitory and the random, for the isolated couple and the single generation and the unfinished, stared-at experience, much of our fiction, much of our televised drama, contradicts and neglects the necessary continuity of our lives, and then the difficult and serious concern which comes only from staying with people, from following the action through. It does not surprise me that millions of readers and viewers turn away from what they feel to be an incidental playing with experience, and towards what the serial, if only as illusion, seems to offer: people regularly and connectedly known; the development of a life-situation; the experience of having to pick up and go on again through pressures which can't be resolved by any stylish cut-off. If we look at it that way round, and stop despising serials, we may get to a position in which the facts of connection and consequence would be written as experience rather than as plot-calculation, and there would be more to think about than a romantic era or the actors becoming household names.

The Forsyte Saga, one-dimensional as it was, commanded attention for just these reasons, though there were also the retrospective costume attractions as now again in The First Churchills. Those names, however, remind me of what cannot be spoken about too often: the resurgence in the BBC of the most banal and naive Edwardian world-view. To start a series like Special Project Air in the first week of "Colourful One" (and on a Sunday too, that religious and settling and classical time) can be seen only as the act of some over-grown boy with the luck of a large desk. We're back east of Suez, in uniform, with an island that's going native (and some of the natives are Chinese). ITV, always sharper and nearer home in these matters, has its Special Branch after the KGB, and has its working-man communist and its references to the Morning Star. Each series is symptomatic, but with a notable class difference, about two generations apart.

I want to mention, finally, the Tuesday Documentary on "Tokyo, the 51st Volcano" (BBC-1). It was of an old kind, but it had some of the virtues of its style: in particular, a commentary so full of fact that many people would call it overloaded and heavy. Among the rush of images was a free theatre group with a dance full of strength and freshness and hope: a welcome experience, with things as they are now.

27 November 1969

A Bit of a Laugh, a Bit of Glamour

Can anything be said about light entertainment except that, more or less predictably, it happens? I have sometimes thought so, often at just those moments when I have been most entertained. If it is watched from outside, without sympathy, in what is supposed (wrongly) to be a critical state of mind, it can indeed be sombre. It can be like watching mixed doubles of male and female impersonators, or desperate men on one-wheeled bicycles, or an elephant prodded into a waltz. An itch for the grotesque has been traditionally served by entertainment, but surely belongs elsewhere. Yet the prettiest, lightest things can be sombre, if the mood is wrong. I remember a theatre in Bayeux, in 1944, when we had come back from a tank battle and got Ivor Novello* singing "We'll gather lilacs in the spring again". In accordance with the notices we refrained from spitting.

A critical view would be different. It would ask questions about kinds of entertainment, from an acceptance and a sharing of its purposes, which would be recognised to be occasional. One of the difficulties in television, where light entertainment plays so regular and so central a part, is that a sense of occasion is difficult to achieve, though it is endlessly and professionally attempted. Things like *Christmas Night with the Stars* or *The Royal Variety Performance* usually achieve the apparently impossible: making a group (they say a galaxy) of very talented people look mutually embarrassed and dull.

Yet, here and there, there is plenty of good entertainment on television. If you were to hunt the channels, tracking down every last musical, variety turn or situation comedy, you could certainly find (as one now finds by accident) some desperate stuff. But then any hunt of that kind is grotesque. Its equivalent, 50 years ago, would be touring the variety theatres all the year round: living out of Bradshaw in the hope of a laugh. I haven't searched at all, and can offer no catalogue. But I have noticed one or two things, of a general kind, which suggest the beginnings of a critical viewpoint. And I think this is necessary: because a lot of entertainment reviewing is now confined to gossip; and because, odd as it may seem, policies for enter-

---

*Ivor Novello, Welsh composer and playwright best known for his lush, sentimental, romantic musicals. Became famous for his patriotic wartime song, "Keep the Home Fires Burning" (1915).

tainment are now seriously and consequentially arrived at in committees and in offices.

Why *light* entertainment? Isn't the conventional distinction between art and entertainment enough for them? Historically, that distinction is one of social class: art in the legitimate theatres (those given a monopoly by the court); entertainment in the unlicensed theatres, where the middle class, and then others, could "take in a show". This division was repeated in the 19th century, between the now respectable theatres and the new popular music halls. In any open and equal society, this could be a division of function. But in a class society it is otherwise, and entertainment there has always included, often without knowing it, what is really popular art. In television, the channels are technically open but many of the old social habits persist. Only this can explain the radical differences of kind, underlying the more obvious and more local differences of quality, within what is still grouped, overall, as entertainment.

I knew this social situation generally, from the history of the music hall, but I saw it more precisely watching *Till death us do part* and *Please Sir!,* and remembering Hancock* and *Steptoe and Son.* In each of these very successful shows (for we still call them that) perfectly obvious social tensions, of a contemporary kind, were being played through with some emphasis. In Hancock and *Steptoe* there was often quite obvious pain. And to go across from that sort of thing to, say, *Cilla,* is to experience a difference of dimension.

Entertainment is said to be distraction, diversion: a bit of a laugh, or a bit of glamour, in a difficult world. But what happened in the music halls is being repeated on television. There, very early on, were the Champagne Charlies and the tinsel and saccharine, and on the same bill the popular entertainers dealing directly, in song and sketch and monologue, with everyday experience humorously, ironically, sometimes bitterly observed.

Each kind, to be successful, must have some popular basis. Glamour is less fun if it is shown where it belongs, in an established class (which through all the imitation—the fine clothes, the settings, the sense of a world at command—is the obvious source). It is most acceptable, because most ideally shared, where it is Charlie or Cilla: when the girl in the expensive dress will still say "Tara."

---

*Sheila Hancock. Actress and director. Appeared in several television comedy series and her own colour spectacular for BBC-2.

I don't often watch these personal variety-and-singing shows, but when I looked in at *Cilla* I was struck by the stability of the form, after a supposed change of cultural generation. Built around one person and "guests", it still includes lots of (scripted?) conversation about how nice it is to have you on my show—no, how nice of you it is to ask me; all old friends together and that's half the turn done; and then really old turns (from a provincial past) in which there are impressions of famous personalities who, in a television world, are at least equally available first-hand; Johnny Hackett, who could have been funny on his own account, doing Tom Jones; Cilla Black and Una Stubbs doing a musical of a Hollywood musical of "Diamonds are a girl's best friend". The skit can be ironic; the "impression", derived from some admired and unreal metropolitan distance, is deferential and impoverished. And then when spectacular mateyness (as in *Cilla*) brings people in off the street and patronises them, in the most down-to-earth way, something needs to be said: not to the performer—to the producer.

There would be more entertainment, as opposed to more show business, if television went out to the many local places of very different kinds—pubs, clubs, centres—where most of the good performers start and where you can have the fun and spectacle without the deference and the sales talk—though, when this was done on Irish television, there was a lot of complaint that one man, enjoying himself, was stripped down to his braces. The petit-bourgeois "show", rigid and gaping, will be with us for some time yet, though the performers to surpass it are already around.

Meanwhile it is worth emphasising the real content of popular television comedy. *Dad's Army* looked a safe old game until one saw how persistently the tensions of brief authority, and of isolated rigidity, were being mocked. Clive Dunn's "Permission to wake you up, sir?" was an exact example of the stock of idiom—following the form but transforming the content —on which this modern popular art can draw. The social disorientation of Hancock, the hysteria and self-pity of Alf Garnett, the bitter deadlock of the Steptoes, the sceptical caring of Hedges, are all examples of tensions explored in comedy, in quite traditional but also very contemporary ways, in which a communicating laughter takes us towards life as certainly as the insulated display of show business takes us away from it. It can't, I should think, be planned. Improving comedy is almost always disastrous. But under that safe and meagre old heading, light entertainment, several useful small things have been done. Looking at the gaps they've come through, and at the contradictions they underline, it's fair to have a bit of a laugh.

25 December 1969

Brave Old World

What sort of a society is it in which the newest technology carries the oldest messages? I expected the first months of glorious Telecolour to be drenched by the colourful past, but it was still a slight surprise to see Ivanhoe on the cover of *Radio Times* and Redgauntlet on the cover of *TV Times* in the same week. "It's Redcoats v. Jacobites as the ITV cameras roam ..." "Will bad King John topple his brother from England's throne?" The rate of regression is becoming alarming.

The Six Wives of Henry VIII suffers from being part of this movement. The production is elaborately colourful and there is some studied acting. But there was a moment in Ian Thorne's *Jane Seymour* when I found myself reflecting that this was almost becoming a play. I mean that briefly, in one or two scenes, an authentic dramatic situation, marked by a sudden deepening of the writing, seemed about to take over from the costume drama and the merely "historical" characters. This had never even suggested itself in the first two episodes, and it is sad that it is in reference to a failure which had serious intentions that one has to underline the limits television is now putting on dramatists. Without the constraints of the series, and the demands for such production numbers as the pig-hunt and the ball, this probably would have become a play, with some active historical sense and with some genuine creation of theme. But what this theme would have been—the entry of a kind and simple woman into that corrupt and brutal court—was directly contradicted, and then constrained, by the external demands of the series itself, in which the surface colour of the court had been accepted for its own sake, as a primary value.

Coal-mining seems quite recently to have acquired just that sense of period which allows it to be repeatedly explored on the screen. It is too early to say yet how the production of Zola's *Germinal* will work out. I thought the first episode suffered from being seen directly after the *Yesterday's Witness* documentary on the Levant mine disaster. What was impressive there was the way the survivors and relatives talked: plainly and powerfully, and with more emotional range (and as it happens more interesting faces) than in any but the exceptional play. The only false note was an obviously arranged reading of a bad semi-official poem on the disaster. In all the earlier talk there had been that still unusual television experience: people speaking as themselves from an ordinary but then never ordinary world; speaking honestly and kindly; also with the real anger again heard only occasionally on the screen—anger about an avoidable and killing accident.

To go from that to the naturalism of *Germinal* was to be reminded that naturalism is a convention. The convention depends, historically, on a way of seeing people as trapped and helpless. Where the experience goes with the convention, as in Zola, the method can be powerful. And I am sure it was right to take the television production to a Durham pit, catching or recovering the look and feel of a mining settlement. What looked like the studio space of the unexpectedly large cottage and pub is another matter. A series of stages was created, perhaps unconsciously, in ways that gave room for acting, and some of this was external: an overwrought impersonation of another class which then, in feeling, seemed almost another race. Much of this, however, is in Zola: it is what scientific naturalism, observing another life, amounted to. And it is still necessary to say that what is observed is so powerful, its specimen language (very well re-created in English) so disturbing, that the point of view can be accepted, at least for a time. To see the life from the centre outwards, in its then quite different rhythms, belongs to a later period, in which observers had been succeeded by native writers.

Neither the scientific observer nor the native writer is at all like the fair-minded professional, doing a job within limits defined for him. This was interestingly illustrated in Alan Plater's contribution, "Standing Orders", to what is now *Softly, Softly—Task Force*. This offered to show how a fair-minded policeman behaves (or ought to behave—there were some touches that suggested a liberal insistence and demonstration, perhaps it will find its way into training courses) during the awkward moments of an unofficial strike. I've been wondering for some time, seeing how much contemporary actuality is mediated in television drama by policemen and doctors, when the image might be used in some genuinely difficult area. This was a possible case, but if so the use was liberal, in negative as well as positive ways. There are policemen like that, one finds oneself wanting to say; and the British police, in that sort of situation, are, when compared with some others ... No. That is the device, the false lead, which pseudo-documentary drama can make habitual. What that world really conveys, as I have argued before, is the inside professional view: other people as trouble, and if drawn up in opposing factions, then probably fifty-fifty to blame. Sensible worker and provocative worker; careful manager and provocative clerk; steady policeman and angry policeman: it's all a question of individuals, in the end. The fact that it isn't, that in and through these men a social crisis is enacted, doesn't have to be seen while the fair-minded professionalism lasts.

22 January 1970

The Green Language

John Clare, John Constable, William Cobbett: to understand these three men is to understand a vital moment of English history. Portraits of two of them, the poet and the painter, were on television last week. Though we needed Cobbett's voice, in its different dimension, there was much to be learned from Clare, through his own words and in his own country. Some of his best verse was missed:

> From dark green dumps among the dripping grain
> The lark with sudden impulse starts and sings
> And mid the smoking rain
> Quivers her russet wings.

But that sense of Clare's impulse, in a sad country, was very clearly conveyed in David Jones's *Omnibus* biography. The main emphasis was on the last broken years. The last third of Clare's life was in an asylum. But visually there was something of the intensity of the early poems—what Clare himself called

> A language that is ever green
> That feelings unto all impart,
> As hawthorn blossoms, soon as seen,
> Give May to every heart.

Spontaneity and its loss: a seemingly universal history. But what was good in the film was that the social constraints on Clare's genius were so clearly shown. Stephen Duck, a labourer poet of a century earlier, became a clergyman and a client of Queen Caroline. His interesting early poems, written while he was working, became polite pastorals as he was eaten by the Establishment. Clare, after some brief attention, was starved by the Establishment. He remained a real poet but was broken as a man. Three times, in the film, this history was tellingly shown: his long and awkward walk through the stately emptiness of a country house, to leave a copy of his poems and be sent to eat with the servants; his awkward exciting meeting with a London publisher, and then the complacent patronising letter of commercial literary advice; his awkward stance, doing field-work in an asylum and being interviewed by a journalist. What Clare hit was the transition from an oppressive patronage to a directing market. His loss of identity—"I am yet what I am who cares or knows"—was lived through with a purity and irony—the delusion of marriage to the girl who was taken from him; the delusion of being Lord Byron, the rich poet—which remains a memorable voice. Freddie Jones, as Clare, had the awkwardness and the tension, though not always the "green language". The film could have been made differently, and probably better, but it was a genuine achievement.

The green language of Constable might have been its complement. *Constable Observed* (BBC-2) was beautifully photographed, in the Stour Valley. And the technique now common in art films, the camera moving over the canvas, added further strength. All that was wrong, one might say, was the sound. "Heart of England" might suggest to some people the trained cadences of Alvar Lidell, but it's just a century wrong: the century of the disaster of the "public schools". I gave up counting the false tones and emphases in that overbearing commentary, and then the voice of the scriptwriter, Ronald Blythe, as Constable completed the destruction. No green language now: quite other words and music. It would be easy to say it could have been saved by switching the sound off, making one's own act of faith in the power of things seen—a power that television, that "visual" medium, so consistently underrates. But it wouldn't have worked.

Clare and Constable. Other things I watched during the week were the first episode of *Doomwatch* and the production of Ibsen's *When We Dead Awaken* (BBC-2). In *Doomwatch* I liked the emphasis on social responsibility in science, and that suspicion of secret research which is now becoming habitual. But I remained puzzled that a virus could consume plastics. As for the Ibsen, it is a dramatic epilogue of an almost purely Expressionist kind. Its themes are very powerful but its conceptions of persons are beyond theatre, and consequently very difficult to realise in production. The attempt was serious. Anything much better would be a masterpiece. But this was a case of fidelity: to an old man in a frock coat; to three acts on stage sets, with interval blanks. What is dramatic in *When We Dead Awaken* is a pattern of voices and images. I found myself closing my eyes, to get rid of the frock coat and the backcloth, and what I saw were faces in a kind of moving sculpture—Ibsen's actual and unrealisable image. And then I have said often enough that film can be moving sculpture: Ibsen, like Strindberg, writing the experience before the mechanical invention. All he could formally write, though, was a play beyond theatre, and similarly a play beyond television in its ordinary productive and reproductive conventions.

James Cameron's *The Sleeping Sword* (BBC-2) was a sharp examination of the development of the Labour Party into its present capitalist orthodoxy. Its strength was the opportunity it gave to non-Establishment figures to articulate their experience and their questions; its weakness its failure to recognise any socialist thinking beyond the style and era of *Tribune*.

Ken Russell's BBC-1 *Dance of the Seven Veils* was an extravagant squib: tearing a comic strip off Richard Strauss. It had its successes, such as the sentimentally grotesque reception of Hitler, and some old English knockabout farce with a Teutonic Salome (not exactly stressing, by the way, that Strauss's source was Oscar Wilde). There were other elements: Strauss's violence and sensationalism were sometimes punctuated with the mock-heroic of superman myths—a reduction of cruel bombast to farce. But it was difficult to feel that some of it was not also enjoyed in its original terms. The slaughter of the cow, the flagellation, the war nightmare, were perhaps only backgrounds. But scenes like the prolonged rape of the hero, by a group of nuns, ritually, and by Potiphar's Wife, in a kind of parody of wrestling—a scissors-grip into the womb—raised different questions. Here, it seemed, was a mind half in love with its own debris, enjoying the confusions of satire and the thing satirised, covering uncertainty with technique.

19 February 1970

The Best Things in Life Aren't Free

It was a serious adaptation of Hardy's *Woodlanders* (BBC-2). So much was in its favour. The novel is defined by its experience of the woods, and this had a precise visual equivalent. Harry Green, who dramatised it, understood the essential action, an opposition of life and exchange. There was no pushing back into an idealised rural distance. The primary values of work and love were shown in the process of being exploited. Everything that was lived and made, by the active woodlanders, was seen being taken from them and used, by the merely cultivated. Mrs Charmond takes Marty's hair and Giles's cottage and Grace's husband: a portrait of a lady indeed. Where Henry James showed exploitation at the end of the line, on that consuming journey through Europe, Hardy showed it at its roots, where the means for the journey are accumulated. It was absurd that this bored and predatory woman should have that kind of power over strong and active people, but that is the power of property, literally a lifehold. There is another, more tragic, internal power: the aspiration, in such a world, to become like that which is destroying you. There is the learning of the woods, shared by Giles and Marty, but the woods are not isolated, and there is an awareness of limitation and ignorance. Grace is pushed into a fashionable education by the social ambition of her father, the timber dealer, at a point in his material success. With Grace as its pivot, half belonging in both worlds, the action moves with a dreadful symmetry through Felice and Fitzpiers, Giles and Marty. Hardy shows the destruction in relentless detail and, through Marty, mourns it. Not the destruction of a rural by an urban world, but the taking of life, of working and loving life, by the indifference and greed and confusion of a possessing and alienating system. Annette Robertson as Marty, David Burke as Giles, were memorable. Felicity Kendal, as Grace, had the intractable difficulty of her divided being, but was often convincing. In the last episode, there was a fault of rhythm, traceable to some elements in the novel but deriving also from compression: too much of the consequent action was left to be hurried through.

I remembered *The Woodlanders* while watching the film of a Gloucestershire village in *The Curious Character of Britain* (BBC-1). What literature has embodied, documentary can observe. The film was a kind of looking with respect, and this was pleasantly surprising when one saw how close the false ideas had come: "a countryside that is lagging a century or two behind . . . that is unsophisticated . . . more primitive . . . almost savage", as it said in *Radio Times*. A girl from a farm was being married. We saw her working, heard her talking, and there was hardly any false note. A girl of 1970, perhaps to the surprise of all those who have only to hear "country" to start a saloon-bar or *Radio Times* free association with "primitive", "unsophisticated", "past". Of course the alien elements were there: the clergyman, in a minor way; the fashionable horse-riding, with nature notes; but above all, those voices that turn country into county with that familiar torturing of the language that is still called cultivation. A man was commuting to Gloucestershire from the Argentine with polo ponies. But also the village had passed into the hands of something called the Duchy of Cornwall, and a sad voice was heard wondering if the Prince of Wales would put indoor sanitation into the unconverted cottages. What was good about the film was that we saw the money passing: people handing over their pound notes—to an agent, of course. The man working his rented farm, the woman worried about repairs to her house, the young couple walking happily through the market-town: a curious character of England, indeed, that overlaid on all that real life is this blithe primitivism of absentee property, this savage cultivation of rents.

In a number of places, all over the country, another past is recoverable: the early stages of industry. BBC-2's *Chronicle* is consistently serious and interesting: a minority programme, perhaps, but at once specialised and general, in ways that used to be taken for granted in broadcasting. Last week was the final of a competition in local industrial archaeology, and the only pity was that so much interesting work had to be subordinated to that alienated prize-winning scheme. Knowledge and work, in this culture, are so regularly presented in a competitive context that the assumptions aren't noticed: the patronage is all. But here, just the same, was real work: the physical objects of tenterhooks and treadmills. A man in Redditch was restoring an old needle factory; another man tracing a canal that had brought down the Derbyshire limestone; another preserving a fulling-mill in Rossendale, first built in 1789. An abandoned slate quarry in Pembrokeshire; an old lead mine in the Isle of Man; a late 16th-century donkey wheel, on the Chalk Downs, drawing water from a 12th-century well; steam engines, from the mills of Yorkshire and Lancashire: in extraordinary variety, and with something more than antiquarian respect, a working country was being recorded by local voluntary groups. The last bit of work was the worst: everybody in suits and the controller coming in with a cheque. But all right, watch the present, even when it's selected. Another man came in to announce the result of the competition for "a song for Europe". "Knock knock, who's there?" As if we didn't know. But the song said "perhaps love", and it's worth hoping. Mary Hopkin looked happy singing "good evening to sorrow", knowing the knock-knock was coming, I suppose. *Grande Bretagne: deux points.*

Fashionable entertainment—show business—is one thing. Fashionable art, it had better be said, is not another. *Review* last week I thought openly sad, though at one point I laughed as much at Eric Morecambe in Wimpole Street. There was a decent brief item on Japanese painting, and a film made by a young Englishman in Czechoslovakia which, given what we already know of the repression there, made some incidental points. But the centrepiece was a Beckett premiere in Oxford: *Breath*, lasting 30 seconds, but by agreement with the author presented four times. It was in Oxford, as it happens, that I first saw *Waiting for Godot*. A WEA group had said most criticism was manufactured: would I go to a play, whatever happened to be on that week, and lead a discussion on it immediately afterwards? The play was so important that the challenge—even the challenge—was all right. And I could go from *Waiting for Godot* to *Breath* and say: yes, that's what happens to stasis, to the despair about language, to that earlier

> Astride of a grave and a difficult birth. Down in the hole, lingeringly, the grave-digger puts on the forceps. We have time to grow old. The air is full of our cries.

Breath was the waking scream of a baby, an inhalation, a silence, a breathing moan, the waking cry again. There are places where one could take that: out on the edge, in the draught, under pressure. But show me a clip of a fashionable party in Oxford, lasting about as long; show me those consuming faces assembled to listen to the cry and the silence, as the curtain rises on a pile of rubbish; show me the academic talking about precision and certified definitions; tell me of the cheque handed over by the rich, impressed Canadian; and then in the middle of that silence I'll laugh, a belly laugh, one of the other life-sounds.

"The best things in life are free," wrote the millionaire songwriters, in the musical of that name, re-shown last week. "Keep your sunny side up": another of their hits, and "hit" seemed the word. Knock knock, who's there? The waking cry of a baby. The pile of rubbish. But actually what made that film, apart from the talent of Dan Dailey, was the moment of composition of "Sonny Boy". Al Jolson was on the line, and he wanted a song. They had nothing for him. They were at a publicity party. And then they thought: why not write a song so bad, so slushy, that he wouldn't use it, but they'd have kept their promise. Long laughs over the whisky as they did their thing. When there are grey skies, I don't mind the grey skies. Staggering out, laughing, and then Jolson singing it. The pianist covering his eyes in shame.

I remembered Jolson, in his coon make-up, as I listened next morning to the Welsh continuity announcer, and there would be snow on the hills, and in the spring, colour was coming to South Wales. Among the early attractions would be *The Black and White Minstrel Show*.

19 March 1970

There's Always the Sport

There's always the sport. Or so people say, more and more often, as they become sadder about what is happening to the rest of television. It's a bit like the man who used to take the *News of the World* for its excellent racing service. But there is some truth in it. The Grand National, the Cup Final, the rubgy internationals, the athletics meetings: only a few programmes, of other kinds, have this openness, clarity and excitement. But there are some difficult questions, just beyond the touchlines. I was sorry I had to miss Brian Glanville's *One Pair of Eyes* (BBC-2). His argument that "above a certain level of performance sport as such can no longer exist," and that the heroes of international spectator sport are becoming victims, sounded timely. Some of the significance given to competitive sport is now clearly a displacement of feelings, from the chaos and stalemate elsewhere. Glanville quoted the indifference of many Olympic athletes, in Mexico City, to the massacre of more than two hundred young demonstrators in a political crisis which could be seen as no more than an irrelevant threat to the final stages of training. I don't now meet many full-time sportsmen, but I meet university athletes and know a little of what he suggests.

All the same, I find more real disproportion in the hangers-on than in the players. Certainly this is how it looks on television. I have nothing but admiration for the presentation of sport on the screen. It is often superb, technically, and for every frantic freewheeling commentator (usually in soccer and motor-racing) there is the informative skill of other professional watchers (in racing and boxing, for example). But nobody can suppose that BBC Sport is just watching people playing games. There is the compulsive talk before and after the event: not invented by broadcasting, since supporters and fans have always done it, but in effect altered by becoming a studio ritual.

I can enjoy it when a lean boxer is flanked by a less lean manager who boasts of what "we" are going to do and have done. But when the dramatic relationship is that of interviewer and player, the effect is different. The player is usually modest, fresh from the bath, and clearly much better at doing things than describing them. It might be the cue for some simple act of hero-worship, the persistent stance of the adolescent fan. But these interviewers, their whole stance suggests, have talked to the lot. With their authorising microphones, they are in charge. There then begins a smooth insistence, past the compliments and playbacks, that the player should translate his own world into theirs. The smiling pressure, often, is cruel. I find I watch the player, as he hangs on desperately to the interviewer's Christian name, which if said often enough might make the squeezing stop.

Interviews just after the event are at least interrupted by the results service. But in the mid-week sessions—in *Sportsnight with Coleman,* for example—time often loses any normal meaning. I've watched plays and features being timed by the second in the cutting-room and in rehearsals. I've seen the relentlessness of the clock in what are supposed to be serious discussions. But in these intercalary sessions, dignified by association with real and interesting sport, there is often an endless dribble of words, a kind of relentless filling-in, as if television were timeless. Last Thursday, in *Sportsnight,* there was a fast greyhound race and a rather subsidiary event of five-a-side football. With other non-events the programme then overran, so that a film in the *Curious Character of Britain* series was cancelled.

Sport, sport... If it had been extra time in a real event, it would have been acceptable. But this is something else. I don't know a name for it, but shortly afterwards we had Michelmore, Day, Butler, McKenzie,* the swingometer and the psephology studio, the representative politicians for up-to-the-minute commentary on the Council elections, and if I didn't get the name I got the pattern. Television is so good when it presents real events that it gains a power which it then abuses: nominally, to set up an anteroom, beside everything that is happening—a budget, a cup final, an election, a horse-race—but actually making the anteroom the arena, the reaction the event, and the commentators the real agents. Players and politicians submit to this process, thinking vaguely and sharply (respectively) of their "public". But from the other side of the box the degeneration is obvious. Politics and sport, in very similar ways, are processed to a desultory ritual, which most of us, I think, only watch because at some point inside this long and mutually boring ceremony the whistle will blow, the result will come up, with incomparable precision and clarity: the kernel of the medium, with this large shell echoing hollowly around it.

Something happens, that is to say, in the end. Or appears to happen. For even here, within the processing, there are so many kinds of result. Real results of at least some temporary interest: matches, elections. And results of other kinds, two or three a night, within staged competitions: *Miss England, Brain of Britain, A Question of Sport, Top of the Form* and so on. I've tried thinking through the difference between these and the "real" competitions. It's becoming harder to be sure. Politics, especially, has the second-hand air, as things now are. Favours and supporters; the modern party system, in fact, contemporaneous with modern competitive sport; the contest more evident than the issues. "Tell me who you're supporting, our side or their side." "Well, David, I don't know. How does anybody choose between an illusion and an enemy?" Next question, or blackout.

---

*A very typical television team covering the Greater London Council elections of April 1970, regarded as a test of the political climate for the forthcoming general election. The team consisted of Clifford Michelmore (broadcaster), Robin Day (radio and television journalist), David Butler (Fellow of Nuffield College, Oxford and author of studies on British general elections) and Robert McKenzie (Professor of Sociology, London School of Economics and author of a well-known study of British political parties).

But then again, it's not every day you'll see a Cambridge don oiling his semi-automatic pistol. Or so the *Radio Times* cover assured us. Our side and their side, the clever stupidity of espionage, the recurrent thrillers (such as *Codename*) in the anteroom of the issues. Can we make an exception for *Doomwatch*? Not always. There's been more than a bit of the old mad-scientist routine, and I've still had no answer about that first plastic-eating virus. But there is this other structure, which even in *Dr Who* (much improved by the acting of Jon Pertwee) is becoming commonplace: official conspiracy, by Ministers and corporations. An alien presence, destructive and dangerous, whether in a business suit or in full reptilian scales. More clearly than anywhere else, at least in popular forms, this sense of an apprehended but indefinable threat, of some intricate and persistent conspiracy against life, is being expressed in science fiction. The spy-cult feeds on it, but has a routine evasion, translating security and threat into national blocs. Science fiction often projects it, into an empty space. And at the edge, undoubtedly, a kind of paranoia is waiting. What does a sane man do, when he senses a conspiracy but has been taught to laugh at conspiracy theories? Explain, I suppose. Explain and keep on explaining the difficulty.

I talked once with Kit Pedler, before and during a *Line-Up* discussion. I think now I recognise his tone. He was a joint author of last week's *Doomwatch* episode, "The Red Sky" (BBC-1). It was convincing, I thought, because it used dramatic concentration—literally, in the tube of a lighthouse—to emphasise what is at the very least a symptom of civilised disorder: uncontrolled and destructive noise. Characteristically, the noise of an experimental rocket plane (to save somebody an hour on an Atlantic journey) was contrasted dramatically with work on nature conservation. There was a wry result: after the destructive noise came the bureaucratic solution—compulsory purchase of the lighthouse and mere suspension of the test-flights. This got remarkably near to the way things happen. But the strain tells. Quist, the sane observer, the far-seeing analyst, was shown as near breakdown before the action even began. The very practice of sanity was shown as being assaulted by unbearable pressures. Even, in a optical effect, Quist and the others saw the flames of hell. It's very easy to feel this almost hysterical strain: hysterical overemphasis in the face of overemphasis and hysteria. The tired mind almost snaps against organised folly. But something real got through, all the same. Much more real, anyway, than the anteroom arranged later in the *Line-Up* studio: a five-man discussion of the problem of noise, in the stale public language of committees and boardrooms. No whistle there. No jet-scream to disturb the public relations. Late at night and tired: a very evident and very general public mood. Still, there's always the sport.

16 April 1970

Going Places

Who first called them travelogues? One of the most obvious uses of the film camera is to let us look at new places. Certainly I almost always enjoy it, but there's just that bit of prejudice. That voice which "said goodbye to beautiful wherever" has bitten into the memory. It's some indication of the power of monopoly that any such voice should have acquired so general a resonance. It's like the more serious case of Disney's way of seeing people and animals taking over a whole sector of civilisation. And then we add to the memory of the voice the commonplace joke about holiday snapshots: another simple pleasure that has become a byword for silliness, without any justification that I can see. Unless there's a feeling that more creative art, more creative television, is being limited by assorted travel. It may sometimes look like that, in the schedules, but I'd rather fight for the creative work on its own terms, without having to do down, by the way, things that are pleasant and easy and within almost everyone's range.

It's necessary, of course, to make some distinctions. A few travel films don't get beyond holiday snapshots, and this is not only a technical point, but more crucially, a matter of authenticity: most of the value of snapshots is that they are personal, family, not a national programme. Actually I've come to think that the holiday snapshots we see most often on television are in all those routine spy-pieces which just happen to have the action in the Bahamas or Italy or the Alps or the Midi. Do your karate bit now, love, and we can all get back and eat. In any case the exteriors which occur in that kind of film are like no place I've ever visited, even when I've visited it. I think I've travelled the whole of the French Mediterranean coast without ever once seeing the film Riviera.

Get beyond the casual trailing and the commercial backgrounds and the more interesting filmed places begin. There have been some important examples just recently. I didn't see all the *Curious Character of Britain* series, but the final programme, along the Tamar, was very good indeed. The river and the valley were beautifully photographed, but there was a social situation inside them that was even more memorable. What was once the largest copper-mine in Europe was there, abandoned, and several little ports with not only the grass but trees growing over the wharves. Hills of arsenic were bare white among the dense woods. An engineer was trying to make the spoil economic. A water bailiff was rowing under the weir, across the wide river, looking for salmon and for poachers. What I liked about the programme (with one or two brief exceptions, like the patronised beauty contest) was the serious, unemphatic, interested looking. An industrial centre that had run out of material, but not a ghost town: a settled and still beautiful valley.

All I knew of the Tamar, before this, was that it is the boundary of Devon and Cornwall. The producer had a meaning in mind, and I didn't really share it—something about the decline of Britain, unless etc—but still the looking was primary. I wondered about this relationship watching Michael Charlton's *The Last of Lands: Australia* (BBC-1). It is his native country and I've never been there, so I'm not going to argue with him. But that Lawrence piece in *Kangaroo*, about matiness and physicality and the lack of any inner life, will bear some questioning, since he said it, after all, about other places too. When Charlton quoted it, and there were long scenes of people on the beach and drinking beer, I lost touch, felt out of sympathy. It's a sad old state when beer and swimming go sour, look questionable. It's not what's usually said about Lawrence, but there's often this fear of actual physicality, in sunlight, and I didn't accept when Charlton seemed to invite us to share it or think about it—I don't know quite which. The camera panned along a line of young men drinking beer, with a voice-over commentary about a national attitude of not caring. The wider issue I can't judge, but at least the beer didn't prove it. Damn standing on beaches and looking at national bodies, or in bars and looking at cultural beer.

Is it a case, perhaps, of feeling some need to apologise? There was a defensive air that might properly be related to political questions, but these weren't really explored. The sequence on the mining towns and on the new boom, financed by Japanese and Americans, was by contrast excellent, and the material on the aboriginals was interesting. Other things I wanted to see, like the cities and the farming, were there only in flashes. The sadly questioning mood was selecting its images. But then, and it came oddly, there were three good lively songs: the mixed children's choir, but mainly the theatre group with the fine shearing-strike ballad, and, over the credits, a lively song about beer.

To Leningrad with Love (BBC-1) was a look at the city through its arts, with side-references to its history. I've got so used to other variants of bias that I didn't feel any shock listening to the official justifying censorship. He sounded like so many other spokesmen for convenience, and if you put him alongside the young Russian getting up in class and reciting his favourite English poem, Kipling's "If", you got a picture of a sort: a new if unlikely International Conservative Association. But the feelings of the film were elsewhere: in St Petersburg really, I suppose, with the palaces and the galleries and the great companies; but then also with Shostakovich, with the young dancers, a continuity of fine art. Much of it was very beautiful, and in the figurative arts and in music it was entirely convincing: the spirit of a city. A young contemporary poet recited his "Leningrad" but all I could really hear was Ian McKellen reading Mayakovsky, in a startling and extraordinarily vigorous intervention. We need new forms of art, but the rest of the film wasn't saying that: it was looking at the great traditional arts in a city that came through like a very beautiful museum.

Nairn's Europe (BBC-1). Nairn in Europe? Nairn in bits of Europe? These grand possessive titles are becoming infectious. But the first programme was interesting: a comparison of Hereford and Bourges. Hereford I've known all my life, and I got the range suddenly. This first place I really knew, out of all the places television had been showing, was now a quick general look. He made one or two good points, about its style and atmosphere, but for a lot of the time he was stuck on the balcony of a bank, looking down over High Town, and I wondered how long they'd been there, with no time even for a walk through the Butter Market or down the narrow streets to the Cathedral. There was little looking from eye-level, from any ordinary viewpoint, and I doubt if he really got the sense of it, the sense I have anyway, of a place in an interim, as sharply transitional, if you keep walking and looking and listening, as any of our market towns; and a bit uncertain, a bit empty too. Bourges I've only been to once; and there he showed a great deal. It's the way it goes. I didn't like the mechanical staring at the great mechanical supermarket: floor-level looks at the wire-baskets and something ominous about the future of France. But in the old town he picked out details of shops and buildings with an illuminating interest, and then there was a grand finale in the Cathedral, stained glass and Couperin: magnificent. Except that there was going to be a comparison, and we didn't get the sandstone of Hereford and the Mappa Mundi and the Chained Library. But I shall go on watching his series. He cares about what he's seeing. Isn't that the distinction we want, to get beyond travelogues and the latest agent in Lisbon?

7 May 1970

Against Adjustment

It isn't surprising that so many people who have got used to this society resist social analysis of literary forms. The forms of accepted analysis, and the judgments that go with them, are part of the deep accommodation to an orthodox consciousness. This doesn't exclude the possibility of local amendment and dissent, which come through as a sort of pragmatic honesty. Superficially, we have plenty of controversy, but much of it resembles what passes for controversy in politics. This last case has been particularly in evidence on television since the election was announced. It can seem extraordinary that at a time like this, and with three available channels, there is virtually no political argument we can turn on and watch. But the absence is overlaid by a surfeit of its substitute: personal display and abuse by projected leaders; selected comparative arguments, in a form that looks like but isn't statistics, at the margins of issues. What is not publicly argued is the basic structure of the society, and the possible policies within and beyond it. But then this is not a failure of technique, any more than it is what some people call the necessary vulgarity of the hustings. The limitation of real argument, and the careful production of apparent controversies, are not technical choices, but real ones. Indeed the form of what during this kind of election is called politics needs analysis in much the same way as a literary or dramatic form, which embodies experience in a very particular way, carrying its own values within and beyond the apparent action.

Wilson and Heath and the others are not limiting consciousness, for all the evident calculation of their appearances. On the contrary, they are limited by it, and could not, if they chose, move to real argument without also moving to a kind of political activity which would go so far beyond their accepted roles that not only the techniques but the issues would have changed. This is what I mean by accommodation. A man gets so used to certain limits and then certain emphases that he accepts a particular form of consciousness as natural consciousness, and then, on that conventional basis, develops what can be called a personality, even sometimes an individual position. Seen from outside, these particular differences are quite evidently variations on a common adjustment; but nothing leads to so much anger as trying to point this out. Indeed, when a limited common consciousness is being celebrated, as in this ritual of an election, any absolute dissenter is in at least temporary danger of losing the possibility of being understood at all.

But there is more resistance, with more experience tied up in it, when analysis of this kind moves to literature and the other arts. Only a very few people, after all, are directly involved with the political false consciousness. Many more are involved, and more deeply, with those forms of action in which primary experience is directly mediated. Over the last 20 years most of our deepest controversies have been cultural and especially literary. The dependent arguments about education have been the nearest political equivalent, though all have taken place within a fundamental conflict about war and its social and political structures: a conflict that, understandably, has carried the deepest emotional charge.

Dennis Potter's new play, *Lay down your arms* (London Weekend) interested me for two reasons: that it was an action within this conflict, and that its form raised questions of an analytic kind which, in television drama, are overdue for discussion. The play was set in 1956, the time of Suez and Hungary, which is now generally accepted as a turning-point in post-war consciousness: the year of the emergence of a new kind of radicalism. Robert Hawk, a grammar-school boy, son of a miner, was doing his national service before going to Oxford. He had learned Russian and was posted to a department in the War Office which monitors Russian troop movements. Within the department, his own most evident conflict was with his officers: directly, in terms of social class; more generally, as the crisis developed, in terms of national and political loyalty—he ends by shouting: 'Up Nasser.' But this is also a crisis of personal identity. The external conflict is shot through by conflicts that appear as internal and personal: problems of adjustment and relationship; habits of fantasy and speculative role-playing. The clever boy who has done well at his lessons ends as a militant anti-imperialist but also as lonely, disoriented, almost desperate.

Now an orthodox analysis is immediately available. Potter is writing (people say) another bit of his autobiography. And it happens that it is representative of a well-known social movement: the working-class scholarship boy making his way into an Establishment which at once fascinates and revolts him. He lets out his anger at a stupid ruling class; even more, perhaps, his educated contempt. But underlying these are the problems of his mobility: an uncertainty, a lack of self-confidence, a mixture of aggression, posturing and self-pity. And then (people say) we have heard all this before. Since the Fifties, really, have we heard anything else? Haven't we by now had just about enough of Our Bob?

I said that this is orthodox analysis, and the reason it is orthodox is that it conceals real content by attention to overt content. It can only do so, of course, if the overt content is capable of being generalised, and if the form of that generalisation corresponds with an element of the orthodox consciousness. What I mean is that explication of a play like *Lay down your arms* is now, in orthodox terms, personal, because any social explication would clarify more difficult issues. I don't mean only the irrelevant ascription of the play to Dennis Potter's personal experience. That's a way of sentimentalising it, or more often of writing it off. I mean the explanation of the crisis in orthodox personal terms, seeing mobility as the problem when what is really important is not the fact of movement but the fact of what is being moved through. There is a very weak but very confident critical mode in which the problem of Potter's hero can be seen wholly in post-Freudian ways: adolescent difficulties of adjustment; his aggressive behaviour a projection of internal tensions and conflicts; his self-pity, the disturbance consequent on the aggression and the shame. This popular mode has the advantage that what is being reacted to, what is there to be adjusted to, what is finally rejected, does not need to come under scrutiny.

But then the interest of this is that the first literature which appeared, with this apparent content, was indeed in the main of that kind. The Movement novelists of the Fifties were, on the whole, preoccupied with problems of adjustment. The contempt and occasional anger, catching up much real feeling, were the functions of finding and asserting a place. The society did not so much have to change as move over, make room (and in the Sixties, of course, this happened, even notoriously). The actions through which the claims were made were always of that kind: finding a job, getting some respect, being left alone.

Robert Hawk was nominally younger than Dennis Potter's earlier hero, Nigel Barton, but the consciousness of his action was older. The apparent themes were familiar, but the method of their realisation changed them. First, and most obviously, the reaction was to the fact of war. We must have seen and read a hundred episodes apparently similar to the opening of *Lay down your arms*. What was radically different here was that this young national serviceman hoisting his kit past the Palace and the changing of the guard was clearly visible as something more than his own awkwardness (the personal reduction): he was a man making his way into a military machine which, seen on parade or more relaxed in the war-room, was a major social fact that could be critically observed. One part of what was critically seen was militarism as such, as in the effective later scene in which there were cross-cuts of the Palace and Red Square and the Red Army marched to the tune of "The British Grenadiers". These were the machines about to move against Suez and Hungary. Hawk's reaction to that was in the full sense critical, and the same is true of his reaction to his working-class home: not just the differences of manners, seen after being away, but the contradictions there (the directly contradictory but confident beliefs of his father about the Army and again about revolution). The problem of identity is then much more than personal: it is a function of social conflict and of perceived social contradictions. The fantasy identification with a Russian goalkeeper was the play stage; the substantial identification with a young Russian soldier, trapped in the same growth problems and in the same kind of military machine, was a way through to the bitter beginnings of maturity. Single plays are now so short that actions can only be sketched. But within these limits *Lay down your arms* found effective images: again apparently those of a mood-play—the subjective experience—but because of the different consciousness going at least some way towards a harder and more critical action.

4 June 1970

Back to the World

It was nice to get back to the world, after the June election trip through the islands.* I don't enjoy feeling distant from my own country, but when I cannot share its definitions and emphases I have no real choice, and this was exactly my feeling during the election. The fighting along the Mekong seemed self-evidently more important, not only to others but to our own future, than those marginal gains and losses. There have been several reports from Cambodia on television, in *24 Hours* and in the News. Many reporters have been in danger, in that uncertain and mobile war, and I would not dream of criticising them. But, so far as I have seen, there has been a failure of commentary and analysis back home, and this can't be wholly due to the obvious difficulty of getting reliable overall information. We are told on the News that "the communists" are attacking or being driven out of this or that town. In the direct reports, they become "the Vietcong" or "the North Vietnamese", but never, so far as I have heard, the Cambodian United Front which is also fighting the Cambodian regime. I see news reports, along different channels, giving the United Front control of most of the countryside, and these remind me of the early reports from Vietnam. Of course they may not be true, and the strictly Cambodian resistance to the new regime may be limited, but given the weight and extent of commentary on matters which are not only less important but much easier to check and to understand, I find the absence of any sustained commentary and analysis disturbing. Much of our view of the world, and especially now of Indo-China, comes from United States sources, but even there more is being published and argued about than British television would have us know.

The instance is symptomatic in the field of news and current affairs. And I have the strong feeling that it is not because reporters

---

*Against most predictions the Conservatives under Edward Heath won the June 1970 general election, defeating Harold Wilson's second Labour government. The radical May Day Manifesto movement, in which Williams played a key role, wished to break the Labour-Conservative hegemony over national politics but itself collapsed over the issue of whether or not to run its own candidates in the election. Williams later developed a sharp criticism of representative democracy and electoral politics, arguing for the more radical demands of a system of direct rather than representative democracy.

and directors are failing to find material. There was a useful *Panorama* report on Mexico, nicely timed for the day *after* the World Cup final. Was that tact or a scheduling accident or a case of the rest of the world being crowded out by the election? Some of the football transmissions were marvellous, but isn't there a strong smell just now, and not only in our own country, of bread and circuses?

Meanwhile, at a different level, some things are being done which can help us to understand the world rather than submit to our powerful local rituals. The *Family of Man* series (BBC-2) was well worth attempting. There was an attractive astringency in the mere listing of this series of communities: Andheri (Himalayas), Colne (Lancashire), Melpa (Buk, New Guinea), Hambukushu (Khegudi, Botswana), Esher (Surrey). This was comparative kinship anthropology of a popular kind, and was consistently interesting, in rather personal ways. I would have been glad to have been given more economic and social information, as another way of seeing the family structures. But whereas the Andheri, Melpa and Hambukushu material, taken on its own, might not be much more than a travel film, the comparative element provoked rather different reflections, and especially when Colne and Esher were brought into the same field. One or two things in Colne looked strange, seen in this abstracted way, but the biggest surprise, for me, was the sense of the foreignness of Esher. I've lived only a few months in the North of England, and have always believed, from discussing experiences with friends, that working-class life there was in some important ways different from my own experience of a working-class family on the Welsh border. Yet again and again, in the Colne sequences, I found myself going along with the responses: indeed knowing most of them before they were explained. But then according to standard popular sociology I have, through educational mobility, become middle-class. Yet the category seemed ludicrous as I checked one response after another against the people shown in Esher. Their use of English was the first difficulty: a stab at what used to be called an Oxford accent, which as a matter of fact I haven't heard in Oxford or Cambridge for the last 20 years. But more than that: I found myself watching their hand movements—a frequent upward baring of the palm, from a bent elbow—with something of the curiosity that was understandable in the case of the physical movements of the Melpa pig-exchanges or the Andheri dancing. It's as if there has been hardly any precise social description outside a few specialised groups for some time, and for the middle class this seems particularly true.

More generally, of this important series (which deserves a reshowing, at *Forsyte Saga* time) I would note only a certain occasional but worrying primitivism. The programme on birth was the most obvious example. It was certainly worth comparing our high level of preparation and care with the very different behaviour and attitudes of the women field-workers in the other communities, but I thought the commentary, which had often been neutral, tipped the scale towards an idea of naturalness which would certainly need more argument (the comparative mortality figures, for example, or what looked like the differential aging of the women). There was something of the same problem in the programme on education. Where was John Percival reacting from, Esher or Colne or some idea of the past or the future?

Another way through to the world was the documentary on India: *The Bewildered Giant* (BBC-1). The scenes in Calcutta and in some of the villages and shanty-towns were, I hope, unforgettable. As for the political confusion, so sharply described, the depression came nearer home. The British interlude in the long hisory of India seemed to me very tenderly handled—railways, justice and individual liberty—and this was not the only case in which I wanted to see Dom Moraes, who had written the programme, standing behind his judgments. There was an efficient orthodox narration by Derek Jones: too fast, on the whole, because the script was too long and had so obviously been written as a narration. I felt I wanted the voice of Moraes himself—the man who had gone back to look at the country in which he was born. Much of the meaning, perhaps, in the more difficult experiences, would have been in the sounds of the voice, or in the features. Past the interesting things seen I felt, as an absence, what Yeats called "the only thing that gives literary quality—personality, the breath of men's mouths".

As an immediate comparison, on just this point, I would mention the second showing of *Craghead* (BBC-2). There the voices and faces of the miners, as their pit was closed, said much more than the formal meaning. The pit might have been kept open, they had been told, if they got production up, yet again, and now to 30 hundredweight per man shift. Much of the recent history of England seemed to me to appear in the contrast between their steady voices and faces at the meetings, offering to be responsible but accepting the

definition of responsibility from a cold system, and then the unfocused eyes, the rougher voices, as the message got to their guts and
muscles, or as they stood in the rain listening to Wilson and Castle*
on fuel policy.

2 July 1970

ITV's Domestic Romance

It can only be prejudice that prevents the general reviewing of those
programmes between programmes that are now so important a part
of television. The other night, for example, I watched a 35-minute
programme (ITV) into which, I do not doubt, as much care and
effort and money had been put as into anything else that evening,
and yet, to judge by what the critics said, it might never have been
put out at all. It is true that it was rather intermittent. It ran in short
snatches of anything from 45 seconds to about three-and-a-half minutes, over the period between 5:45 and 10:30 p.m. Nevertheless, it
was an interesting blend of naturalism and fantasy, with some clever
photography and a few good if recurrent tunes. And it was centred,
clearly enough, on domestic issues.

When you think of all the study and research (much of it drawing on the services of professional psychologists and sociologists), of
the script conferences, the negotiations on timing, the search through
the casting agencies, the rehearsals, the editing, it seems a bit hard
that there is no considered reaction at all. Some people say, of
course, that the ads aren't art, though they have probably forgotten
that every group making them has its creative department, which is
even, to prevent misunderstanding, known and referred to as such.
Moreover, there is a good deal of mutual voyaging between programmes and commercials. Some of our best directors, it is said,

---

*Williams had been critical of Harold Wilson when he was a junior politician at the
Board of Trade in 1947. He resigned from the Labour Party in 1966 because Wilson's
government was collaborating in the process of reproducing capitalist society rather
than attempting to create a socialist society. Barbara Castle was First Secretary of State
and Secretary of State for Employment and Productivity in the Wilson government.

make little programmes about products between their bigger programmes about processes, and many popular performers seem as
willing to appear smoking a cigar or eating an ice-cream as doing
anything else—murder or detection—that the current script may
require. The acting skill needed is in any case approximately the
same. Certainly there are plenty of girls who can be guaranteed, after
rehearsal, to manage to look coy *and* sultry in the same lingering
glance. But try casting a housewife who can repeat "biological" as if
it were a faintly improper suggestion which she's naturally a bit wary
of but is by no means certain to refuse. Or the ordinary man, just
home from the office, who's depressed thinking he's going to get
tinned food for supper and a few minutes later is delighted and affec-
tionate when he gets it out of just the right kind of tin. That, brother
(as they say in the trade), is skill.

I want to try then to make amends for this too-long neglect. All
this work, all these people, deserve some critical response. It is true I
shall have some difficulty in recounting the story-line. It isn't that it
wasn't there, but there was this profusion of surface detail: by my
count five beers, a cider, four patent drinks, three wines, a tea, three
patent medicines, three disinfectants, a flykiller, a hairspray, a toothpaste, five deodorants (though three of these were identical in what
seemed the *leitmotif*), bath salts, a bra, high-speed gas, petrol and
oil, a razor and two kinds of blade, two newspapers, a paper towel,
sweets, two dogfoods and a dog medicine, cigars, tobacco, paint,
film, a gardening centre, bread, butter, cheese, a breakfast food, two
ice-creams, three kinds of biscuit, salad-dressing, condensed milk,
potato mash, chicken pie, tomato ketchup, canned ham and fruit and
risotto, two soaps, a washing-powder, and a bottle of washing-up
liquid that one of the guest-stars autographed. Describe, describe, as
Virginia Woolf said, ironically, about the novels of Arnold Bennett.
But then that is where, with this kind of art, we can all very easily go
wrong. Perhaps six or seven of these varied things were what you
could call described. This feature of the art was indeed almost incidental. What was really there was what happened in the novel after
Bennett, when things, objects, became instrumental, active; when it
was the life that flowed through and around them that came to
count. Take the patent drinks. One, it is true, was being mixed to be
drunk. But in the others the flow of feeling was different. A young
man and a girl were running by the sea, in the cool spray, and then,
in one of those characteristically rapid modern associations of idea,

the drink was good, also, for morning sickness. Consider the subtlety of that.

Some people have objected to commercials as the signs of a materialist civilisation. Nothing, on this evidence, could be further from the truth. Most of the objects are charms, talismans. A materialist civilisation would insist on properties and quantities. The world of this art is different. A girl gets off a plane, and throws up her arm for the photographers. Embarrassment. She goes back, gets the product, comes out again, throws up the other arm. Happiness. But meanwhile our hero (I think it was he) is flying his falcon and drinking his cider (of course, in that order). They meet, after she has run through the woods, and they run together by the sea. When the baby comes they give it a magical cheese which, for boys, could lead to a future as an Olympic athlete, for girls Miss World. They do not forget to wipe its face with a paper towel with a pretty pattern, and you sing while you use it. Nor do they forget to keep theirs a safe home, killing all known germs with a variety of disinfectants. Yet the strains and pressures of living mount. Though she sometimes waltzes round the kitchen, in delight at a new powder, she has trouble keeping him at home until she finds a magic can that opens at both ends, and confesses, another night, when she has bought a prepared chicken pie, that it is making a dishonest woman of her. She keeps using deodorants, hairspray, a toothpaste that gets you noticed and another that gives you confidence, but still she gets pain in those tension areas in the magical map of her head. He, meanwhile, does nothing to stay attractive but shave, though with the most craftsmanlike devices; he is usually, in fact, off on the beer or the cigars. He can sometimes be playful, even imitating a dog to get more tinned food, but though when she is out at the shops she refuses all substitutes (even two for one), he remains hard to please, and she is continually worried that she is not attractive enough or doing enough or her home isn't safe enough. Still, through the troubles of life, you can always dream. Buy one brand of ice-cream and bearers carry you through the jungle or into a sheik's tent. Buy another and you don't even leave home; put on sunglasses, a sunhat and a sunlamp—of course not forgetting the ice-cream—and even though it's raining outside you're on holiday. A last whisk with the flykiller and another anxious, happy, magical day is done.

A story of the way we all try to live now. It makes its effect, really, just because it is intermittent. "We'll take the break now," say the ITV news-readers, as if under the weight of the world they need to slip out for a drink. But what the break is really for is this persistent domestic romance: the long suggestive massaging of a skilfully calculated art. What effect does it have? It is impertinent, perhaps, to keep considering effects. Indeed, it comes as a surprise to discover behind this young art—this art of the childhood of the mind and of the childhood of a kind of society—hard and precise calculations about profit and impact. In a new paperback* there's an essay by Peter Masson called "The Effects of Television on Other Media", and the surprise is not only that the central concern is the effect on the advertising media, but that the study is more precise and professional than anything else in the book (things like arts, politics, social behaviour). It seems a long way from that Olympic cheese, but that, perhaps, is how creative art now relates. Behind the scenes, calculation, but in front the pantomime.

30 July 1970

Breaking Out

The *Panorama* programme on poverty, directed by John Gau, was excellent. But it was also, in my experience, very unlike *Panorama*. Often, after the loud music and the fixed stare, I switch off. But the Establishment, it seems, is on vacation, and one of the advantages of this is that a quite different conception of politics can occasionally emerge. Instead of a studio full of the usual figureheads, or the regular reporter making his rounds, we were given the chance of seeing men like Peter Townsend and Ken Coates** talking and presenting evidence from the centre of their working lives. And poverty, as it happens, is a case where the need to get away from orthodox political argument is especially urgent. In more ordinary times we could

---

*James D. Halloran (Ed.). *The Effects of Television* (Panther Books, 1970).

**Peter Townsend is a professor of sociology with a special interest in poverty and social policy. Ken Coates is a social researcher and political activist on the left of the Labour Party. He was expelled from the Party in 1966 but mounted a campaign for his readmission which Williams supported even though by then he himself had decided that it was impossible to work for radical social change within the Labour Party.

have expected the usual battle of percentages between Labour and Tory spokesmen: "In the first three months of our administration we spent 8 per cent more—8 per cent." Or, again in duet, "we are the compassionate party and but for the economic crisis for which your party is responsible we would have done even more, and when we have got things right will do even more, though of course it would be premature to give details now."

These routines are more significant than grouse or Cowes.* They represent the kind of evasion which is now systematic. The point the programme made about poverty is that it is a shifting social definition: not a failure to reach some fixed and abstract standard, but a complex deprivation in terms of the normal lives and expectations of other people around us. What might be called traditional poverty was still evident enough in the streets of St Ann's, Nottingham, which Ken Coates has studied. There were the decrepit houses, the washing in the treeless streets, the children playing in a brick desert, and going to moribund schools which made the idea of equality of opportunity a bad joke. But there were other less familiar and so less visible cases. The deprivation of the unsupported mother, for example, as against the widow, or the wage-stop applied to the father of the large family, or the bare but tidy survival, by great effort and planning, of the tailoring worker on £13 a week. This radical case, about what poverty now means in Britain, was so clearly presented that one became aware of that other kind of deprivation which the party-political consensus enforces. Balance, there, is between authorised spokesmen, representative official figures. What remains unbalanced, by the sheer force of orthodox political thinking, is the selection of issues, of approaches and kinds of evidence.

Roy Minton's *Sling your hook* was repeated as the first of a series of six earlier *Wednesday Plays*. I had not seen it before and I found it consistently interesting. The coachload of Nottingham miners, on a weekend outing to Blackpool, was at first as expected and as described by some selected reviewers: "earthy, human, extremely funny". But the theme was more complex: the disintegration of a community. Only the landlord who had arranged the outing made the journey back to the mining village. The others had all gone their unexpected ways. The tight photographic realism of the earlier

*Cowes is a yachting centre on the Isle of Wright. Annual sailing regattas culminate in Cowes Week, a major social event held in early August.

scenes had given way to the kind of fantasy which was grotesque as much as funny, and in which "bursting with bitter" meant more than the beer. This started when two of the younger miners broke away almost at once, and the tone was exact: "Spider and Hooray have pissed off with the Flower People." "We love everybody," said the pliant little girl on the beach. The union militant whom they called Stalin's Batman (a memory, obviously, from an earlier period) settled down with a nice ex-prostitute to run a bingo hall. He had been "rattling" for years about a different life: now he could at least bring in the customers. Lol, with the old rolling songs, got a contract as a pub singer. Cossack drove off with a comfortable widow to a bungalow in Harrogate. Roland, who had called himself Dylan, married into the haulage business, on a ring guaranteed not to go green in two days. Most of the others got signed up for a football team, by a fat man with three factories who said it would be no trouble at all to absorb them.

This indeed was the fantasy of the break-out. With the bitterness of pits closing behind them, the miners went, in every sense, into a Blackpool world. It began as the tone of *Saturday Night and Sunday Morning*—the rush to beer and fun in a brief interval from work, but with the sense of the next working week still involved in the definition. The Blackpool break-out was different: more like the wistful if boisterous dreaming of old army songs, where the high-born ladies line up to be lived off. The play was full of jokes about actual outings (like the old shoes put out to be cleaned that get thrown in the dustbin), and of this quite different and ambiguous wit in which an underlying idea—a social movement which may never quite visibly happen—was dramatically projected. "They'll be back," the landlord said, on his own in the coach home, settling down to the crates of beer. It was the play's last word and it carried all the bitter humour. These projected figures would not be back, they had really slung their hook. But in the empty seats of the coach, it seemed, the real men were still there. Only the wishes—the understandable wishes—had got clear away.

24 Hours, the next evening, had a second-anniversary programme on the Russian invasion of Czechoslovakia. There a real break-out had been stopped and dragged back. I find the political argument about the Prague Spring very difficult to resolve, but it happened in this programme that one of the slogans —"socialism with a human face"—coincided with the face of Dubcek in an unguarded moment: the mobile intelligent face so saddened that "human", as a description, took on a quite different sense from the political definition, and was of course a whole world away from the commercial use, as in the *Sling your hook* trailer, to mean easy-going or boisterously fallible. Now, looking back, this face is still what I most clearly remember.

27 August 1970

Between Us and Chaos

I got back from prison in time for the television police. While we were being introduced to the new Alsatian, and given a few brisk sketches of who was boss around here, I found myself settling reluctantly to what is now the domestic police routine. At the admittedly limited level of casual recognition, the police in *Softly, Softly* are indeed much like the police I normally meet: sensible, restrained, rather resigned; a kind of organised and very conventional common sense. TV scriptwriters, in series like *Softly, Softly* and *The Troubleshooters* and *Special Branch,* seem extraordinarily pre-occupied by questions of authority: who exactly takes the decisions and gives the orders. Since the world they know best is presumably that of the television authorities, it is tempting to suppose that we are getting a series of objective correlatives of Television Centre. But I doubt that. Modern management, which is now the characteristic form of authority, seems to me rather different, in tone and style, from these snapping egos taking responsibility, taking over, glaring and rasping at each other. I haven't experienced any institution, including the army, which could survive the cold snubbings and chronically overt power declarations which our televised institutions seem to thrive on. Of course I may have been lucky. But I think it is probably a case of inexperienced and rather isolated men having fantasies of how they would run things, and decorating them with what I expect they would call themes of dramatic conflict: the journalist's eyeballs-to-eyeballs. More experience of a kind seems to go into the British police series than into their American counterparts, but as far as I can see it is the British series which most regularly act out the crisis of authority and command. Ironside, for example, is a sugar daddy compared with the growling, insecure, status-conscious lot at Thamesford.

Still, one main trick has been turned. In *Softly, Softly* the police have been domesticated: your friendly local Coronation Street force. And most of us, I suppose, have enough good will to go along with it, in a relaxed, relatively inattentive way. But then suddenly, near the beginning of the episode, there was an almost throwaway line: some slob of a student had got away with a fine of three pounds for hitting a policeman. I confess that while this was being said I was still mainly remembering the prison, where I had been visiting a student who had got nine months for doing what still seems to me much less than that. It wasn't necessary to the story, which moved on, sensationally enough, to a psychopathic escaped convict about to blow up a chemical factory. But that is how it all happens. In cases like that, which occur from time to time, and in thousands of other everyday cases, it is easy to feel this kind of sympathy with the police; even to see the world from their point of view. Outside political demonstrations, I have invariably found the British police as good as they are said to be, and I have had several easy and pleasant acquaintances with them. Even on most demonstrations, they are quite evidently different from the riot police and stormtroopers we see in action elsewhere. I stood on tiptoe at Twickenham last December wondering just what would happen when the pressure of the crowd behind threw me, as seemed inevitable, straight at a police line. I guessed it would depend on the luck of the draw: whether I got the one in fifteen or so that I have noticed at ordinary demonstrations as quick to be aggressive. Again, I have probably been lucky. Some very bad things have happened to people I know and trust, and in any case I am white, Celtic, agnostic, and in professional employment—quite apart from being as old as most superintendents. It is very far from easy to take any single, settled attitude, because we have an all-purpose police force, operating in vastly different communities. "Law and order", I find, is as crude a slogan, on most lips, as "the fuzz" or "the pigs".

It was to this complex of difficulties that the *Tuesday Documentary*, "The Jolly Copper" (BBC-1), tried to address itself. It had an honestly inquiring tone, and worked hard at being various and specific. But there was an undertone of something different—something hysterical, one might even say. "Between us and chaos" stands this police force. The phrase stuck in my mind. The versions of people that seem to have soaked into orthodox sensibility, even liberal sensibility, are still very surprising. All right, we see, too often, that thin blue line spread out over fields looking for a missing child or the victim of some psychopath. At the other end of the scale we see traffic control and similarly obvious and useful regulation. But "between us and *chaos?*" What do our scriptwriters and commentators really think people are like? Are they judging from themselves, or from ordinary experience? One of the most interesting scenes in the film was the reception of a train at a seaside resort: all the skinheads were turned out, searched and warned. But then a group name like "skinheads" is often the way to chaos. What some boys dressed like that have done, what some of them carry, is dangerous to any society. But then the whole group was in effect guilty, on arrival. One young man was protesting that he'd had a button ripped off, and in the pushing and shoving one saw the thing happening:

> You get along, sir, and behave yourself.
> I've had a button torn off me. I haven't done anything.
> Now you go along and be quiet.
> I tell you I've had this button torn off me.
> You get in the car and come along to the station.

I know nothing more than that, and the words are approximate. But if we're talking of chaos, this also was it. The pressure building up now to avoid certain conspicuous styles of dress, certain kinds of conspicuous protest, is not law and order, in any generally acceptable sense. Words like "peril" are being glibly inserted by judges, who ought to know better. The difficult borderline between law and repression is more in question, it seems to me, than I can ever remember. In the training sessions at the police school, and then on a demonstration at which the police were being ritually insulted before anything (at least that day) had happened, we saw most of the practical difficulties. Television won't solve them, but does the BBC—in its fiction rather more than in its documentaries—have to put itself so simplemindedly on one side of the argument: not even as bias, or commitment, but as naturally, as casually, as, say, it supports King Hussein?

Perhaps it's better to laugh at a lot of it. That thin blue line, at the end of "The Jolly Copper", coming up out of the grass to be looked at by those really coarse faces on the reviewing stand, had all too clear a link to the ministry of Silly Walks sketch which followed, almost immediately, in the new series of *Monty Python's Flying Circus*. Swinging your arms that high, some inches higher than the Guards, would wear anybody out: even John Cleese, wildly extending his legs before authorising an Anglo-French research and development project on a new silly walk.

ITV's *Special Branch* is getting so lovable that I'd willingly settle for Chief Inspector Jordan to keep my file and listen in on my phone, in between his affairs with the girl captain in the KGB. They did the CIA down, jointly, last week, so you never know. It's curious that this light fashion-conscious knockabout has survived into the era after Deighton and Le Carré and the very interesting (because sceptical) *Callan*. Only its crises of command, more lightly handled, link it to the new police quasi-realism. But then the same nagging thought comes back: this lightly domesticated Special Branch, and meanwhile the actual Special Branch and the rest of that underworld: two million files on us, didn't somebody say? Anyway, coming back from the prison, I didn't feel much like laughing.

24 September 1970

The Decadence Game

The young man with the cross bore down on the camera. "Satan, get ye behind me and be gone from this place for ever." It wasn't one of the ritual damnings of television. It was a *24 Hours* piece, inquisitive rather than inquiring, about some desecrations in Highgate Cemetery. I suppose the piece wasn't typical but it certainly had the half-hearted, middle-minded air which now fails to distinguish such programmes. This particular image, though, remained in the mind. It shows some technical sophistication that the camera could thus be willed to be absent: a convention that in many circumstances is necessary but in this case only succeeded in telling the viewer to go round the back. I wondered about the co-operation of the exorciser. People are usually co-operative enough, all their amateur acting instincts rising, when they are asked to play this particular game. Indeed it is the break of convention that now attracts notice. An exceptionally pointless discussion between the television critic of the *Financial Times* and the editor of *Review* (BBC-2) was made momen-

tarily interesting when the man from the *Financial Times* said there
were about nineteen people in the room, filming the thing, and that
this made a difference. Not so much a medium, I suppose, as an
exorciser. Taking the spirit out of it all.

Television, I would have said, was too new a medium, had so
many obviously important things just waiting to be done, to be
showing those first signs of decadence which consist of a turning
back on its own conventions. It is to be expected that such decadence
elsewhere will be observed and reported, but it need not be com-
pounded. Having Norman Mailer speak straight to camera about
Norman Mailer making a film about a man played by Norman
Mailer making pornographic films and running for President of the
United States is probably more than a game of public relations. In
some frankly commercial show like *The Frost Programme* it is to be
expected that Norman Mailer, visiting in the first half to talk about
making a film about a man making a film etc., will be called on to
give the last word in a discussion about British trade unions. That, as
they say, is business. It is much more serious when what is offered as
an arts programme gives currency to absurd confusions between a
spectator and a voyeur: a critical decadence rationalised by the
scraps of theory which are floating about in that half-hearted,
middle-minded world from which television now so notably recruits.
There is a moment in many cultures, and in many art-forms, when
the concept of the mirror suddenly becomes exciting, and a wave of
confusion and excitement suddenly breaks. Most people, within its
area of influence, start thinking of watching themselves in mirrors
watching others watching others—a keyhole art which till then has
stayed in its place on the pier.

I turned over to Michael Parkinson's *Cinema* (Granada) too late
to see what I wanted: a trailer of *The Reivers*. The mirror game was
in full swing: a television programme watching a film in which the
guests at a party were watching, on internal television, a couple who
had gone off to the nursery and who unless I was mistaken were
putting on a show for *somebody*, posing as each garment came off.
When a sense of identity and of reality breaks down that far, it is
necessary for somebody to do some thinking, but running "spectator" and "voyeur" together doesn't help. The intellectual wreckage
of the post-Freud, post-McLuhan era is serious enough in its own
terms, and will take long enough to clear up, without anybody making half-art about half-art about it. I get the strong sense, also, that it

is a hypocritical world: that it includes people who would, say, sympathise or even identify with a serious writer like Solzhenitsyn, because political accident has floated him their way. I think about that case too, but the most pressing problem I can see, in the matter of art and society, is understanding what is happening in our own culture, after the failures of the Sixties: not decadence—that is more complicated—but the decadence game, the respectable and money-making decadence game; half-hearted, middle-minded, too bleached even to believe in itself.

What then do we seem to believe in? There was an interesting ambiguity in a *Chronicle* programme, *Marx was here* (BBC-2). The title makes some of the point: the edge of the game, after Kilroy. And Alfred Marks as the voice of Karl Marx: did somebody think that would be funny? Much of the narrative was a loose kind of gossip, with a few bitsy images. No respect, no real sense of the work, but then one hardly expected that much. Except that suddenly, in two notable cases, there was a very different and apparently radical vision. As it happened, I had just been writing an article about the Hyde Park affair of July 1866, when the government illegally closed the gates on a meeting to campaign for the right to vote, and a number of people very properly proceeded to take down the railings. This was the central "anarchy" of Matthew Arnold's *Culture and Anarchy,* which I had noticed being quoted so often in our own late Sixties. I argued that to understand the response we would have to translate Hyde Park, now the site of "immemorial" democratic freedoms, as (though it is not really the same) Grosvenor Square. I had thought this might be a difficult argument for some people to accept, but then in the middle of this reductive and rather patronising programme about Marx the Hyde Park affair was narrated with accompanying newsreel film of Grosvenor Square, and Marx's response to the Commune was described with pictures of the May 1968 events in Paris. In a radical programme I could have understood it, but in this one, with its chat about boils and a possible bastard, it seemed odd.

Can we say, perhaps, that at a certain level, given the right kind of rather distant figure, anything and everything is believed simultaneously, up to the point where it produces an effect? This is a state of mind sometimes known as professionalism. Actually I would be very much happier to think that it was the product of some real tension, inside the programme: different people having different ideas. But I could find no external evidence to support it.

In the middle of all this, two modest short programmes. *Look*

Stranger went to Nuneham, in Oxfordshire, where in the 18th century a village was pulled down to improve the view from a new house: what some people call one of the stately homes. Arnold (to get the balance right) used to think of these houses as "the great fortified posts of the Barbarians", and since I have known anything about those 18th-century placemen and agrarian capitalists I have found the description accurate. It was good to see that the house is now a teachers' training college, but watching the children from the displaced village being taken on an educational visit to the monuments of the family that did the displacing stirred rather different feelings. The question was raised whether this was the source of Goldsmith's *Deserted Village*. It is one of the possibilities, in the quite regular practice of engrossing:

> the man of wealth and pride
> Takes up a space that many poor supplied.

But there are others. What Goldsmith described, in his neglected poem, was a social process and not an isolated incident, and from internal evidence his scene is various:

> Along thy glades, a solitary guest,
> The hollow sounding bittern guards its nest.

Before clearance and draining the bittern may have been more widespread, of course. Now, in *Survival* (Anglia), we saw it getting by accident as far as the parkland of Stansted, where it was at last filmed booming. Hollow-sounding, perhaps. It was in close-up a curious eructation, with what looked like vomiting movements to match. A strange sound to accompany Goldsmith's hope

> That trade's proud empire hastes to swift decay.

But at Nuneham or at other places, one could still take his point.

22 October 1970

A Very Late Stage in Bourgeois Art

It has been a strange experience watching *The Roads to Freedom* (BBC-2), which in its sixth part reached *The Age of Reason*. There is a very difficult problem of convention in any relation between text and performance. Take any novel written in the first person singular.

It is often difficult to decide whether to say that the novel or the character is self-centred. The very act of performing such a work creates a certain inevitable objectivity. We see the character from outside as well as listening to him. More important, we see for ourselves (or so we think) the other persons he meets and can compare his reactions with our own. The film of *Room at the Top* can be said to be better than the novel on which it was based because this element of objectivity allowed and even compelled us to face certain problems about the central character which the subjective form of the novel had seemed to evade. The fiction of special pleading—the self-explaining, self-justifying voice which is the only real voice in the narrative—is often very powerful but on certain major issues requires, and in performance gets, this other dimension. And it is then difficult to say that *The Age of Reason* is not self-centred. Mathieu's self-consciousness actually organises the novel, and that he is in the ordinary sense self-centred isn't likely to be doubted.

It is important that this is not so much an ethically distinguishing characteristic as a representative condition. Many of the other characters are similarly self-centred. What can be called their relationships—Mathieu, Daniel, Boris, Ivich, Lola, Jacques—are like the collision of billiard balls, causing movement this way and that but without any effect beyond the surface. What we cannot see, though we are invited to infer it, is the player of the game—the larger social history of which they are part. And it then won't do to find the characters flat or boring, the general atmosphere casual and listless. It is easy to see why people want to make these comments, and they are not to be dismissed—as in mid-Atlantic criticism is now increasingly fashionable—as "moralism". The real problem is one of convention. The moral statement is in the demonstration of a condition. Some people reacted to Bergman's *The Lie* (BBC-1) as if a play were a kind of "at home", after which, under the excuse of criticism, they could make what remarks occurred to them about the furniture, the conversation, and the moral status of their hosts. And it is of course entertaining to see intellectuals using long words to express what in short words would be recognised as the naive reaction of liking (or not liking) a play because one liked (or didn't like) the people in it. ("Never could stand that Hamlet. Now Laertes—*there* was a decent young man.") But the neutral bleakness of *The Lie* or of *The Age of Reason* raises a problem nevertheless. Sartre's theory in the novel was a rejection of reflection: in immediate terms by the characters or generally by the author. Moral reflection by the characters, and then by the author, was held to be false. What was needed was literal reflection: the flat view in the mirror. I don't think it worked there. The novelist's organisation of material gave an inevitable perspective. And it could then be said that the perspective was inadequate; not enough was shown; the gestures to history were no more than suggestive.

Watching the television version, I at first saw no reason to dissent from this. Of course, something different was happening. The song at the beginning and end of each episode gave us an explicit moral and historical signpost. The characters' responses—written to be flat—were acted with some intensity, jerking them into an unintended emphasis. Yet what they were and did remained flat; the adaptation, in general, did not falsify that feeling and condition. But I began to feel that the very act of performance, of presentation, was achieving an objectivity that was much closer to Sartre's original theory than the novel itself had been. We were being allowed, and indeed compelled, to see more for ourselves. The maker and organiser was more truly absent.

Take a simple piece from the novel:

> "It's funny," he said, "when I now think of Lola I see her as a nice old thing."
>
> Ivich laughed shortly and Boris was shocked: he added, in an attempt to be fair: "She can't be feeling very cheerful just now."
>
> "That's quite certain."
>
> "I don't want her to suffer," he said.
>
> "Then you'd better go and see her," said Ivich in a sing-song voice.

The author is undeniably there, whatever his original intention or subsequent rationalisation. "He said", "he added", "in an attempt to be fair", "Boris was shocked" or "said Ivich in a sing-song voice"— the direction leads us back to the author's strings. In performance it was different. The things were said and done, flatly, and we saw the whole grouping, the negative relationship, coldly laid out. Strangely (but it happened also in *The Lie*), something like neutrality was achieved, but a neutrality which permitted real analysis. The characters' own explanations of what they were doing hung in the air as gestures and attempts; nobody would take them as definitions. We looked at the screen as at something better than a mirror—something that didn't reflect but simply showed.

Many questions still remain. Neutrality is willed, and like all non-intervention is, of course, a moral position. It is a fact about a culture when a particular convention, in fiction or drama, embodies this sort of reduction: seeing others from some low, and indifferent point in one's self. Bergman and Sartre are representatives of a very late stage in bourgeois art: a stage very far past its creative confidence, but also past pretending that any confidence of a received kind is possible. Most television drama now is, like the rest of the medium's content, deliberately forthcoming, usually with derived and stereotyped offers. Some of the best work is reaching, within obvious limits, for new and active responses. But the received high art, of the modern era, is of this other cold, neutral kind. I have reacted against it, so strongly, over a generation, that I was surprised to find myself thinking that the Sartre work, now, had become fixed and past, but also that one could see it more clearly. I felt there was no need to fight it, any more than one need fight Wycherley.* It is no road to freedom, in any but a negative sense. There's a different, historical feeling: that is done and over, and is there to be looked at. It stands very like a monument of, and to, the end of an era: distant, solid, cold.

12 November 1970

Galton and Simpson's "Steptoe and Son"

There have been one or two surprises in the new series of *Steptoe and Son* (BBC-1). There was a by-election in which, unsurprisingly, Harold worked for Labour and Albert for the Tories. There were the usual anguished arguments and manoeuvres. But then, for once, Harold won. He succeeded in wrecking his father's reception of the Tory top brass: a bucket of whitewash set in the lavatory for Heath found almost as acceptable a target in a double-barrelled man from Central Office. Or again: they were trying to move house, into middle suburbia. The prospective neighbours raised £500 to buy them off, and Albert beat them up to £750, against protests by Harold that he was selling his class. Yet they then worked together for once, with real enjoyment, on a prospective move into upper suburbia, in the expectation of an even higher bribe to keep away.

*William Wycherley. English dramatist (1640-1716). Admired during his life as a satirist.

I haven't, over the years, seen all the episodes, but these two seemed unusual for another reason: there was more or less direct contact with the world outside Oil Drum Lane. Ordinarily, that world is merely reflected, by example and allusion, in the enclosed and bitter conflict within that extraordinary living-room. I wonder if it is an accident that the patterns are different when the outside world becomes, however briefly, actual.

For there is evidently a problem in the comedy of *Steptoe and Son*. I have often asked myself, watching its bitterness and frustration, what exactly is funny about it. In a way it depends on a very old pattern, in the drama of the last 100 years. This is the pattern of men trapped in rooms, working out a general experience of being cheated and frustrated on the most immediately available target: the others inside the cage. What began as tragedy, in Ibsen and Strindberg, was already ambivalent in Chekhov, and in our own period, in Ionesco and then in Osborne and Pinter, is a kind of comedy: at once absurd and sinister, a kind of desperately comic raging. Is it simply a case, then, of something beginning in tragedy and ending in farce? It's very difficult to say. The convention of serial characters but self-contained episodes, now so common in television, prevents any full working-through. The form allows endless evasion and opportunism: hints and temporary effects. Some of these are successful just because the pattern is deeply known, and we can read into the episodes more than is really there. But then the pattern that is known is not mainly or directly the dramatic tradition: it is the experience underlying it—the continuing experience of a trapped and frustrating society.

An ordinary tension between father and son can acquire, in this pattern, a clear social resonance. And obviously, at the surface of the Steptoe sketches, this is directly contrived. Albert is seen as an old social world: the war, discipline and deference, and inside this a rooted habit of cheating, conniving and covering up. Harold's aspirations are confused by the opportunism of the form. If memory serves me, he has been socialist and orthodox Labour, frustrated connoisseur and frustrated petit-bourgeois, book-reader and supplement-reader. In the looseness of the form, what he wants can vary from real aspiration to illusion. This uncertainty, I think, is part of the self-protecting trick that keeps the series viable at about its existing level. But what is interesting is that any and every kind of aspiration is frustrated and defeated, by the cut-down worldliness of the father.

Inside the laughs, the recurrent defeat. I don't find it pathetic. It often makes me angry. It belongs, I think, to what we can now see shaping as a period, from the late Forties to the early Sixties: a period dominated and symbolised by Orwell's conviction that it is all a swindle, good and bad alike: a despair that was wrought into viable commercial forms, superficially tough-minded and demotic. When I now read late Orwell or Braine or Amis or Pinter or Osborne,* I have the sense of a past, and the Steptoes, essentially, belong to it. But I don't underestimate the general experience that made many people believe this was new and important work. Indeed the external evidence for just such feelings is perhaps stronger now than when the pattern was first formed.

But it's never primarily a question of external evidence. It's the feelings we bring to the evidence that count. I was reminded of this in the by-election episode, when Albert and Harold sat facing each other across the living-room table, each using a typewriter to address election envelopes. It was like a pair of scriptwriters, with actors standing in. I can't imagine anyone in his senses using a typewriter to address those prepared envelopes, and as so often there was no real question of verisimilitude. Harold was tricked into delivering Albert's pile, but in Parliamentary elections they go through the post. It isn't the detail, it's the trick that matters.

The whole fascination of the series has been this kind of error: more precisely, an anachronism. The contemporary scrap men, with their vans and lorries, are a full generation beyond the Steptoes, and yet the anachronism is not some failure of observation. As so often with the work generated in that period, childhood memories of an earlier period are drawn upon. But it is more than that. A crazy style is demanded—to keep the feeling at a certain pitch, and of course to protect it. The living-room with its skeleton and other assorted junk is not so much a room or a remembered room as a studio in which props are arranged to create an impression, as in the rooms shown in advertising photographs. Albert's mittens and grimaces, his calculated vulgarities, are not the impersonation of any old man but a style to screw the nerves to screaming pitch, and the easiest form of a

*Williams's unconventional assessment of the "Angry Young Men" of the 1950s, including John Braine, Kingsley Amis, Harold Pinter and John Osborne, is that they represent a continuation of the mood of entrapment that characterizes George Orwell's writing and not a genuine breakthrough appropriate to the late 1950s and 1960s.

scream is a laugh. Somebody has said that this was old working-class habits being exorcised by comic exaggeration. Somebody said the same about Alf Garnett. That sense of distance is the source, I don't doubt, of many of the laughs. It is crucially different from the Muir and Norden Glums, who were the old *Punch* working class, seen from above. But it's then necessary to add that there isn't any exorcism, any more than there was with Garnett. The ranting and the wheedling, the old ideas and the old cheating, win. The projected horror acquires sympathy or authority. Harold's disgust is understandable, but it's only an aspect of his despair.

When Albert sends Harold to a dancing competition having taught him only the woman's steps, it is inevitably funny—the way he and his partner, at the signal to start, move stylishly away from each other to opposite ends of the floor—but it is also the kind of emasculation, behind a sentimental screen, which is a real and painful English history. Laughing at those old codgers is part of a familiar popular deception though it's also a necessary stage. But to laugh at the frustrated illusions of the son is something else again: a submission that isn't made acceptable by some tone of universal recognition or complicity.

It remains a fact that the insinuating power of the writing, and the more evident power of the acting, have led to an extraordinary success: not just by head-counts but by the degree of emotional reaction. When Harold and Albert turned together against suburbia, it was like a victory, but I don't suppose it will last. The thing to set it against, just now, is *Please Sir!* (London Weekend), which is a full generation on. The movement of feeling between Hedges and his pupils in 5C is in a mobile as opposed to a static world, and the caretaker, Potter, the latest in a series of sketches of the old order, is in a new and welcome way on the defensive. When he was stripping wallpaper to an army rhythm—sponge, two-three, strip, two-three—in the wrong flat, while the others worked happily and easily next door, there was a sense that the old cheating and regimented orthodox deformity was at a healthier distance than in the wheedling and broken-down Steptoe, and that the young had enough confidence to run rings round him instead of staying and arguing and raging and almost crying. I hope so anyway, for this ought to be where we are. It would in any case be a new and welcome kind of comedy: the laugh on the run rather than the rueful laugh in the trap.

17 December 1970

Being Serious

It is always useful to propose a definition of what is serious, and in television now this is especially necessary. So we can be grateful to Paul Fox (*Listener*, 7 January) for quoting and discussing the official BBC definition: a programme "whose primary intention is informational, educational or critical". I would like to examine this further, with reference to last week's programmes.

But perhaps I ought first to say that I do not seem to belong to any of the three groups who, according to Fox, write about television. I am not in his first group: those who do it full-time. I would be in his second group, since I have two other full-time jobs, except that I am not, in the essential part of his definition, a television executive *manqué*, though I don't know how I can prove this except by saying that I would regard that sort of job as about equivalent to a prison sentence. And then I am not in his third group either, of those inside television: I have written two television plays and a feature programme, and taken part in more discussions than I can remember, but always occasionally. I suppose I can only hope, as a way of hanging on to existence, that these definitions are less reliable than the definitions of seriousness.

What is wrong with the official formula is obvious enough. It is the same old utilitarian proposition which was imposed on public libraries, in the distinction of seriousness between fiction and non-fiction. When I was not in a university, and had to borrow most of my books through the post, I felt the weight of this quite practically, since I had to pay the postage on a novel but had it paid on anything, serious or not, which had that "non-fiction" guarantee. I used to wonder about being subsidised on *How to Build a Garden Pool* and not on *Anna Karenina,* and I find myself wondering now about statistics going through to all sorts of committees, based on the proposition that, say, *About Anglia* is serious and *The Roads to Freedom* is not. So I can agree with Fox up to a point, in his inclusion of drama, though the form of his new definition is hopeless: a programme "whose primary intention is informational, educational or critical, whether it be in narrative or dramatic form". A utilitarian bias, supported by old academic inertia, produces that limiting version again and again, and people who want to justify a policy take it up in the same spirit as a phrase like "prestige production". There can surely be no priority, for example, in "critical" as against "creative". "Education" usually means what it says, but "information" is a very doubtful category, not only because it can be very important or very unimportant, but also because it normally includes angled presentations which are serious only in the sense that they need to be seriously watched. I am sure we have to get away from the paternalist idea that instruction, of one sort or another, backed by what is called informed discussion, is the only really serious broadcasting. But what we also have to get away from is the idea that we can judge the seriousness of a programme by its *intention*.

I can see some use in statistics by category: not that they throw very much light at the time, but over a period they can be significant. I went through last week's programmes on the official formula and on the Fox formula. I took 6 p.m. to 11 p.m. as more reasonable hours. On the official formula the result, in percentages, was BBC-2—48, BBC-1—35, ITV—28. About what you'd expect, though BBC-2 was perhaps higher than usual because of John Napier's six marvellous Christmas lectures for children. Then on the Fox formula: BBC-2—55, BBC-1—43, ITV—30. Again about what you'd expect, and the point is not only the difference between BBC-1 and ITV: it is the marked difference between the two BBC channels, by any definition of seriousness you like to take.

I then applied a quite different method. I took the programmes that seemed to me serious in another sense: that looked as if someone had successfully meant something in making them, rather than simply slotted them into a market, though I didn't exclude established programmes (like *Match of the Day*) which, however familiar, represent a serious use of television. My judgments are my own, of course, but I tried not to exclude things I had little personal taste for, where it seemed clear that in its own terms the programme was serious. The results, for what they are worth, were: BBC-2—60, BBC-1—29, ITV— 22. Nobody need be surprised that these are much more like my own normal estimate of the quality of the three channels than the other figures. But then I wasn't judging by abstract category or by intention. Of those I included, on BBC-1, *Monty Python, Match of the Day* and, for once, *Panorama* went in above the line; so too did *Z Cars*, now normally better, because less personality-ridden, than *Softly, Softly*. Just on the line, but still in, was the *Omnibus* programme on Eliot, where the only serious bit was the fine performance of part of "Sweeney Agonistes", with music by John Dankworth, while the rest had the resources of television—the photographs and filmed reminiscences—but was based on an idea of the relation between the life and the poetry which seemed to me naive and tendentious, which one certainly wouldn't accept from a first-year undergraduate and which is perhaps made not better but worse when built into a powerful television production. On BBC-2, above the line, *Chronicle,* with a fine programme on Viking ocean ships; *Europa,* with a superb Polish film on Siberia; *Disco 2; The Roads to Freedom; Laugh-In,* not as good as it was; *The Money Programme,* excellent on the press and dreadful trailing round the rich of the Bahamas; a Japanese film on New Guinea, in *World About Us,* which in its closely observed funeral ritual could hardly be casually watched; useful short programmes like *Look Stranger.*

One final thing that struck me was how few officially "serious" programmes seemed anything of the kind: *Nationwide* and so on. And neither *Play of the Month* nor *Play for Today* could be taken very seriously. A suitably confected *Hassan* can be put down as experience.

14 January 1971

Billy and Darkly

It is always interesting to see how younger dramatists work in and through the conventions of their predecessors. Two interesting television plays gave some evidence of this: *Billy's Last Stand* by Barry Hines (BBC-1) and *The Bequest* by Carey Harrison (BBC-2).

Billy's Last Stand was familiar, structurally; a duologue centred on the arrival of a sinister stranger. Billy has been scraping a living by shovelling coal from its delivery point on the pavement to people's coal-houses. Darkly arrives, watches him and persuades him of the need for organisation: Darkly will get orders and set up a regular rota; Billy will hump more coal and earn more money. This goes along until Billy's back gives out under the increased work load. And then there is competition—from a younger man, Briggs. Darkly persuades Billy to join in an attack on Briggs, after threatening to leave and organise him instead. Back in Billy's hut, Darkly insults his shame and his pride. He throws Billy's souvenirs around, smashing the place, and for a long time Billy does nothing. Then at last he picks up one of his lumps of coal and kills Darkly.

About ten years ago the arrival of a sinister stranger, and the passage of violence, had acquired what was in effect a metaphysical status, only thinly disguised by an extreme and studied colloquialism. What interested me was to see Hines taking this form and restoring its human substance. The lively and convincing common talk was not a theatrical cover, but the slow creation of a world of work and precarious survival. And the stranger came, not from an undefined area of threat, but from a real social condition. Everybody else had been organised, Darkly explained; Billy was one of the few casuals left. But for Billy this was work, as opposed to employment. An old miner, he had chosen this way of running his own life, taking his own time, relying on the fact that people knew and trusted him. What Darkly was taking away was the freedom and self-respect of that kind of work, and he was doing it in the name of the modern idols: increased productivity and a rising standard of living.

Barry Hines didn't have to force any superstructural meanings. He had created a situation in which all the necessary meanings were direct. And it is a mark of his fundamental quality as a dramatist that, having dropped the theatrical cover, he was able very quickly to let the substance of the experience come through. There was at once immediacy and resonance: the facts of labour and of human identity, the destructive intrusion of a familiar alienation.

The Bequest also began from a familiar contemporary convention. Again a duologue, this time of father and son, it was centred on what used to be called non-communication. This also, some ten years ago, had acquired metaphysical status. Everyone knows, from experience, how difficult speech and understanding can be, under ordinary tensions and pressures. But this was built into a convention, in which people began from the abstraction and then proceeded to talk about it: an unanalysed rhetorical fact which was meant to set limits to human understanding, but in terms of recognisable immediate experience. The final gesture to the incommunicable was a conventional gesture to the irrational.

Carey Harrison worked inside this convention. The opening scene, in which the father appears to be talking to his son but is only desperately rehearsing, was of that kind. But when the son came, the difficulties of speech and understanding acquired a flow of a particular and comprehensible reality: the limits of *this* communication, between *these* people. Moreover, as the talk continued, there was a real clarification through all the indirections and hesitancies. The actual experience began to come through, and in terms of a questioning of the theatrical convention itself. What was wrong, between father and son, was the mutual prediction of roles. Slowly, past this, they began seeing each other as men, not for any easy solution but at least in real recognition. Human speech, as so often, broke beyond the dogma of the incommunicable and the determined.

By contrast, the first episode of the adaptation of *Jude the Obscure* (BBC-2) was an unexpected disappointment. I was delighted that it was being done, and the problem of dramatisation didn't seem especially difficult, but what happened was a curious reduction to staged scenes, and an apparently deliberate avoidance of some of the most dramatic moments. So much that is important in the early consciousness of Jude is necessarily internal: an aspiration that is as intense as it is confused. A different convention, of voice-over reflection, could easily have been used, but the chosen method was the invention and connection of expository scenes, with Jude's consciousness minimised and his aunt's commentary exaggerated. Some part of this seemed to be due to a received interpretation of Hardy which few serious readers now accept: an isolation and overemphasis of inherent fate. For how, otherwise, could an adapter avoid such essential moments as Jude alone in the ugly wide field, bird-scaring, or the journeys to see Christminster in the distance—the mirage, the smoke, the city throwing light into the sky—in which the real tragedy—the modern tragedy—is being prepared?

Yet there was also misdirection of another kind. On the wedding night with Arabella there was the by now obligatory strip, just as there had earlier been the obligatory roll in the field. A friend of mine visiting the studio during production was told he could not go in yet: there was a naked actress in there. But this apparent (though protected) openness was an evasion of something more difficult, emotionally and physically, to the conventional mind. In the novel, when Arabella gives herself to Jude, she takes a cochi egg from her breast, where she is hatching it, and says it is natural for a woman to want to bring live things into the world. It is an extraordinary moment, of the kind Lawrence learned to share with Hardy, and I think it is significant that in its real intimacy and physicality it was avoided, in favour of the invention of the nude pose.

Whenever an adaptation is criticised, one is asked to remember the difficulties of compression, but this adapter took plenty of room for his own scenes, such as the quite unnecessary and misleading invention of Sue meeting Phillotson in the Christminster shop. Quite apart from its superfluity, this got the film to a conventionally spired

Oxford well ahead of Jude's arrival: a timing that is directly contrary to the movement of the novel, in which he arrives at sunset and explores his vision and the reality in darkness and shadow, and alone. We shall have to see what is done in the remaining episodes, but on the evidence so far this is the worst kind of adaptation, in that it is organised to replace the novel.

11 February 1971

Programmes and Sequences

It is difficult to choose between two kinds of writing about television. It is possible to isolate particular programmes and try to analyse them. This is not necessarily what some people call reviewing: looking at details of performance and direction. For these can never be isolated from the essential character of the work, which is not an object to be judged by its transmission, but a particular structure carrying meanings and values. Yet, in quite another direction, one of the most obvious elements of television is its quality as sequence. We can switch on and off for particular programmes but in some ways the programmes are conceived as a whole and they're often received as a continuity. I have come to feel lately that the kind of analysis we most need is of this general flow: of the organisation, the methods and the values within and through which particular programmes occur.

But these, for many reasons, can be very difficult to see: above all, because we aren't used to them. For example, last Friday on BBC-2 I watched a series of programmes from about eight until past 11. At various times that evening there were four solo pieces for which we don't quite have a name: Peter Cook in a parody of Rod McKuen and his dog, Alan Bennett in a fairly conclusive parody of Kenneth Clark's reminiscences of Bernard Berenson,* William Rushton announcing a brave mock-expedition to get away from a British mood which he described with great accuracy, Bernard Braden performing Mark Twain on Fenimore Cooper. In between these pieces, there were three short films of India, Georgia Brown singing Brecht, the News and an episode of *Jude the Obscure*.

---

*Bernard Berenson. U.S. art critic especially of Italian Renaissance art.

The internal effects of this sequence were remarkable. Cook and Bennett were parodying very recent television programmes which were still clear in the memory, Braden's cue was the current adaptation of *The Last of the Mohicans*. Rushton's mock-expedition followed an announcement of the BBC/*Sunday Times* expedition to Everest and was itself followed by an interview with one of the members of the expedition, who by this time I could hardly listen to because of the prolonged sense of double-take. After Georgia Brown singing the Brecht-Eisler parody of a sentimental ballad, there was a low-keyed discussion of how to prevent expensive paintings leaving Britain while remaining expensive. Capitalist art-dealing was taken for granted and then its marginal consequences worried about. Alan Bennett showed us the conversion of art objects for use in the "Civilisation" game. Next, as a commercial break, the link man showed clips from the week ahead, incidentally playing what was meant to be a sophisticated game with Percy Thrower's gardening programme. Then, following Cook as McKuen, there were two apparent discussions with an American woman on her scheme of physical exercises and with three oddly assorted people on (somewhere, vaguely) Women's Liberation—in which Cook managed to reduce the television interview to the kind of impromptu and sceptical inconsequence on which his own normal performance depends. Then Part Four of *Jude the Obscure* and the edited bits of the News.

What, then, ought really to be said? That this was an ephemeral structure almost instantly parodying itself: a kind of frantic consumption of shadows and responses? But it was not the frequency of parody that was wrong. It was that most of the things being parodied seemed even more insubstantial and artificial than the parodies themselves. Or could one say that the only solid thing there was the attempt on *Jude the Obscure*? But this was television *using* a major English novel with what seemed a quite structural indifference: an object to be adapted and transmitted, the latest classic serial. To pull back and say that Robert Powell was giving a fine performance as Jude, or that the scene at the country wedding (it was actually a town wedding) was pleasant and nicely directed, would be easy but evasive. Deep in this adaptation, the extraordinary and challenging unity of Hardy's theme had been taken apart and put together again in a much smaller action and consciousness. It would be too much to record every minor distortion, every major omission, every gratuitous insertion. Anyone who knows the novel well will have noted them already, and in any case it is the novel that will survive. The real point is the way in which a very difficult and powerful structure of feeling has been made over, as a job, into passable television. The connection with the rest of the evening's events didn't seem too remote. And did it then seem significant that Germaine Greer, in a reduced and disintegrated discussion, could say less about freedom and marriage than even this unrecognisable Sue Bridehead: a voice from 80 years earlier?

Or take the fact that Cook and Rushton in different ways referred to the previous evening's television prize-giving at the Albert Hall. That has certainly provoked some related thoughts, not so much about television as about the paradox I've been trying to get at in its current English usage: this air of mutual congratulation and habitual self-consciousness within a sequence of basically impromptu acts; a brave and busy improvisation through a series of dissolving gestures and images, with just a few steadying shots of the past. Of course I was glad to see Keith Michell's virtuoso performance as Henry VIII applauded. And Eric Morecambe, since his kind of disintegrating scepticism carries the memory of innocence and good will. But it was interesting looking past the synthetic pomp to try to work out the median date of the current show-pieces of English television: *Civilisation, The Forsyte Saga, The Six Wives of Henry VIII*. It can be done on several projections, some alarmingly far back, but I think the latest and most accurate would centre on Clive Bell, Galsworthy, Korda/Laughton, which I make about 1925. Of course all three are in pictures now. Superb, impressive, etc.

The television I find interesting is very different and there was some of it in the same week: *Man Alive* and *World in Action*, the ice-skating and the tennis and the rugby, René Cutforth's helicopter views of Wales, another case for my private dossier on police series in the *Softly, Softly* episode on demonstrations, an interesting *Talkback* on the reporting of strikes, two or three news films. These programmes tried to deal with events and places that belong to our own world. The *Europa* films of India, though sketchy, belong here rather than in that strange BBC-2 evening. These are programmes within the present real limits of television, and above all, they were not confused by the residual power of other art forms. There was a parallel stage in the evolution of the cinema to what has happened in television. Some of its controllers sought artistic respectability by the transfer of cultural objects that already had prestige:

adaptations, famous theatre actors, show places and galleries—and of course the comedians at once parodied them. The real potential of film was meanwhile being developed more directly elsewhere.

I think there is now enough evidence to say that the present controllers of television, after the difficulties of the Sixties—difficulties of genuine growth—are turning more and more to the received values of other forms. A work like *Jude* is too resistant for them, it still cuts directly into their own consensus. But the Grand Tour, the Edwardian bourgeoisie, the rollicking and colourful English courtly past: these are static experiences, ready to be upholstered, given the tickets of prestige. A younger generation can do little but mock them, for its own original work is forced out more and more to the edges. The parodists survive, the makers just hang on. But if this is the sequence, I do not see, given everything else that is happening, how it can last much longer.

11 March 1971

Remembering the Thirties

If there is one thing certain, it is that the Seventies will not be like the Thirties. Several people have been saying recently that they are getting an ominous impression of the Thirties coming back. The reference is usually to the rising unemployment figures. But that kind of retrospect is like those stories about the future which depend on projecting a single trend. It offers a simplification which usually has the effect of reducing our awareness of the real present.

But there is indeed one way in which the Thirties are coming back. Many students, in my experience, find it the most interesting modern period, and are beginning serious work on it. And on television, just lately, we seem to have been getting an unusual number of memoirs and revivals in which the Thirties are significant. Here, it's the variations of viewpoint that may be what really matters.

Most treatments of the past, in current orthodox thinking, manage to isolate particular figures, and everyday television, of course, lends itself to this. Within two days I watched Walter Greenwood, of *Love on the Dole*, talking on *Late Night Line-Up*, and the fine Tyne-Tees film on L. S. Lowry. On its own, each programme was interesting, but I thought of Greenwood in Salford, Lowry in Manchester, at about the same time, each making a characteristic but very different kind of art out of Northern industrial life—I felt what I really wanted to see was the two brought together: perhaps to talk, for they were both good talkers, in much the same dry undertone; more critically, to get a discussion and comparison of the two kinds of art: the representative naturalist play and the crowded friezes of Lowry's mill paintings.

It may well be that they never met, just as in the Manchester of the 1840s Elizabeth Gaskell and Friedrich Engels do not seem to be recorded as having met, though within a short distance of each other, and within three years, they were producing works as closely related and as interestingly different as *Mary Barton* and *The Condition of the Working Class*. I suppose a period becomes history, in the full sense, when we begin making different relationships: between works rather than persons. I have often wondered if three young men, living not far from each other in the England of the Thirties, ever happened to meet, or even pass each other on the pavement: their names, then, were Eric Blair, Christopher Sprigge, Leslie Mitchell. It would not in any case have been the same as it now is for us, when the names are Orwell, Caudwell and Grassic Gibbon. But whereas, until recently, we were using figures from the Thirties only to suit the mood of the Fifties, some wider and more properly historical range is now beginning to open.

The adaptation of Grassic Gibbon's *Sunset Song* (BBC-2) is especially welcome. It is extraordinary how completely his work was neglected, except in his own region. And I am sorry, even now, that we are only getting *Sunset Song,* for the other two books of *A Scots Quair* are equally interesting, and *Grey Granite,* in particular, catches elements of the Thirties that are not so well expressed anywhere else.

It was also welcome to have the BBC-2 classic serial returning to its normal high standard, after the wilful failure with *Jude. Sunset Song,* I would have thought, was much more difficult to dramatise. The problems of language are considerable. But in its essential spirit, and more visibly in its directing, acting and setting, this *Sunset Song* seemed to me to begin well. And for so long as we are interested in our native literature, this succession from late Hardy to the Lawrence of *The Rainbow* and to Grassic Gibbon's *Scots Quair* ought to be seen as important.

Yet the most memorable single work on television last week came from abroad: the production of Arthur Miller's *The Price*

(NBC:ITV). I haven't yet been able to find out when this was written: it seems relatively early, though it was not in his volume of *Collected Plays*. The dramatic date was in any case around 1950, and the characters were remembering the early Thirties, in a familiar Ibsen kind of retrospect in which the slow revelation of the past is a way of defining the significance of the present. The theatrical conventions of that kind of play were very evident. There was a strong curtain line before each end of an act, to carry us through shoving for a drink or the more insinuating Seventies commercials. The characters were stuck in a theatrical unity of place and time, or more strictly, in a fully furnished set: the room where the father had sat and died—a remarkably preserved room, after 20 years, with the mother's dresses still bright on the hangers. The dealer arriving to give a price for the furniture had to be sent to lie down in an adjoining bedroom so that he could reappear, from time to time, whenever the action needed him again. All these features of that kind of naturalist drama are now very obvious and rather difficult to accept.

But the point, when such drama is serious, as in Ibsen and again in Miller, is that the fact of being stuck in a room, and stuck in a present still dominated by the past, is much more than a theatrical convention. It is what that kind of life is essentially taken to be: probability, in spite of the surface, is a secondary consideration. The importance of this trapped, static quality was brought out, negatively, by the recent restless production of *The Wild Duck* (BBC-1). I have only recently been noticing, in television drama (though it used to happen a lot on the stage), how superficially many directors understand movement. In one short speech an actor is often made to run a kind of race against time: how many positions, chairs, drinks, postures, rooms he can get through before the bloody words run out. But whether sitting still and feeling trapped is now acceptable or not, it is what Ibsen, in that period, and Miller, in *The Price*, were writing: a precise experience in a precise rhythm. And then the Miller production was very powerful, with the actors allowed to be slow and involved—an opportunity they brilliantly took. I don't know how it got through to most people: I read only one review, which got it spectacularly wrong. Miller has written of his "secret drama", in which the characters are "logically brothers" and where the "search for relatedness" carries all the feeling. This was even more true of *The Price* than of any of his other plays. The "success" of the brothers is, of course, contrasted: the one has lived, the other careered. But the roots of this are in knowing the truth of the past: Walter, who thought he knew, became cynical; Victor, who thinks he didn't, has a more general truth, about a responsibility to others that overrides circumstances. The knowing and affluent Walter, a true figure of the Fifties, is suddenly seen, when the whole past is known—not an isolated event but a general history—as radically weaker than the tired Victor, who even in error made a commitment to others which will now sustain him.

Some people want only to say that Miller is dated, but with what is now happening they are merely outdating themselves. The figure in Miller's writing was as clear, as simple and as absolute as one of the Lowry figures we saw the old man tracing, past his guarded, dry talk: the finger on the paper, a few deliberate strokes, a feeling and a history.

8 April 1971

Open Teaching

Any Sunday morning, at the press of a button, we can drop in on some of the Open University's lectures. It will be interesting to know, eventually, how many people do this, over and above the registered students. One of the important effects of having this work on television is that some aspects of the real work of universities are available for direct public observation. Nobody could say that universities haven't been in the visual news in recent years, but I often wonder what image has been built between the poles of student demonstrations and quiz shows like *University Challenge*. At least here, in the lectures, we are getting some of the preponderant routines.

It must be said at once that the television lectures are only a part of the teaching. There are also the radio programmes, the finely produced printed material—in course units and background books—and beyond these the whole system of assigned written work, study centres, tutors and counsellors and residential schools. As a combined exercise in educational communication it is genuinely experimental, and we shan't know its results for some years, until more than one generation of students have gone through.

What is being shown now are the Foundation Courses, in Social Sciences, Mathematics, Science and Arts. A good deal of work at something like this level is already transmitted on television in other ways. Interestingly, though, this other work is mainly science and arts. In economics and mathematics very little professional work ever penetrates beyond the educational programmes. And yet it is not, for example, that economics is not endlessly discussed. On *The Money Programme*, on *Panorama* and *24 Hours* and *This Week*, on the Budget Specials, there is what often seems a perpetual economic conversation. But the number of professional economists who take part in it is very small. Political and financial journalists, and a few rather regular politicians, industrialists and trade-union leaders, go through discussions which, whatever else they might be, are never educational, in any sense. Difficult and controversial concepts are tossed along those studio tables in what has to be seen in the end as a sort of national game. Like much of the press, *The Money Programme*, for example, has included more and more share-tipping and company gossip, in a quite open way. I've calculated that in proportion we would need six or seven hours a week on the more popular form of gambling with pools coupons, though it's fair to say that the racing spots, on sports programmes, keep the expected ideological proportion between the sight of horses running and the calculation of chances and starting prices.

Such considerations are crucial in reviewing one obvious problem, which affects the relation between television education and general informative programmes. Ideology, in the form of known kinds of communicator and audience, gets into the general programmes quite frankly. But this is sometimes rationalised as not wanting too many bloody dons. It is a fact, for example, that a different kind of economic discussion, in the general programmes, could be quite easily arranged, if economists rather than journalists were more regularly invited. But think of watching it, people say around the studios and the offices. I do, and I also think of the party gossip we now get as a matter of course: some of the most boring television ever made or conceivable.

What ought to be happening, on the Open University courses, is something more serious, more sustained, more open. In general science and arts programmes we do usually get people with more real things to say—more authoritative people, if you like—than in the general political and economic discussions. But, in the hazards of programming, the subjects are often random, or a single subject is dealt with in one big programme, where genuine understanding might require a different method: more orderly, more progressive, more sustained. This, then, is one of the ironies of some of the Foundation Courses. Offering an introduction to a very wide field, they can result, as last week, in John Dankworth on the instruments of the orchestra followed by an analysis of Bernini's *Ecstasy of Saint Teresa*. The Science and Mathematics programmes, as I understand them, are teaching basic units, concepts and procedures. So, it might be said, are the Arts and Social Science courses, but at what seems to me a rather different level. There is a problem of deep theoretical penetration from which alone any really founding introduction could follow, and it is a fact about our culture that some of this has been achieved in mathematics and the physio-chemical and perhaps biological sciences, while it has not been achieved in social sciences and the arts. So it has to be said that some of the Arts programmes, and in a different way several of the Social Science programmes, have been useful in particular ways but also in quite enclosed ways: that there is nowhere to go from them, towards the discipline as a whole. But then it must be added that the Open University is no different, in this respect, from other British universities. The whole problem in arts and social science faculties in recent years—and it has underlain a great deal of what has been stupidly received as Student Unrest—is precisely this question of relevance.

I watch the Mathematics and Science programmes as a layman. I am often baffled by details but I do get a sense of where the exposition is going. Last week I tried to follow a problem in the geometry of surfaces: introduced, by way of good will, with a film of an oil survey and then moving, by way of some instrument readings, to what were to me some truly formidable equations. Only duty kept me watching, but then the teaching began: a series of visual demonstrations of problems of minima and maxima, becoming more complicated but with a warning that it was involving simplification; and I then found to my surprise that at some different level of the mind a new way of seeing certain physical relations was beginning to form. I am sure I would have needed to follow it up, with exercises, but the working models and mobile diagrams seemed a clear advantage of television teaching.

Similarly in the Science programme on cells, where I already knew rather more. The detailed unpacking of a model cell, with very flexible visual interpretations of its structure, was clearer than anything I had previously seen or read. And the second part of the programme, showing procedures for getting actual material for analysis, took this beyond spectator science and at least some way towards the idea of an active discipline.

In some elementary economics, of the M=PQ/V variety, there was also a good use of diagrams, but as so often in that field there was an element of abstraction of a quite different order from that of, say, the surface geometry. The Social Science course in general has been very orthodox, and another way of saying that (in any university) is bad. Some terms—there was an early example in a demonstration, actually a misunderstanding, of "cognitive dissonance"— have been presented more as instruction towards a phraseology than as analysis towards an understanding.

In the Arts course, John Dankworth's theme composed to demonstrate the various instruments was more interesting and clearer than several similar programmes I had previously watched. There were good earlier programmes on, for example, the use of primary historical materials, and on some of the elements and conventions of visual composition and recognition. An early programme on the Yorubas, offering to make a point about culture and cultures, was less successful, and like other things in this course, was not seriously followed up, at least at this stage.

As I've already said, the difference about these courses is that everybody can drop in on them. I think we are all in debt to these teachers, who are working right in the open. The use of television for real education has barely begun, and most of the signs are that it will be a real expansion of our resources, not just as a transmission system but in actual modes of understanding.

6 May 1971

Terror

Last week I found myself wondering if I had ever been frightened by a television programme. The occasion was paradoxical: half-way through a play in the *Out of the Unknown* series (BBC-2), which the linkman had introduced with some remarks about its being spine-tingling—or was it spine-chilling? It's difficult to remember that this conventional physical vocabulary is supposed to relate to real dramatic effects. There must have been people whose hair stood on end as something dreadful appeared to have happened, just as there must somewhere have been somebody reading a book who found that he couldn't put it down. But it's just as curious to meet people who denounce violence and say how much they enjoy a good crime story—a juicy murder, to revert to the conventional language. So it's interesting to wonder about this wholly respectable terrorisation. Some people who talk about a really good thriller aren't at first sight people you would expect to hear talking about thrills in any other capacity. And what is it that produces, in a culture dominated by business and by its versions of common sense and practicality, this persistent taste for the conventionally irrational, with its local repertory and dialect of spooks, creeps and chills? There are traditional arguments about purgation, about discharge or reconciliation, through a play. But they seem rather a long way from the television set. There, the deliberation of the entertaining intention to frighten can come through as chilling in quite another sense.

Out of the Unknown used to be mainly what is called science fiction. In the current series the operative word seems to be "psychological". "Welcome Home", which provoked these reflections, used an internal dramatic viewpoint to persuade us that the man coming home after an accident was the husband and doctor he believed himself to be and that the husband and doctor he found there, with the same—his own?—name, was some kind of impostor. Every convention was then spoken about: invasion by an alien species or a hostile foreign power; the fingerprints of a man who had died two years before in the West Indies (voodoo!); sinister mind-bending drugs. Or it could, take your pick, be paranoia, as everyone including his supposed friends seemed to be part of the conspiracy, though since we had seen the other man apparently committing a murder, with local dramatic effects suggesting furtiveness, we were still inclined to take the conspiracy as objective. As in the end, rather hurriedly and in a different way, it was: the field-trial of a new suggestibility drug, to give the man an identity that would be preferable to his past. Though why the alternative identity should be that of one of the doctors treating him wasn't exactly clear. Unless—but of course: the irresponsibility of science. A clear case for *Doomwatch*.

What would it be, I wondered, that could come anywhere near

fulfilling the conventional promise of desirable frightening effects? I'd better say, as a check, that I've been startled often enough by footsteps in empty houses, strange figures at windows, shadows, knives, abysses, mirrors, wrong faces above the pram. Mostly in print or the cinema: I can't remember an instance on the box. When the figure at the window turned up in "Welcome Home" I found that I was looking at almond leaves through our own blue venetian blind. Perhaps the frame is too small to enclose us dramatically; the world around the frame too insistently present and domestic. I've often noticed in the cinema those moments when one comes back from enclosure in the frame; when through the half-dark one sees the clock again, and the red light for Exit, and the signs for Ladies and Gentlemen. Usually the film is still going on, but for a time not easily measured—and when measured still qualitatively different—there has been no conscious space between the absorbed eyes and the moving sequence of images. I don't know how many people ever find this happening on television. For me it is less frequent but not unknown. Yet the dominance of the images—for it is also that—never seems to occur when it would be useful to people trying to entertain us out of our wits. Horror and terror still run in the cinema, with old images of vampires, bats, pterodactyls, mad scientists, automata and the walking dead. Television by contrast is silvery and cool.

Is it different in televised "science fiction"? The difficulty there is the wide variation that description now covers. A sharply written play a week earlier in *Out of the Unknown*—Edward Boyd's "The Sons and Daughters of Tomorrow"—had us assuming some murderous coven, with strong smells of traditional witchcraft, and then revealed a community of telepaths and energy-throwers. Mutants, an alien outpost, a Tarot seminary? One wasn't encouraged to make any final identification. But this is a world away from, say, the adventures of *Dr Who*, where odd things regularly happen and there have been some memorable monsters, but where there is also Brigadier Lethbridge Stewart and some familiar office politics and a general air of suffused charm. Not much of the best science fiction has yet got to the screen. Its critical themes are identity and culture-contact, and in many ways it has advantages for the exploration of these, not only over realism but over the medieval and romantic repertories. Visual realisation, however, is a complicated matter. Watching *Yesterday's Witness* (BBC-2) on how the talkies came to

Britain, I was interested to see how the sound-effects man used to suggest dripping blood by tapping the back of his hand, but something else was also happening which was much more dramatic. There were some conventional dissolves from the faces of the men talking to their younger faces, and then back again. And this was strangely powerful, in ways that pushed past the abstractions—time, change, identity. I could hardly listen to what was being said as these dissolving images recurred. Nothing to do with the spine or the hair but an arrest, a disturbance: something out of the known.

3 June 1971

Cowboys and Missionaries .

Who's for Europe? Who's for tennis? But the interesting programmes last week were about more serious questions. *Chronicle,* for example, looked at what it called, not altogether fortunately, *The Fastest Con in the West* (BBC-2). I suppose we have always known that the Wild West of art is not the Wild West of history, but interpreting this as a con begs too many questions. Presumably the title couldn't be resisted, but the programme was more serious. It is an important cultural problem: why this particular structure—the Western—became in the 20th century the most potent example of popular art. I remember seeing film of clubs in France and Germany where people went at the weekends and dressed up as film cowboys and took their drinks in a film saloon. More recently we got a glimpse of the thriving industry of Italian-made Westerns. And of course for as long as I can remember Christmas has been marked by the appearance of children in gallon-hats and chaps, flourishing tin or plastic Colts. A phenomenon like that isn't analysable only in terms of the distance between "truth" and "fantasy".

The *Chronicle* programme, written and directed by Lucy Goodison, had one advantage over other inquiries I have encountered, in that it had its own visual power. There was a pleasant sequence in the Boot Hill graveyard at Tombstone: a tourist attraction since the local Chamber of Commerce put down some new graves. But what was interesting even there was the facility with which the dominant convention had been imitated: the inscriptions on the crosses had the authentic laconic humour of the film style. The real visual power, though, was in the old photographs of the period: the actual cowboys, log-cabins, covered wagons. These were like poverty anywhere: historical photographs from the steppes or the slums. The photographs of outlaws had that flat, brutalising prison-photograph quality. There was one exception: the series of photographs of the Earp brothers and of the men they shot at OK Corral (or somewhere nearby, until the legend started). There the opposition looked like entries in a family album: tidy, settled and pleasant faces. The Earps and Doc Holliday looked altogether more enigmatic. We heard the varying accounts of the shooting alongside the official reconstruction: the cut-out figures more like Disneyland than film.

The simple point was effectively made, but hints of the more difficult question were always present. Gunfights, for example, are staged in the streets, in the tourist season. A week after the reshowing of *The Plainsmen* we saw this street-theatre version of the last minutes of liberty of Wild Bill Hickok's murderer. Some of the people who had been watching were interviewed. One girl thought it was not the murderer but Hickok himself. Estimates of the number of men who finally held him varied from two to four. There was an extra twist on the truth-and-fantasy question, as people saw even the plain facts differently: the plain facts, that is to say, that had been agreed on for the show. There was a comparable exercise in a sequence of four versions of the death of Billy the Kid.

The fastest con? Only an extraordinarily naive view of the nature of imagination and of art could support any continued posing of the question in those terms. The real question is often glanced at, but I haven't seen any satisfactory approach to an answer. What impresses me is the Western's fusion and conversion of two traditional structures: the rural idyll and the brigand. That the real cowboys were wage slaves is relevant but not decisive. The critical history is of an art form, from Charles Russell and Charles Siringo and the first Western movie in 1903. It looks to me like Robinson Crusoe in an occupied and competitive land: the last stage of a great bourgeois myth, intensively explored in a strange and varying combination of celebration and doubt. Perhaps *Chronicle* or some other programme will return to it some time: not to distinguish the history but to inquire into the much more important structure of feeling.

Other versions of Americans on the move were on television last week. There was a fine account in the *Disappearing World* series (Granada) of Catholic and Protestant missionaries among the Maku and Barasana Indians of North-West Amazonia. The Catholic mission was all bells and lines and table-manners and dresses and alphabets: a traditional mix. The Protestants, disguised as the Institute of Linguistics, were altogether more curious, though only superficially more alien. They had a God who had a time-table and who paid the bills. With hard businesslike precision they occupied the tribes and sought "Satan's ugly face" (and here the camera, exploring the conference, was cruelly ironic). Three young Cambridge anthropologists made all the relevant points about these coarsely dominative intruders. But there is a question beyond that: the recording, participating scholars had also dropped from the sky; so had the unseen production team. In one way or another I would expect "the last primitives" to be our persistent, gentle, liberal myth. But if so it will have to keep flying further. I respect even those crude missionaries more than, say, the substantially similar but more overtly destructive American advisers in Laos, on whom Max Hastings reported for *24 Hours*. Their frustrated attempts to make the people into soldiers, in an alien war, were much more damaging—killed and uprooted many more people—than the missionaries, who had communicated only two concepts—sin and laziness. Of course in Laos they had bombers to help them.

Three brief notes, finally. Dave Douglass, the young Communist miner, was impressive in *Where do I stand?* (BBC-1). *The Uninvited* (BBC-2), though in the end very flat, had some moments of physical effect which ought to be noted as qualifying what I said about terror on television. And then Arthur Miller's *The Price*: I said it felt early, though it wasn't in the *Collected Plays*. Someone wrote to say that this wasn't surprising, since the date of *Collected Plays* was 1958 and of the publication of *The Price* 1968. I was arguing, and still would, from internal evidence, but though the 1968 text begins "Today. New York", I have now been told on what seems reasonable authority that it was first written in 1951 and only later put out.

1 July 1971

Careers and Jobs

What is the difference between a job and a career? There is no more up-to-date riddle, but nobody yet seems to have thought of an answer. In the *Panorama* programme called *Starting Work* I thought I heard a figue of 70 per cent of adults in Britain in unsuitable jobs. It may well be quite accurate, but are we to suppose that if after proper guidance we were all shifted around, any reasonable majority of us would find ourselves in careers? This is only one of the unanswered questions that crowded in my mind as I watched this interesting programme. Moving away, as it now sometimes does, from superficial high politics, *Panorama* had arrived at a central social problem. The immediate cue was the difficulty of school-leavers finding any jobs at all in this year of high unemployment. The central focus was then on the kind of advice that is given between school and employment. Passing from cue to focus already involved a contradiction: between the fact of scarcity and the illusion of choice. But this faded behind the more massive contradiction: between the facts of most work and the illusion of universal careers.

The dominant tone of the programme was one familiar in liberal journalism: an engagingly baffled but inquiring rationality—"surely if this problem is seen it can be put right." Thus we were taken to a meeting of the National Association of Careers Teachers, and heard that it was a scandal that only 10 per cent of schools had adequate careers advice facilities. Headmasters needed convincing that this work was important; teaching colleagues often thought of it as free time. Local authorities and the Department of Education and Science needed to give much more weighty support.

Over then to a school in Bristol which had a proper careers department. Job-identification and classification from photographs; a library of pamphlets and brochures; a visual aid to identify the most important person in this whole business of careers—the mirror: you. Also a kind of Dutch auction about how many careers there were. One girl suggested a million but the answer, it seemed, was 80,000.

This was convincing as far as it went. In many places children get no more than two hours' advice about kinds of work in their whole school lives. There was an interview with a young man formerly in the top stream of a grammar school who had fallen behind because of illness and was now stacking and sweeping in a supermarket. His school hadn't worried about what work he would ever do, and now he was in what he called a dead-end job. Getting some O and A levels would have been useful, especially for after 30. Or again, there was the young engineer who with his time over again would have stayed on at school and taken some exams and become a draughtsman.

Square pegs in round holes, or however that phrase now goes. But not quite that, surely. There are so many more factors than careers guidance in the difficult process of sustaining an education through the long and uncertain years of adolescence. For example, in the model careers department, a pleasant girl came to say that she wanted to leave school and not stay on for exams. Her friends were in jobs and she wanted more independence. The advice? Well, she had difficulty writing letters of application. Cut to a letter-writing class. Remember to mention sex, age, qualifications. One polished exercise managed to mention the progressive policy of the firm being applied to. The letter ended: "Yours faithfully, Mr Michael Quinn Esquire."

And indeed we had been told at one point that faulty careers guidance led to adolescent cynicism and disillusion with the society. A man from the Schools Council said that it was a difficult transition from school to work: from a place where you smiled, did tasks, played football, to a place where you were making a profit for someone else. As this range of problems comes clearly into view, we begin to see the limits of the simpler advisory routines. Given the examples of the supermarket boy and the young engineer, what, or what else, should have been said to that girl? And what, if we are really talking, should be said to the owners of the supermarket or the factory? What, finally, can be said to the great majority of people who in this kind of society will have jobs like that and never, ever, a career?

This is the contradiction within the whole "careers" philosophy. It makes sense to have better advice and selection, and this can be rationalised as "making the best of yourself". But past the known muddle and ignorance there are the deeper constraints: of an employing, hiring and firing society; of an economy where people are thrown out of work for the sake of financial orthodoxy. And beyond even these, facing all school-leavers from now on, are the structural changes in industry, where labour saving and productivity bargaining are now major goals, leaving the certainty of a growing minority who will not find work at all, let alone satisfying work.

Panorama or some less official programme should come back to these questions. It's all very well showing the clip from *Kes,* with an idea of freedom highlighting the bureaucracy of youth employment. But it can't be had both ways. One of the careers people said the object was to bring the young down to earth without stifling their dreams or ambitions. Someone else used the word "instability" to describe young people who went through five or six jobs in a year. That gives an odd idea of what stability may be, or of what learning is preparing us for, in an increasingly mobile and flexible society. Education can disregard work altogether in ways that derive from a class situation in which people didn't get jobs, or at best got positions and had careers. Or it can be reshaped, against the stubborn instincts of many good teachers, until it is from the beginning a part of industrial training: all round pegs in round punch-holes. Or, may we not still say, it can try to teach the whole truth about work: a history and a society; our own skills and those of others; the realities and the possibilities of choice. *Panorama* touched the edge of these questions, but television, of all media, with its unrivalled opportunities, should go, and repeatedly, to their centre.

29 July 1971

China-Watching

It was a good idea to put together the films on China made by Max Hastings for *24 Hours* and show them as the *Tuesday Documentary: Ping-Pong in Peking* (BBC-1). I had seen them before and found most of them interesting. The beginning was not promising: pointing the camera at everything, in a kind of tourist swing, and riding the alliteration of ping-pong, pandas and pagodas. But when he was given wider filming permission, he made a serious short study of a family on a housing estate in Shanghai, with scenes of work, school, club and shopping, and then went on to Canton and the Red Guards and a factory and a university and a hospital reformed by the Cultural Revolution. It was all fairly solid reporting, with some detailed information and an attempt at interpretation.

I say "attempt" critically. I think it was bound to be difficult. I have listened to experts, just back from China, with interest but with only partial understanding. I could have done without Hastings's remarks about the "deification" of Mao and the "revolutionary

delinquents" of the Red Guard. But in the first place the contradictions are very striking, when seen from outside, and the snap judgment is tempting. Hastings gave a reasonable account of the philosophy of the Cultural Revolution, but it remains ironic that a movement designed to stimulate popular participation should have produced, side by side, such positive features as the neighbourhood and
factory committees and such blatantly negative features as the
massed chanting, the ubiquitous portraits, and the reduction of
thoughts to quotations. Similarly, there was a contradiction between
the relaxed and graceful life of the apartment and the street and the
park (the slow and beautiful morning exercises staying in the mind)
and the sudden sharp marching of children in and out of school. I
noticed these contradictions everywhere. Traditional opera, for
example, had been replaced by revolutionary opera, and we saw an
excerpt from *Taking Tiger Mountain by Strategy*. But what was
interesting was the fantastically skilled traditional swordplay of the
fight and then, marching into it, the uniform and the pistol and the
flag. From which opera, I wondered, were the old men in the club
singing pieces? Or again, the children in school were doing a rifle
dance, and they managed to make every movement but one graceful
and natural: the exception was the ritual stamp for the bayonet
thrust. To feel one's way into all this was so genuinely difficult that it
is no surprise that the short visit and the pressing commentary often
seemed shallow.

But the second reason is harder again. In nearly everything I
have heard about China in the last five years I have been aware of a
particular and very complicated challenge. In its central intention, or
at least in its declared intention, the Cultural Revolution seemed to
me one of the most hopeful things that have ever happened in the
world. I don't share the commentator's hope that it is all settling
down again, unless I can be sure what it is settling down to. I wondered about the "extremists" reported as exiled to distant com-
munes. But this was still interest: a relatively distant interest—
China-watching. What I have called the challenge is something else
again.

It comes when the sense of a new life and a new morality really
begins to connect with oneself. There was a simple instance when a
factory boss confessed his errors—failure to work with others and to
relate as an equal. It's easy to draw back and say we dislike or suspect confessions: a whole record of arranged public recantation is in
our historical bones as a warning. But what if it is also in our bones

as an evasion? Through the stilted jargon of the manager's translated statement, what was being said was remarkable, but only if we at once apply it to ourselves. In the factory it was relatively easy. The management had been reduced from 800 to 200; decisions were made by workers' committees; all executives did physical work. But it strikes home more closely when it is a matter of education and the universities, and of the general life of intellectuals. The requirement to go to the country and do physical work is not, for me, the difficulty. In very different conditions I find I have to do it to keep sane. But the interview with the professor of engineering who had changed his emphasis from theory to practice, and who taught a different kind of student—workers, peasants and soldiers—reached into the heart of our own difficulties.

The change can't be judged in isolation. It depends on what kind of society and what kind of economy is being served. But revolutionary intellectuals in the West, who are still mainly humanists, have to face in this Chinese example their most difficult questions, and not abstract questions either. At the worst moment of the difficulty I felt the pull of the commentator's language: not only his habitual identification with the manager and the professor but the easy point about Mao-worship and conformity: true as far as they went, but also screening the harder questions. We can build the easy points into something like solidity: the paradox of the unwanted theorist, the unwanted free intellectual, in a society in which even the simplest practical operation is preceded by a theoretical proposition quoted from one man. At that level the resistance holds, and must hold. But I have to say, finally, that in its attempt to abolish the divisions between intellectual and physical work, between town and country, between the executive and the operative, between theory and practice, China is or ought to be searching our hearts and minds, in a way that hasn't happened with comparable power in my lifetime.

Some unintended miracle of planning led to Chairman Mao being immediately followed by Chairman Watts: "our Chairman, Mr Arthur Watts", head of the family which has started and owned most of the factories in the small Gloucestershire town of Lydney. BBC West, usually a good region, is putting on a series called *Their Town*. The next in the series is Street, "home of Britain's largest private company". It might have been interesting, but this naive and sycophantic little film was a disgrace to any public broadcasting service. There were endless public-relations interviews with the Watts family and associated managers. Nobody below the rank of family or manager got a word in at all, and of Lydney we saw virtually nothing except the family's assorted enterprises and benefactions. They used to run Red and White buses, and the Labour Government gave them £41/2 million's worth of compensation on nationalisation. It had been profitably invested. Once, on the edge of this "Royal Forest of Dean", there were the Bathursts or Bledisloes, landowners; then the Wattses. In the future, the commentator wondered, would there be such benefactors? Mightn't the money for public purposes have to come from the rates? I ended by wondering where they think, in BBC West, any money comes from. Perhaps they think it grows on trees in the Royal Forest.

26 August 1971

An English Autumn

An English autumn? In one of those hollow moments before the picture comes up I thought I heard a voice say: "An English autumn, a prelude to winter, a reminder of a new season of drama on BBC-2". Driving down, later, through the heather and gorse of a Welsh autumn, I wondered if the English Broadcasting Corporation had meant the announcement as a promise or a warning. But the set I had access to didn't get BBC-2, and whenever that is the case the television world shrinks. Most of what I saw on BBC-1 suggested images of recurrence, though Barlow of *Softly, Softly* was on special duties in a sort of Wales: coal and coast, weak and corrupt local police, a homosexual borough surveyor, and Islwyn and Ceirwen the young nationalists who had been after the English road-signs and were hinting at worse. Hint, glare, suggestion, scenery, aggression, complication: it's quite slick, going down—it's only later you realise what you've swallowed. Mind you, though, the source of the corruption was an Englishman.

In an English autumn, and presumably in others, the evenings draw in. But then that usually means, on the majority channels, that they are very long-drawn indeed before there is any serious television. On the other hand, there was time to get rid of the taste of the Barlow pottage before the start of the new short series, *Double Vision*. The first programme, on Hull Docks, was interesting. The idea of the series is to get two people of opposing views to show us, in turn, what the world in which they are in conflict looks like. Here, in an order settled by the toss of a coin, a port employer and a docker showed us how they saw Hull Docks. I write "showed" and "saw", because that is how the programme was offered, following the special emphasis on vision in the title. It's a common dead metaphor, but it made me think again about television as a "visual" medium. Each man, we were told, had been asked to make his short film as he wanted it: he was of course given the usual technical facilities. The offer seemed wholly genuine, but it is interesting how it had been interpreted. For suppose the director had said: "Each of you can make a speech on television and suggest some pictures to accompany it." The films would not have been much different, though the unusual bare face of instruction would have contradicted the televisual code. This raises the characteristic problem of how far a "point of view" can be embodied in things seen and shown.

Suppose the sound had been turned off. How readily would we have known which film was which? By inference, undoubtedly, from some (though not much) explicit content. There were two moments I remembered from the employer's film: when he was sitting at his desk talking into an intercom (though the sound would have to come back to make the full point, as an anonymous subordinate voice floated through the instrument to announce that no work at all was going on); and, in the same mood, when he walked in wide shot along an empty quay and looked up at an immobile and obviously expensive crane. Against these, two moments from the docker's film: a shot of unloading, one of the few moments of the actual work process in the entire programme; and a ring of men in their working clothes, discussing and arguing. Beyond these, there were only occasional moments in which the meaning was being carried by the images, and with these I wasn't sure if I was seeing or being shown. For example, the two sides of the negotiating table and the immediate contrast not only of clothes but of ways of sitting at the table: the employers set at it, firmly, a possession and self-possession; the workers in a more uneven line, a bit away from the edge, one half-turned as if ready to get up and go. There was more deliberation, perhaps, in a long steady camera-look, from the workers' side, at the employers' faces: groomed, prosperous, sour.

But at the level of the ordinary argument none of this was primary. The voices carried the meaning, mostly in slabs of generalised content. Each view of the world was highly structured by ideas and by underlying abstract attitudes. This is not a complaint but a recognition: not only that this is true, and must be true, even in a world of very practical men; but also that it is very rare, in film or television, for the eye alone to do much viewing or embody a point of view.

What points of view were then given by speech? This programme was different from others I have seen about industrial disputes in that the tone of the worker, Wally Greendale, was, though firm, more shaded and more relaxed than that of the employer, Geoffrey Cullington. It took one back to Barlow's simulated asperities to keep up with Cullington's flow of judgments: "deliberately sabotaged", "agitators", "not prepared to do an honest day's work". Of course, even this tone was better than that of the visiting authority who after a question for camera said "purely mischievous" in a plummy voice that I had thought (and hoped) I might never hear again. But put it this way: Cullington was there in his office; he was exasperated; he had his reasons (the docks were making a loss, though his firm had made a profit). He took his chance on television—he said his piece. But if he said it at all often like that I wouldn't have thought we'd need television to tell us there was trouble. And if he really believes, as he said in the later discussion, that the dockers are "the most privileged people in the country" I can imagine, as they say, some scope for further divergence in points of view.

It is a complicated industry, the docker insisted, as quietly as if he had been to a business studies seminar. The stewards (agitators) were elected by the men. The dockers had been exploited, and were still being exploited. They remembered the "fathers of the men who employ us today", but today's disputes were about modernisation: that crane, if activated, would put most of them out of work; some of the new container traffic was being handled by non-registered labour; they had not made the changes but were expected to adapt to them; the only solution was for the docks to be run by the men who do the work.

Brian Redhead, chairing the subsequent discussion, did his best to get down to cases. The idea of workers' control brought from Cullington a remark about anarchists and a constitutional remark from Greendale that town clerks weren't in the hands of anarchists. The books could be opened and inspected "if you'd behave like responsible people"—which would come about if the books could be opened and inspected. A complicated agreement "didn't mean that". Your "breach" was our "very specific definition". Fade-out. It was well worth trying, and is well worth following up.

I got back to my own set in time to see Jim Allen's new play. I've respected all his work from *The Lump* and *The Big Flame* to *The Rank and File*. *Walt, King of the Dumper* was an anecdote from the vernacular tradition, a laugh before a curse at how we get fooled. The writing was sharply convincing and the familiarity of the moves—impressing the barmaid, digging her garden, being cut out by the boss, dumping his trench full again—reminded us of the still barely touched power of that whole submerged world, at once lively and resigned, in which work is mediated and tempered. It was well directed by Jack Gold and particularly well played by Dennis Waterman and Paddy Joyce.

23 September 1971

Judges and Traitors

Perhaps it was the sudden bad weather but there seemed, last week, more to watch on television, and a number of programmes to go on thinking about. There was the repeat of the sober inquiry into the Katyn Forest massacre.* There was the continuing "search for the Nile", which for all its gaucheries has some oblique documentary value: a lake is discovered when a black man tells a white man where to find it; Speke and Burton,** for all the *parti pris*, are interestingly contrasted eminent Victorians. Or take the case of the unexpected resemblance between the television adaptations of Sartre's *Roads to Freedom* and Huxley's *Eyeless in Gaza*. Huxley and Sartre, in their whole work, leave very different impressions, but here there was a central correspondence of movement and feeling: a passive intellec-

*The Katyn Forest massacre. Mass execution of Polish military officers during World War II.

**Sir Richard Burton (1821-1890). First European to discover Lake Tanganyika. Traveller, linguist and writer, he was an outsider and sexual radical in England. John Speke was an officer of the British East India Company. He joined Burton in a search for the source of the Nile but their collaboration ended in disagreement.

tual is moved indirectly towards commitment; the relationships and failures of relationship through which this happens are characteristically cold and willed. This made me think again about one of the strangest false conjunctions of our period: late Huxley (mescalin), late Sartre (revolution): not as a matter of ideas, where they are easy to distinguish, but as a structure of feeling made actual in many contemporary and supposedly new personal histories. That is a labyrinth to be explored only with more resources than we now have, but the two adaptations and, more important, the two original works may be a starting-point.

There can be no doubt, though, where the main thrust of serious television now drives us in Britain. It is towards exploring one of our own subcultures, which only here, I suppose, could have been called the upper middle class. That is the real tension behind the excuse of the Nile, and it was, after all, the intellectual fringe of the same group that played at being Samson in Huxley's *Gaza*. But there were two more direct approaches: Bryan Magee's attempt to investigate the judges (Thames) and Dennis Potter's play *Traitor* (BBC-1).

Magee didn't get anywhere. Perhaps he didn't expect to. He reminded us of some disturbing recent judgments (Garden House, *Oz*), but since he wasn't allowed to interview serving judges the inquiry had to be general. Were the judges an unrepresentative, out-of-touch social group? Yes and no, meaning yes and yes. It was the bland frankness of the judges' answers, confessing and justifying what they are and what they do, that stood like a glass wall: transparent enough, but knowing all the time it is reinforced with highly refined and very strong metals. It's no wonder people keep on coming up to look, and Magee put his questions with a quiet rationality, as if talking to philosophers. It is very difficult to believe that you can live in the same country, or, as an intellectual, in the same universities, as men like these—judges, civil servants, other kinds of professional men—and know nothing about them—nothing that matters, that is. It is the combination of those quiet voices, those composed manners, those relaxed drawing-rooms, that keeps suggesting there is nothing whatever to hide: all is the purest rationality and normality, whatever cruel or stupid (as well as reasonable) acts they may happen to be engaged in. The appearance of frankness, of that cool but always available politeness, is the most efficient collective disguise I have ever encountered, and for my own part I have given up asking it questions. I look for the answers in what they do.

Dennis Potter, in his play, put the boot in—or that was one way of taking it. For it's an undoubted irony that the same subculture should have produced a few traitors who appear to have relied on some of the same qualities: the confident transparency, but with a different thing to hide. I know that I could never imagine myself into the skin of such a man, and I share enough, in real kinship, with Dennis Potter to wonder how he thought he could. I waited for *Line-Up* to hear him talking about it, and the same question remained. He said that he wanted to put a question mark after "traitor", and I see that point. From within that system it was possible to revolt. The newsreels of poverty were one kind of reminder: newsreels of fascism and Appeasement might have been even more apposite. But where I hesitated was when Dennis Potter confirmed, as some of the writing had suggested, that he had given his Foreign Office traitor some of his own things to say. The matter is very complex but I can perhaps put it briefly. To defect from that class and that role seems to me not dishonourable. To defect in that way, to another state system, seems to me characteristic of that group. But as a matter of feeling I can never get over the consequent and very damaging confusion between a revolt against fascism and poverty and that cold, alienated method and destination. Just because, like Dennis Potter, I feel those causes in my bones, I cannot stand that cold flesh that attempted to grow on them. And the effect of the play was then even more complex, for the private wounds were seen as the source, and what the visiting journalists met in Moscow (until the very end made it clear that this was the private truth, not the public show, but by then it had been given all the weight) was not the cool self-justifying public transparency but a whining drunk who devalued everything he said, leaving only the pathos which exists on the far side of error. Certainly the play was powerful. An edge of the glass wall was smashed. But whose truth then came through?

21 October 1971

Sesame Street

"No one wants to be a two-and-sixpenny father." The English toy manufacturer relied on this "psychological fact". Travelling to see *Sesame Street* (Children's Television Workshop: London Weekend), I kept remembering this phrase. I had been told that this children's programme was American and commercialised: "clever, of course, but not our cup of tea". And soon enough, in the intricacies of learning to make a jelly-and-peanut-butter sandwich, I saw one of the local difficulties. But commercialised? Don Haworth's documentary, *Something for the Children* (BBC-1), had been marvellously informative about that. We've been watching rather a lot of children's television since we've had a grandchild in the house, and noticing the apparently endless series of whimsical animations and puppets, for the most part set in that English dream world of the small community full of helpful tradesmen and officials, or the middle-class family complete with gardener. Then we heard, through Mr Haworth, about "character merchandising". A puppet was no sooner lovable than he was a soap, a woolly toy, a jigsaw, manufactured on licence.

"No one wants to be a two-and-sixpenny father. He wants to be a £10 father, a £15 father." There's a dreadful context to this "psychological fact". There was a *Horizon* some time ago about working-class children in a Northern town. They were educationally deprived because in the critical early years their parents didn't play teaching games with them. The £15 toy would be no remedy for that. But is children's television a remedy? *Sesame Street*, quite obviously, is a response to the fact of educationally deprived children in a poor urban environment. And then the first thing to say about it is that the response was made. Most English children's television, by comparison, assumes a slower, more leisured, more protected world. But while there are differences of degree between the two societies, I think this difference of emphasis follows mainly from the social character of the producers. *Play School* and some of the other English programmes are often excellent, but there would still be room, where most producers don't live, for an English *Sesame Street*.

Children enjoy the Woodentops and the Mayor of Trumpton. In my experience children enjoy most things that move and make a lively noise. There is one *Watch with Mother* which just shows film of farm animals. I saw it watched with fascination by a child who had just been seeing the same animals outside. The perceptually simplified cartoon, the puppet, the jingle are responded to at once, whatever their adult content. I can still myself recite, like any other childhood poem or hymn, a composition beginning:

Hurrah for Betox, what a delightful smell,
The stuff that every self-respecting grocer has to sell.

In the same way I have seen children delightedly watch and learn to repeat the beans jingles, the biscuit slogans, the Fairy Liquid responses. *Sesame Street* has taken these conventions to teach letters, numbers, animals, urban noises. To call its methods commercial is an abuse of terms.

There is more to it than that. The young teachers (in contrast to their counterparts on most English children's programmes) begin teaching games and then the emphasis passes to the children. The main teaching of "B" and of "4", for example, was done without an instructing adult in sight. Actually—and it leaves room for thought—most white adults, and especially the middle-aged, appeared only to be incompetent and to provide some of the cue-mistakes. This special kind of child-centredness, and the basic identification with a poor minority-group community, would be enough in itself to disturb our very different aunt-and-uncle-and-garden world.

My granddaughter, at 16 months, watched 80 per cent of what seemed, for young children, a very long programme. She turned round and said "B" after the "B" sequence as happily as she turns round and says "Woof" whenever she sees Dougal. In the lively figures of four and in the strong beat of the count to ten I found myself joining in. The magic glasses to identify noises were delightful.

There are so many good schools and children's television programmes on British television that I don't want to be understood as saying that *Sesame Street* supersedes them. But it is doing a vital and particular job, for the educationally deprived, which with allowance for age-groups and different school-starts is much more generally useful and enjoyable. I don't say "Buy it," like the £15 father. But I say: "Think about it."

18 November 1971

Three Documentaries

Three documentaries: *Public Poison* (BBC-1), *Willingly to School?* (BBC-2), *There was this fella* (Granada). It's worth noting that these were on two nights of television last week, and that on one of the same nights there was a fourth. This steady flow of reports needs remembering when we are trying to make any general judgment of British television. It can be said that as a rule it is safe ground, and that rather a lot of people know how to cover it in a workmanlike way—as opposed, for example, to the difficulties of genuine experiment. But it is still at the centre of ordinary serious television, and I think it is right to acknowledge it.

Take one obvious comparison first. On the magazine programmes there are many small documentaries, but in some reports and almost always in the studio there is steady adherence to that less effective convention of the visible intermediary, putting questions "on our behalf". In the conventional documentary, *Public Poison* or *Willingly to School?*, there is a linking exposition and commentary, but with admirable economy—because of the editing—answers come through reasonably straight. In the magazine programmes it is much more common to see interviewer's itch, in which the secondary sufferer, the man likely to have something to say, is lucky if he gets through two consecutive points and in some cases lucky if he gets through one. We are now so used to seeing day-to-day public issues refracted through the same few minds that we may have given up protesting, so for the record let me say that the "come-back-to-that-in-a-minuters" (they often don't) and their brothers who remark, "That's very interesting," (expression of harried distaste) "but could we just deal with this"—my—"point?" are a bloody nuisance in television. The only wonder is whether they acquire their anti-skills by mutual imitation or by training.

A documentary gets preparation time: magazines are rushed on the air. But that only partly corresponds to the division of interests and subjects. More could be done to improve this kind of television by pushing back the magazine empires and extending real documentaries than in any other reasonably ready and simple way.

Public Poison was about industrial pollution, especially by mercury, lead and cadmium. In Japan a catalyst used in a chemical factory had poisoned, killed and deformed many people in a fishing village on an enclosed bay. On a lake in Canada, accessible only from the air, mercury from a paper-bleaching process had worked its way through a network of rivers to poison the fish. There was some useful and balanced argument on the natural incidence of mercury and on its danger levels. Similarly with lead poisoning: for and against estimates of pollution by lead as a petrol additive, and scenes of foul water coming out of old lead pipes and of poor children in St Louis picking and eating peeling lead paint. The pictures of people ill and deformed from these kinds of poisoning and from a cadmium case in Japan were painful but necessary. Written by John Lloyd and directed by Michael Blakstad, this was a steady, responsible public-service programme. Almost its only false note was a gesture to melodrama in the introduction of a Japanese doctor (as yet unidentified) who was called "notorious", and said to need a bodyguard and varying routes to his work. So far as I heard, this wasn't explained, and it created a false image when he stopped in his car and a terribly bent woman got up from a pool and hobbled to defer to him: by most dramatic conventions he was by this time the poisoner rather than, in fact, the diagnostician and healer.

Willingly to School? was a *Horizon* look at new kinds of infant and junior teaching: a decent and timely explanation, with good examples. Its best things were the poems and commentary by the pupils of Christopher Searle, the suspended teacher, and the Piaget learning-stages demonstrations by Joan Bliss. Its worst thing was a potted history of 19th-century elementary education: several of its points were fair, and the overall emphasis was right, but it ran different periods together, missed the fact of some early project-learning, and in its reference to Dickens made Gradgrind a teacher: more off the point than usual, since in the illustration M'Choakumchild was standing beside him. I remember Gradgrind the theorist as I listened to some of the expert phrases in which creative practice and practical learning got embedded as educational theory. "Organising the imagination" and "organising the child's emotional life" (I quote from memory) seemed curious descriptions for what was actually going on, and they raised odd echoes.

On the obvious public-service issues—education, science, health—the BBC has the tradition and the edge. But Granada followed up their *Comedians* series with an interesting, exploratory and flexible programme by Gus Macdonald, *There was this fella*: not the standard serious topic but a socially-extending look at an area of popular culture—the part-time comedians of the Northern clubs. We can be glad that Macdonald did it, with the skill and respect of looking in, taking part, sensing the subtle and interesting interplay between the life and the entertainment. It's not my locality, and there was more than I'd want of a fat eye on the cash looking or trying to look like down-to-earth bluff fun. But I came very much to respect the audiences (unless the editing misled me). They delighted in what seemed if not the real thing then the best thing: a Liverpool teacher, Tom O'Connor, son of a docker, telling more new jokes and improving more old ones than most professionals we now see—all of them based on the life of the docks, many overheard from his father and his children at school. His "winged chicken" foreman was very funny popular art, and his audience, sharing the same life, were with him in ways quite different from show business.

16 December 1971

The Question of Ulster

It isn't often that a television programme becomes a matter of intense controversy even before it is shown. For this if no other reason *The Question of Ulster* (BBC-1) requires some extended notice. Coming as it did in the middle of an important controversy about the politics of television, it was bound to be a landmark. The news report that the Home Secretary had decided not to use his powers to prevent the programme being shown must have reminded many people how precarious and critical the situation in communications now is.

The BBC showed a necessary firmness in going on with the programme. Since I am saying this in a BBC journal, I ought to add that I think the BBC has in general, and especially in recent months, a less than honourable record on the reporting of events in Northern Ireland. Earlier pressures have taken their toll, until the point has been reached which marks crisis for anyone seriously concerned with communications: when some views are excluded because they are *prima facie* abhorrent— the charter of censors anywhere in the world. I do not have to approve of the bombing of a pub in Belfast to want to know why it was bombed.

Thus a victory for the censors had already been gained before *The Question of Ulster* was announced. Nobody from the IRA was to be heard, in whatever form (one can see that for practical reasons it would have had to be recorded). The trouble with that kind of exclusion is that it gives provocation to others. Mrs Whitehouse is reported as asking for a legal ruling on the participation of Bernadette Devlin.* In ways like this an atmosphere is created in which the whole case for free speech has to be restated and fought from the beginning.

Free speech is only a difficult issue when the matters to be spoken of are indeed disruptive. Historically the reaction of Ministers was reminiscent of campaigns against the press in the late 18th and early 19th centuries. That period, like our own, was one of democratic transition, in which the character of political discourse was changing, ideas of "the public" expanding. What had been permitted within a closed circle was found offensive and dangerous when anyone who could read could follow the argument and arrive at his own opinions. The current anger about politics on television is a symptom of the same process at a further stage.

It isn't easy now for authority to say that the public has no right to hear the arguments of an opposition or a minority. But what can more easily be said is that they must never be heard without immediate reply from ruling or majority opinion. Since it is that opinion which we in any case most commonly hear, the appeal to "balance" is usually less than candid. But it can also be used, as in this case, to try to exercise a practical veto: if *they* are speaking, *we* will not—so no balance and no programme. It is an event of some importance that in *The Question of Ulster* this bluff was called. The refusals of Mr Maudling and Mr Faulkner** were dealt with by a substitution of filmed reports: perfectly fairly, in my view. Indeed, this happens all the time to ordinary citizens, in more local cases; or when someone has refused to appear, the fact is reported and only the other side of the case is heard.

But these, the reply seems to go, are Ministers. They were being asked to speak in a programme which had something of the appearance of a "tribunal". I agree it was unfortunate that this word "tribunal" was used by the press. It was only the familiar Establishment device of the three wise men, but some people may have thought of it as giving a verdict. The tribunal that mattered—and it is a real

---

*Mary Whitehouse. Co-founder of the "Clean up TV Campaign", 1964. Bernadette Devlin (now McAliskey). Student activist, Queen's University, Belfast. Youngest Member of Parliament when elected for 1969-74 term.

**Reginald Maudling. Home Secretary from 1970-1972 in Edward Heath's Conservative government. Brian Faulkner. Northern Ireland Premier until direct rule from London was imposed in 1972.

tribunal—was the viewing public. Before them, before us, Ministers have to appear, and this is more likely to be useful if it is not always on occasions and in circumstances of their own choosing, but side by side with their critics and opponents, and given no privilege or authority which they cannot themselves earn by the weight of their arguments. Behind many recent controversies this has been the real issue, and it is the central point of historical significance. There are many arguments for and against representative democracy, but the central argument, now, is about its claim to monopolise and exhaust the political process, to a point where all other substantive political discussion can be made to appear impertinent or even illegal. It is this tendency which it is the duty of any public television service to resist.

The pressures are obviously intense. The *Telegraph* had a cartoon of a song-and-dance show by the Devlinettes. But if a television programme is planned to run for two and three-quarter hours of quiet and orderly discussion, the "entertainment" slur is absurd. It is also contemptible that when the programme has gone out at this length and in this temperate manner, some of the same people can turn and jeer that it was boring and dull.

Or take the other objection, that it was "trial by television". This is a phrase that got into currency for quite different events: the hostile questioning of an individual or a group in isolation from other kinds of evidence and process. It cannot be fairly used of a programme which, if it had gone out as planned, would have questioned representatives of all major positions except the IRA, and which, as it in fact went out, was a series of statements and questions designed to elucidate differences of opinion and possible areas of agreement.

Short of an extreme political reaction, which if it comes will of course be resisted by all possible means, the authorities cannot effectively control the content of television or explicitly limit its capacity to make different views in the society visible and audible to all concerned. All that can now be done—and it is being vigorously attempted—is to create a climate of fear and anxiety, in which people and institutions will begin to censor themselves. Some effects of this attempt were evident in the very programme on which, to its credit, the BBC had taken its stand.

It is right that people should carefully consider what they say about a dispute in which other people are being killed. But responsibility is not only that kind of care: it is also an insistence on rising to the level of the events themselves. The most relevant witnesses were those who, from different points of view, spoke this kind of substance: Bernadette Devlin, describing the facts of the society and understandably impatient of external constitutional deals; Mr Paisley, Mr Bleakley and Mr Cooper,* offering other views of their day-to-day experience and drawing different conclusions. By contrast, Mr Maginnis, Mr O'Kennedy and Mr Blaney** seemed lost in what passes for politics. The three members of the panel were similarly contrasted: Sir John Foster asking questions which would make a political point about the witness; Lord Devlin trying to elucidate conditions for talks; Lord Caradon, not the lawyer but the international negotiator, trying to persuade participants onto some common ground. This necessarily dramatised some of the uncertainties of the programme. If the object, as was said at the beginning, was to seek "not conflict but conciliation", Caradon was the only likely starter. Lord Devlin ended with the implication that the Opposition's conditions were unwise but did not mention the other conditions and restrictions of agenda. Sir John Foster, clearly embarrassed, tried to summarise what all the others had clearly said. But if information rather than conciliation was the object, then that object was achieved. I read all I can about Ireland, but I learned several new facts and heard two or three new arguments.

What then was the final objection? That it had hardened attitudes? It seems a ludicrous comment when we look at what is happening in the streets, but what was meant has an important political significance. Mr Fitt† is being pressed to enter talks while internment without trial is still in force. Speaking in front of his constituents, it has been said, he had to be harder on this than he would

---

*Rev. Ian Paisley. Presbyterian minister and member of Northern Ireland Parliament. David Bleakley. Social scientist and politician. Minister of Community Relations of Northern Ireland Parliament, March-September 1971. Ivan Cooper. Member of Parliament of Northern Ireland (Independent).

**Ken Maginnis. Member of Ulster Defence Regiment 1970-81. Ulster Unionists party spokesman on internal security and defence. Michael O'Kennedy. Irish Republic politician (Fianna Fail party). Parliamentary Secretary to the Minister for Education, 1970-72. Neil Blaney. Irish Republic politician (Fianna Fail party) and strong supporter of a unified Ireland.

†Gerald Fitt. Member of Parliament of Northern Ireland 1962-72. Later founder of Social and Democratic Labour Party (SDLP).

otherwise have been. I would doubt this imputation, but what is more important is the perspective it gives on what is supposed to be politics: presumably, getting a representative out of sight of his constituents and then trying to persuade him. Some people may see dangers in open television politics but these are as nothing compared with the dangers of backstairs political bargaining, and our only defence is the power of publicity, in television and the press.

A final word about the production. I was surprised when the first clips and stills came on while statements were being made. Clearly there is room for dispute about their selection and effect, and the point can be conceded that they gave a different impression from current news bulletins. That cuts both ways. It is a long time since we have seen, in any regular way, what it is like to be at the receiving end of the actions of the Army and the Police. What we are now regularly shown is the injury and damage caused by the bombs. The rest of the production was unobtrusive and well-sustained. On other subjects, as urgent though less bloody than the tragedy of Ireland, the open-ended programme should now have come to stay.

13 January 1972

Culture

"We don't watch television," said the young Italian professor. We were at the end of a seminar on contemporary British culture and I had said that in several different ways television had to be part of the evidence. "It's quite true," someone added: "Italian intellectuals don't watch television." I tried to think back to when I had last heard something like that said in Britain: I guessed ten years. But it started several trains of thought. Some people explained the difference between the two television services: the Italian was much more controlled. I had no way of judging that. The one free evening I had in a fortnight was a Sunday and apart from a news bulletin and a quiz show it was all football: I noticed in the after-the-match interviews that players lined up with the same hung heads, the same good-natured inarticulacy on unanswerable questions, as in *Match of the Day*. The other thing I noticed, and liked, was the more frequent appearance of women announcers and presenters.

As a matter of fact, I knew that the point about Italian intellectuals didn't hold universally. Several professors and writers had seen

the newsreels from Ulster and the very good Italian report on the
crisis, of which an extract was shown on a useful edition of *24
Hours.* It will perhaps be no surprise if I add that those who had
recently visited Britain and watched the home television reports on
Ireland were dismayed by what they saw as the evident pro-
Government bias. Travelling back through the Alps, catching the
occasional glimpse of the blue screen in the houses under the snow, I
wondered how much our controllers and their supporters realise,
even yet, the international character, the frontier-crossing power, of
television and film. To keep someone off British screens seems really
ludicrous, even in terms of a bland *realpolitik,* when he is quite certain to be seen and listened to on the screens of several continents.

Nevertheless, a problem remains. Have British intellectuals simply drifted with television? Have we forgotten, or half-forgotten,
some necessary discriminations and standards? After a break, always,
I find I turn this question over. I came back to the cold set and the
first thing that rose in the glory of colour was an English actor wrap-
ping his mouth round some words of Italian charm which were to
delight, as I remember, an English actress about to wrap her mouth
around some chocolate or other. I went and unpacked my cases.

And it's no answer, I suppose, that the next time I switched on
there was that jumpy fanfare of the News and a man came round a
street corner carrying a white cloth and crouched over a stretcher.
That Sunday in Londonderry came through with quite terrible
power, like the street television of the Tet offensive in Saigon. You
can read all about it. But "a man was shot" is different from a man
being shot. The immediacy was extraordinary and can be claimed to
have forced a different kind of attention.

Other evenings followed. The question isn't to be settled by that
kind of crisis. So I went back to the starting-point of the argument.
What relevant evidence, of a cultural kind, can television offer?
Negative evidence is of course admitted, by intellectuals everywhere,
whether or not they watch. The simplistic sociology of what is called
"mass communications", "mass media"—academic jargon that stops
thought—has made terrible inroads everywhere: as certain a
symptom of uncertain standards as anything, even the worst, on television. But positive evidence? Is there any?

I was talking, it must be remembered, to serious men. I couldn't
offer them the publicity hand-out, now perhaps permanently set up
in type: *Civilisation, The Forsyte Saga, The Six Wives of Henry VIII.*

What I could offer, tentatively, was certain structures of discussion and certain forms of documentary drama, though the interesting thing about these is that neither of the older terms, nor their conjunction, defines the work quite closely enough. It is a difficult argument, and impossible without comparisons. We have to look at what else has happened, in the received high cultural forms: contemporary theatre, for example, which is still widely taken on trust. Anyway I was still thinking about it when *Review* put on a discussion in a Manchester cinema immediately after the showing of *Family Life,* and Tony Garnett and Ken Loach and two of the actresses talked about the film and its subject with the audience.

First: it is important that this was done, and done in this way: a world away from showbiz. "We want to open these issues up," Tony Garnett said, "get people thinking critically about these issues they're involved in." It's always said, but here it was meant. Garnett's record in doing just that is part of the positive evidence.

Second: "documentary drama". Brecht said that to get people thinking critically we had to alter dramatic form; move away from imposed single meanings and the selective organisation of sympathy; promote complex seeing within the form and not leave it to subsequent discussion. Some real contradiction, then, undoubtedly arises between the dramatic form and the dramatic intention within which it was held. This contradiction was evident here.

Third: language. When Tony Garnett or I say "politics" we mean "society". When "politics" is said to most general audiences in Britain it means Wilson and Heath.* One girl asked (twice, because she wasn't understood) where you went, in this society, after a human psychological treatment. And it's a real question, though I know one of the answers ("fight the system"). It wasn't answered. Did the dramatic form retain its hold? Suppose one said contemporary capitalism is breaking down the last social ties that are inconsistent with its kind of mobility: the family, the local community, provincial settlements. Who then is being liberated into what? And the

---

*Edward Heath. British Prime Minister 1970-74, a period marked by strong class conflict and opposition to his incomes policies. Even though he had broken with the Labour Party, Williams briefly supported it in the 1974 election when Heath was looking for support to break the trade unions. Having lost the general election Heath was replaced the following year as Conservative Party leader by Margaret Thatcher.

question was there, but the form couldn't answer it: it had set it up the other way round.

Positive evidence? I still think so. Outside a very few books, and even fewer university courses, these questions don't get raised anywhere with the clarity and openness we still sometimes get on television. These young men facing an audience they had to some extent brought into being, too quickly defensive but keeping on with the offer: that, among other reasons, is why television matters, why it is part of our serious culture.

10 February 1972

Old Times and New: on Solidarity

The most powerful sequence in Ken Ashton's film, *We was all one* (Thames), was of life in a slum tenement, plagued by rats, and it didn't have to be reconstructed, or taken as a clip from the library: it was only a bus-ride from where the rest of London is living. It was like, and yet curiously unlike, comparable sequences from the documentaries of the Thirties: the same squalor and debris in which crowded families have to grow up, but the young women trying to cope with the dreadful conditions were dressed in today's clothes and had hairstyles much like the other young women who in the unnatural commercial break were simpering about chocolates and detergents. That made it much worse: the survival of that kind of slum among the images of affluence. It also gave a necessary perspective on the rest of the programme, which was lively reminiscence of the old days in Bermondsey. The question that has been central for the last 20 years was again put: has anything been lost, in neighbourliness and community, as the material conditions of the majority have been altered and improved? The older people who spoke about the past gave a convincingly specific and varied picture: the hunger and poverty came through with the assurance that there was then a more active solidarity, mutuality; that they all helped each other, under the constant pressures; that "we was all one."

It isn't an easy argument, and the film offered questions rather than conclusions. There were some conventional visual contrasts between the spaced impersonality of the tower blocks and flyovers and the warm, singing friendliness of the pub; the young, in this version, were all standing crowded, passive and wide-eyed at the strip-dance. But a more fertile question was put once or twice: was the tower block the only alternative to the old streets? Couldn't the existing houses have been modernised, keeping neighbours together? That was qualified by facts about changes in locations of work, but it is still a real question. It's easy to be distracted by a contrast between "squalor" and "affluence" presented in conventionally materialist ruling-class terms. The real point is that the people who needed better housing were never asked what kinds of house, what kinds of community, they themselves wanted. They were planned *for,* and there was then an inevitable confusion. We are all so uneasy about a possible betrayal by nostalgia, and at the same time uneasy about the brittleness of many adjustments to a planned consumer society, that we swing this way and that and miss the hardest question: why we allowed the terms of change to be so imposed—what it was, in representative democracy, that permitted the gap between people's feelings about life and what was done in their name and with their money?

I couldn't connect, directly, with the people remembering their old life in Bermondsey, except at one incidental point, the hop-picking, which from a different place my family also used to set out for. But I listened to the stories and found myself thinking back to that other version of Cockney life in *Steptoe and Son.* Of course, the period there is ambiguous. When Harold took the horse and cart through a carwash, this was even part of the joke. The first two episodes of the new series were in a familiar mode: Harold's ambition, first to write, then to act, frustrated, compromised or simply upstaged by his father. That is the painful nerve that keeps being touched. But obviously a lot of the success of the series depends on a certain detachment from older ways of living. The bizarre junk, the hand-to-mouth manners, the pronounced and self-conscious roughness of language: these mediate the tensions of transition which *We was all one* faced directly.

Low life is traditionally a middle-class joke, but I wondered what kind of a joke it was in the third episode: one of the rare occasions when father and son go out together against another group—in this case the rest of the Steptoe family at a funeral. The sketch was a compendium of working-class funeral jokes: the beer on the coffin, the family rows. But set the feeling of "we was all one" against the fierce conventional rapacity of this contrived family—the race back from the funeral to get the best things from the house, Albert's cunning capture of a piece of 18th-century porcelain—and you get another ambiguity: this rapacity is a traditional working-class joke, but past the caricatures of Old Cockney types there was the unmistakable accent of a different kind of rat-race—the socially ambiguous world of the Sixties. Perhaps it is only that *Steptoe* is all things to all men, but there is a necessary question about the transition from the traditional internal stories of a community to the same material as general entertainment.

One of the old ladies in the Bermondsey pub told a story from hop-picking times: how they were 14 (I think) in a bed, women at the top and men at the bottom, and in the middle of the night they would sometimes get mixed up, a man not knowing which was his wife. Some of this, I expect, had already improved in the telling, but as I heard it I could also hear, like an echo, its translation—see Wilfrid Brambell's Albert-face telling it, with a leer very different from the tolerant laugh—and it struck me how different the feeling then was, how the presentation altered it—from our life to low life. And yet I'd bet you could play it back, to the original audience, and it would be accepted, perhaps rightly, as popular art, in the confused feelings of the general transition.

Something of the same process was consciously seen in an interesting episode of the *British Empire* series: the rural history of Australia. The song "Waltzing Matilda" was taken back to its presumed origins, in a sheep-shearers' strike, and the episode was re-enacted, for an audience and cameras. I found the facts of Australian rural labour important evidence for my growing belief that in spite of the flummery the *British Empire* series is letting through a lot of hitherto suppressed history: suppressed, that is, at the level of ordinary popular accounts. It is necessary to remember how the idea of Empire was sold, to three generations, and how much of that confusion still lasts, if we are to give a fair account of this very mixed and properly controversial project. Even *The Regiment* (BBC-1), the latest piece of costume drama, is letting things through about Rhodes and the social structure of the Army.

At a distance, of course, we can see more clearly. A beautiful film about the Spanish Empire and its silver in Bolivia, *The Treasures of Chuquisaca* (BBC-2), had not only the force of an exotic and memorable history but also an awareness of contemporary struggle there.

16 March 1972

Hardy Annuals

Every month I mean to write about the small programmes which make up so large a part of decent television. Again and again other more insistent events seem to take priority. But that, in itself, is characteristic of experience in this society: an experience which in its own ways television underlines.

They are very mixed, these small programmes. Take *Gardeners' World* (BBC-2), which has come again with the Spring. Almost always it is simple, honest visual instruction, especially at this time of year when it is more concerned with planting than with display. At times it strays off to the country-house circuit which the social sensibilities of planners and the facts of training of most professional gardeners indicate. But these last two or three weeks it has been at its best, showing the details of sowing and planting. Anyone who has done much gardening will already know most of the advice being given, but it needs unusual steadiness to realise that this, in many ordinary matters, is the cultural point: a certain necessary recurrence, and the needs of new people doing something for the first time on their own. What impresses me about the programme is that it avoids a familiar impatience. Percy Thrower, planting and pruning, with almost every verb a present participle, sticks to the job as if it had never been done before. If this makes him vulnerable to a certain kind of mockery—which is in any case always latent, in this society, in anything to do with the land—his persistence is in the end that much more impressive.

Take, as a contrast, *Going for a Song* (BBC-1). There, too, in the idea, is a simple enough need. It is painful to think of the number of well-made and interesting things that have been neglected and thrown out: indeed there are still many in what are called the junkshops. But *Going for a Song* has for the most part given in to a formula and an ideology. There is enough ideology in gardening: not only the old country-house point of view but the new instant mail-order amaze-your-neighbours huckstering and confidence tricks. *Gardeners' World,* for the most part, steers clear of both, in their worst forms. But the ideology of antiques is more total. Historically it is built on a ratification of Georgian and Regency taste: indeed its constant propaganda is a major element in the myth of "taste" in those dreadful years. More critically it is oriented to the sharp accents of the contemporary fashionable auction, like the News bulletins which only mention art when it has been turned into sales-room money. *Going for a Song* had the advantage, in Arthur Negus, of a man who could brilliantly explain many of the details of craftsmanship, especially in wood, and it has had visiting experts who have given a great deal of similarly interesting information. But the programme then made two choices. First, to encapsulate this into a sort of quiz game, with an intervening chairman who in himself has had an effect on its now cosily lacquered tone. The competing guests, significantly, win points for the auction price rather than for, say, the style or the date of the pieces. Second, and connected with this ten-dency, it has drifted towards the top of the market: so much so that at home we now call it *Going for an Opera*. It can be said that many of the most beautiful things are bound to be expensive, though that relation is by no means constant. But the real point is that the high prices are visibly enjoyed, and the offer to the viewer is that as well as learning about valuable objects he can take part, mainly as a spec-tator, in what then becomes vulgar display. It is as if Percy Thrower, instead of telling us how to plant blackcurrants and sow lettuce, went straight, in every programme, for the peaches and the orchids. But as it happens there is a more immediate comparison in *Collec-tor's World* (BBC-2), which is also often punctuated with the ring of the cash-register but which on the whole is more open, more varied and more genuinely public.

The areas of interest in which these short programmes are put on are significant. There is the evident pull of the past: *The Craftsmen* (BBC-2), for example, has an excellent range and is a fine series. And on recent Saturdays (the association with weekends is another part of the ideology) there have been two or three interesting and curious short films from Wales: a harp-maker and ship-model builder; a forestry worker who carves ram's horns. Through each, as from Cardiff Arms Park, came the sound of choirs; and there was the russet of bracken on the Glamorgan hills and the green of the woods above Dolgellau. Perhaps someone soon will go to the isolated Welsh tapestry mills, now again producing to capacity. There was a compa-rable film, in *24 Hours*, on the ending of the slate quarries, again with a choir. I had driven, only a few days before, through the black valleys of the slate spoil, and past the deserted lead-mines above Llanidloes. It was easy to share the sad mixed feelings of all these beautifully-made films, and the pleasures (though rather externally seen) of a film about Black Mountain sheepdogs in the admirable

Look, Stranger series (BBC-2). But the sense of just that title is disturbing, as in so many small programmes. They are done so well as visits, glimpses, but as you take their full weight you know they should be composed into a connected history, a connected way of seeing, that would include the real present. Meanwhile, however, no Britain (except, as in the ideology, assorted Tudors and Churchills); but of course continuing, and already being repeated, *The British Empire*. I'd put in a supporting word for some of its episodes: the programme on Singapore was again illuminating. But I have now seen the programme on Indian independence, *The Long Farewell*, and I can see why many people are angry, though for me it went beyond anger. The pictures were there; most of the facts were mentioned, within the ordinary limits of summary. But the tone of the commentary should become a set text: I only wish I had it in front of me, for some proper analysis. For it was so deep a ratification of the original power relationship: deep enough, as can happen (see almost any White Paper), for the language to be moderate, all points of view apparently represented and weighed, and yet the result is the bland reassertion of the white man's "burden and responsibility", as against the ambitious and quarrelsome Indian politicians. Fortunately, to go no further, we had recently seen a good filmed interview with Indira Gandhi. But it wasn't just India that made the tone important; it was the extreme persistence of what are called moderate points of view. And I should have noticed this, I think, even if the tone—the moderate-sounding extremism of the conventional politician—hadn't been there all week, from all the English political parties, about a new phase of our history: the struggle in Ireland.

6 April 1972

Where Does Rozanov Come In?

"Suppose Masters's real point in letting the girl come to see us was to get us to think that Richardson is the sleeper. But follow that through. If Richardson *isn't* the sleeper, how do we decide between Bate and Mrs Anderson? And above all, Charles, where does Rozanov come in?" Snatches of intricate reasoning of this kind seem to fill the air waves. The spy story has taken over from the detective story as family entertainment. BBC-1's *Spy Trap* has the added complexity of being divided into episodes. One keeps being told, by disillusioned politicians and communicators, that most of the public can understand very little, but it doesn't seem to hold for these plots. Or is it that the pleasure comes from watching the sharp investigator going through his pirouette of names and motives and possibilities? In the most popular kind of detective story that was undoubtedly so. His style when unravelling, but also his style when baffled, was so carefully created that even Bate and Mrs Anderson became, by comparison, shadowy figures: a ballet of ghostly categories, but the dancer was marvellous. We can look at an old instance in the serialisation on BBC-1 of *Lord Peter Wimsey: Clouds of Witness*, where the literary allusiveness seems to have been lost in the adaptation (finding a clue in *Manon Lescaut* seems almost incidental), but where there is an attentive reconstruction of aristocratic period charm and in the leading actor a strong reminiscence of Bertie Wooster.* A contemporary equivalent, I suppose, would be *Jason King* (ITV): the stylish novelist who turns up, as if with "Fascinator" in his passport, on an island full of rumours about revolution, and to work out his plot asks for a likely place to land guns. Things happen, but in the end he brushes the dust off his sleeve.

The investigators in *Spy Trap* do not set out to charm. They are doing a job, as if they were in *Softly, Softly*. Something must be allowed, I suppose, for the direct inclusion of contemporary international politics. None of the old thriller Ruritanias or shadow Balkans: usually the Russians, the East Germans—if you watched many of these stories, in the numerous series, you might be forgiven for imagining yourself something of an expert on the KGB.

It is all now standard commercial entertainment and there is perhaps no more to say, though what we take as standard and seal off as entertainment may in the end tell us something about our culture. But I have found myself more interested in just one of these series, *Callan* (Thames). It is interesting in an obvious way because it belongs with Deighton and Le Carré to the kind of disillusioned spy fiction which became popular in the Sixties. The unwilling, the suffering, the deceived agent: the distant debt to Graham Greene and beyond him to some important late 19th and early 20th-century liter-

*Bertie Wooster. Amiable young gentleman in stories by P.G. Woodhouse.

ature is fairly obviously there. But Callan, I find, is very much the most interesting psychological figure. Some of the earlier examples have an abstract scepticism: international politics and international espionage are a dirty game, on both sides; the professionals recognise this and can respect each other more easily than their manoeuvring and deceiving employers. This abstract cynicism is important, but less so, I would say, than the accompanying reversal of values and styles. From Holmes to Wimsey* (and in a survival like King) the agent is all glamorised intelligence, of an upper-class kind; his professional aides are usually plain, limited men. This emphasis has been reversed in police stories like *Softly, Softly* and *Z Cars,* but the change in spy fiction has been very much sharper. Glamour moved down till it got to James Bond, but in *Callan,* for example, our introduction to the agent is not in Mayfair or Crete or the Bahamas, with careful allusions to exotic literature or exotic drinks, but in a bleak flat where he has a cold and is trying to clear it with a towel over a basin. At the office there is intricate reasoning, and anyone, by ordinary script mechanics, may ask: "Where does Rozanov come in?" But the interest is not there: it is in a dull, inescapable job, which happens to be killing.

I can see the case that might then be made: that this anti-romanticism is merely, as elsewhere, a romantic twist; that it makes the whole thing worse by taking the glamour out of espionage and the secret police and yet retaining killing as normal—showing it as just a job. The other week it happened that I switched over from *Callan* to the *24 Hours* special report on Bloody Sunday and Widgery.** I noticed how different the dead looked. Anyone who sees even a moderate amount of cinema and television must have seen thousands of actors die, and every kind of simulatory skill has been used. There were very similar shots in *Callan* and the Londonderry newsfilm: a view from above of a murdered man lying in a pool of his own

*Lord Peter Wimsey. Aristocratic hero of mystery novels by Dorothy Sayers. The reference to King is unclear but seems to be to the author Francis King whose novels, many with foreign settings, are marked by a cool and ironic detachment.

**Bloody Sunday. Thirteen civilians were killed and others injured on January 30, 1972 by troops during a Civil Rights demonstration in Derry, Northern Ireland. An official inquiry under Lord Widgery found that the troops had been fired upon first but that those shot by the army were not handling guns or bombs.

blood. And it wasn't only the context: it was the image that was different. No actor that I have seen has yet come near to simulating the untidy crumpled emptiness of the real victims of violence.

We remain, you could say, on the right end of the gun. But that is almost incidental, or is made to seem so. What comes through in *Callan* is a different feeling: an overwhelming, inescapable but unaccepted alienation. It is there even more strongly in James Mitchell's original book, *Red File for Callan*—once called, in an older style, *A Magnum for Schneider*—so it is not just Edward Woodward's compelling acting. The trapped irony is indeed quite internal. Callan has a criminal record, a conventional policeman complains. Where else, he replies, would you recruit from? When he has killed some less professional gunmen, from a London gang, the office version is that he has killed thugs: not like us, Callan says, we're civil servants.

It is this corroding self-deprecation and irony that may be the real significance. *Callan* is, I am told, exceptionally popular, for all the strength and variety of the competition. It would be easy to say that this is because it is very well produced, on an interesting variant of a safe entertainment formula. But I think it may be more. Through this improbable channel (which may, it is true, allow just enough for fantasy when the killing starts) what flows is something that might, in different circumstances, have been expressed more directly: a contempt for the system in which he is trapped and in serving which he knows he is destroying himself and others. Not a principled contempt: more a contempt in the guts, as the only residual language. Isolated contempt, from the bottom of the system: the employers are self-evidently trivial, stylish, unfeeling and dishonest, and this is a plain man's job, but not a job to respect. Residual impulses of kindness and loyalty, which may or may not get in the way of the killing, but that is the only way they come up.

It is worth thinking about. Because if that is the feeling, and if it gets through so widely, it is significant and desperate. And you can see why it is covered by the usual apparatus of projection and by asking as if it mattered: "Where does Rozanov come in?"

4 May 1972

The Golden Lotus

What is the difference between a classic serial and a drama series? That with the classic serial we already have the book? But as often as not that doesn't help with the television adaptation. I don't mean only that if we have read it we already have visual images of our own: some directly derived from the text; others, inevitably, a distillation from more general experiences of reading. Some people would say that "the classics" shouldn't be adapted, that television vulgarises them. But the answer to that is not only that there is evidence that these adaptations send thousands of readers to books they might not otherwise have heard of, and send other readers back to them: it is also that to see a work in a new version and a new medium is always potentially illuminating. This is essentially what happens, after all, every time we go to see a contemporary production of *Hamlet*. The real problem is deeper, and it is interestingly illustrated by the current adaptation (BBC-2) of Henry James's *The Golden Bowl*. I watched the crucial third episode within a day of watching the fifth episode of *The Lotus Eaters* (also BBC-2). "Episode", of course, means different things here. A few central characters appear in each episode of *The Lotus Eaters*: the people at Shepherd's Bar in Crete. It looked at the beginning as if the series would be the usual hybrid of an exotic setting and a spy story: Ann Shepherd, the flashbacks remind us, is an agent waiting to be assigned, and sooner or later, I suppose, she will be. But meanwhile it is a string on which separate stories are being threaded. A nasty thing happened to that Major at the corner table: his wife had a breakdown and thought she saw tarantulas, including one on his face, and camera and props collaborated in seeing and killing it and, incidentally, him. It had seemed a long way from Henry James.

Then in the fifth episode, again a separable story, we got what can be described as true "drama series". I don't mean only the sense of insertion: the golden girl washed up in the motor-boat being seen as Aphrodite, in the same spirit as the stylish Greek lettering of the titles. I mean that habit of taking (the trade word is "creating") an interesting situation, involving complex problems of character and ethos, and playing it fast, presenting all the sharp details, including the various characters' attempts to describe and understand it, and resolving nothing. It was quite genuinely interesting: two young women, school-friends, whose relationship could be seen in several ways: the tart using her simple friend, or the cynically intelligent woman trying to preserve the physically insatiable "Aphrodite", or a mixture of both. It was in that stylish mode where it all happens fast and that's the product. This explains the evident connection, in direction, camera-work and acting, with commercials. Who can say or understand anything when the golden girl arrives on the beach? Nobody, while that's happening, wants some analyst, some moralist, prosing in. Have a drink, catch a plane: it's all happening and that's life.

Professional reasons? To some extent. If you're not Henry James and dead, you don't get that much time to explore a situation: you get your idea into the 50-minute slot in a series. But cause and effect, in this current mode, are more complicated than that. It *is* a way of seeing life: transitory, unresolved, unavoidably multiple; very disturbing, very difficult, but unavoidably ambiguous or opaque. And don't the textbooks say something about Victorian moralism and the outdated "omniscient-author convention"? In the trouble-shooting, lotus-eating, spy-trapping Seventies, better travel faster and lighter than that.

Henry James had the habit of mentally rewriting every new book he read. He once thought of rewriting Wells's *First Men in the Moon*: that must be one of the strangest lost books. Watching *Aphrodite,* I could sense that rewriting ghost of James: it was just the ambiguity, of how people use and depend on each other, in interlocking but often contradictory ways, that would at once have held his attention. But it wasn't, as he would have said, *done.* And if we look at *The Golden Bowl* we see what doing may involve. Look at one sentence from a scene that was directly adapted: " 'Yet you're not'—Charlotte made the important point—'too different from me.' " An adapter drops the author's underlining intervention: to advantage. The written conversation, in all its scrupulous qualifications and then its suddenly startling directness, comes through very strongly on its own, when it is allowed to: more strongly than James, after long experience of misunderstanding and neglect, believed possible. Some part of his anxious direction is a despair of being understood, and it's too easy to say that he should have had more confidence: that kind of energy is quickly sapped and to keep going in his own terms, driven back on himself and anxiously refining what was already pure metal, cost enough.

It isn't there that the adapter is serving him badly. It is in trying to find some equivalent to the running analysis of a more general kind. The device used is taking out Colonel Assingham—"what he said represented the limited vibration of which his confirmed old toughness had been capable"—and having him um and ah and wonder where he'd better begin, from the depths of his armchair in house or club. That won't do, in any terms. It can't touch the real James complexities, and as television drama it is only bearable—no, it is not bearable—as pure "classic serial": the leisure, the leather-chair storytelling.

Opposite poles, then: classic serial and drama series, in extreme but significant cases. Perhaps the polarity is the real point: the assumed and separated cultural categories: gracious living, fast living. But between them, struggling, occasionally getting through, is the drama that matters: life seen, rather than merely observed or rehearsed.

Down to Earth (BBC-1), a weekly magazine, uses every way it can think of to present problems of the environment: just enough of it works. So too did the two substantial programmes, by Paul Ferris, on *The Press We Deserved*: a repertory of techniques, some of them controversial; a good deal of visually interesting historical material; and in the second programme some film inside newspaper offices that seemed to me to reveal more than any analysis from outside could, though it quite memorably confirmed it. Fast dialogue, fast images; an interpreting, controversial mind.

1 June 1972

Hassle

"I noticed a couple of red hairs sticking out. Trim 'em." This was part of the amiable advice given by a trade-union leader to the McGovern organiser inside the Pennsylvania delegation to the Democratic Convention. The nominal subject was the organiser's beard. In the end it was the old leaders, full of such homely advice, who got trimmed.

Or so the narrative ran, in Granada's *World in Action Special* on how one delegation organised itself and its voting. The technique of the programme was almost continuous close-up, with only a minimum of explanation. "We're going to have a hassle," the trade-union leader was saying, as if privately, to a friend. "Now we don't want a hassle," he said, unpersuasively, when he started negotiating on the phone. The programme was full of people in action in just this local sense: the naked looks, the impulsive words, the hot intricacies of bargains and rows. As such it was intensely engaging: an unusual television experience, though *World in Action* has given us things of this kind before. It was a world away from the ordinary presentation of politics: the prepared public appearances. American openness and American political procedure made this possible. The roughness and confusion were not specifically American in any other sense. I have taken part in British political meetings which were much rougher and more confused. But this was inside one of the major established parties, and everyone seemed to agree that it was not just the ordinary rough-and-tumble of the day-to-day struggles for power, but a historical turning-point, a new direction in American politics, opening up a basic ideological choice. The programme was called *How to Steal a Party*, and in line with other commentaries saw the new people, the McGovern people, moving in and through the toughest political struggles establishing a new kind of politics.

I haven't the evidence, and I certainly haven't the desire, to dispute this interpretation. It would be marvellous if it were true, but my doubts are steady and harsh, and this programme did nothing to remove them. People have to move, and at other levels than a deal or a vote, if there is to be any real change. Presumably this happened somewhere, but we saw it only indirectly. What we really saw was indeed a hassle, and of a kind to make its ordinary television facsimiles look pale and contrived. But this wasn't the politics of what are called the grass roots. It started several joints up the political stem. As I watched, I felt two contradictory responses. An intense involvement with the outcome, for the dramatic closeness was so powerful: "as if," a friend said, "we didn't already know from the papers who won." At the same time, a questioning, a need for perspective: a need to know how the delegates got there, before the hassle started.

Stealing a party, after all, is not new politics: it is the central history of most democratic, radical and socialist movements. Stealing it back then? We have to hope so, but on this evidence we can't say. The programme noticed the contradiction between the partisans of open politics and their practice of local manoeuvre. There was an evident respect for just their toughness and smartness, beating the old bosses at their own game. But there was one woman delegate who clearly believed in open politics, as something more than a slogan, and her face, intermittently seen, silent and puzzled among the contending and swaying groups, had its own testimony.

One last point about the programme. It was an extraordinary achievement, even given American openness, to get so close to a process, in contrast with the ordinary current affairs programme which offers only the product, or even the packaged product. In its extraordinary vitality and record of vitality it made its own contribution to a new kind of politics, if only in its reminder that we don't need leaders and interviewers to be tough, concerned and persistent for us: we can do all that, given procedures and opportunities, for ourselves. Whatever I may think, or hold in reserve, about the particular outcome of the Convention, I find myself wishing that British politics, in their central processes, were even a quarter as open, as active and as public.

It was an accident, I dare say, that two other programmes I watched were so English and so quiet. A more relevant comparison, but it wasn't at sufficient length, would be the *Panorama Special* on the resignation of Maudling.* No edge or vitality there, except briefly and significantly in the openly hostile questioning of Paul Foot,** who may, in *Private Eye,* have started it all. He answered well and solidly, but he was treated as an outsider. Between interviewers and politicians the tone got back to the normal low-key disagreements of an essentially consensual group. With respect, as they say, offering their modest divergences. With respect to some.

Cradle of England (BBC-1) was the first of a new series which is trying to use archaeological evidence to reconstruct early social life. It came on around midnight—it deserves a much better time. It wasn't England then, of course: it wasn't even Britain. But past the simple gestures of a suggested continuity, which is probably only physically real, the inquiry was interesting. One very cool specialist picked up bone after bone and showed the stature, the diseases, the violent deaths of these men and women. The reconstruction of one of

*Reginald Maudling. Home Secretary in Edward Heath's Conservative government. Resigned following allegations that he had received money when in Opposition from architect John Poulson who was at the centre of a major corruption investigation.

**Paul Foot. Radical writer, journalist. Granada Television Journalist of the Year, 1972.

the big round houses, inside the oak palisade, and the calculation of the acres of forest that had to be felled to build them, were very illuminating, especially as one saw at the same time the stone and bone tools with which the work was done. This added a dimension to the twisted and damaged spines, the scattered anonymous bones, emphasising the short lives, the heavy lifting, the damage of child-bearing.

The programme on Graham Sutherland, in another series, *The New Masters* (BBC-2), was intermittently illuminating, with some useful montage of natural objects and particular paintings created from them. But much of the camera-work on the pictures was of the kind now habitual in art programmes: moving over the details of the composition and creating, often interestingly, an essentially different visual effect. John Berger, in his useful recent series, pointed out what this method does to the art of painting, and one of his other points, the characteristic adding of another artistic dimension by accompanying music, was again fully exemplified in this film. It makes for a successful programme of a kind, but I wish what Berger said could be more attentively met.

27 July 1972

Natural Breaks

Holidays seem a good time for thinking about natural breaks. Like so much else that is artificial, conventional and man-made on television, the natural break for commercials seems to be becoming part of a way of life. People who question it, or television advertising in general, must run the risk of being met with "Not that again," or of being told that to persist in such thoughts is to declare oneself a member of the new cultural Establishment. Meanwhile, the Establishment that turns out the commercials is palpably, if sometimes ridiculously and annoyingly, present: it is in this way more real than any possible criticism of it—it has, in a word, become natural.

I was reminded how far this naturalisation has gone while watching a film the other night on ITV. It started, after a natural break, at a few minutes past seven, and at 7:25, 7:43 and 7:55, when I switched off on some remarks about Britain's best-loved medicated shampoo, this film, itself highly commercial, had experienced natural breaks that even Hollywood had not thought of. (It is some indication of how far things have gone that in the cinema, under the most intense commercial pressures, we could and can watch a film straight through, before the adverts come up with the ice-cream.) Given the nature of film editing, at times with several breaks a minute, the possibilities seem endless, though I notice that we are allowed a fairly long first run to get us interested, after which the frequency of the natural phenomena that are called "breaks" seems miraculously to increase.

It is worth considering how this situation was created. A correspondent has recently sent me an illuminating exchange of letters on this matter with the present Chairman of the IBA. When the 1953 White Paper was introduced in Parliament it was said on behalf of the Government that at no time would "interruption" of the programmes be permitted. A month later it was said that there would be "no interruptions at all unless they are in what are called 'natural breaks'." That was the loophole through which, as a Member of Parliament observed at the time, a coach and four could be driven; and of course has been. One of the early examples of what a natural break might be was between the acts of a two-act play, "especially if the first act had lasted for an hour and ten minutes". A later example was between the scenes in *Hamlet*. (One catches the high-cultural atmosphere in which the business was being done.) As things have turned out, with many endorsements and ratifications including the Act of 1964, the fiction of the natural break has come to mean almost anything that can be made to occur, or, as it were, to stop occurring, at an evening's average of three times an hour. To go on calling them natural breaks is, even for advertisers and their friends, straining human nature too far.

Yet of course, as most of us know, the real problem has to be put the other way round. There are presumably people in Commercial Television who sit watching old films for natural breaks to happen. "When she goes out and slams the door, Bert. Or when he staggers and there's that cut to the vultures." Whatever creative possibilities these moments may suggest—deodorants? catmeat?—have never been systematically tried: most authorities don't wait for nature—they make it happen. Producers and their writers and performers are given their time slots—as in all programming, but with the difference that within programmes there will be this predictable alien material. Many people put up with it as they put up with the weather: any powerful social system seems to acquire that natural weight. But it is so far from being the only way it could be done that somebody has to keep insisting that it's natural.

My correspondent complained particularly about commercial breaks in a film of a mountaineering expedition and in a concert from St Paul's. He was told, in effect, that advertisers often sponsor expeditions (though these weren't the advertisements complained about) and, of course, that "the great mass of our viewers" are not offended by breaks for advertising or by the advertising itself. Perhaps there is evidence for this, but if so, it is significant that the calculations for profitable insertion are so fine. If people accepted, or even, as has been said, positively enjoyed, advertising, there would be no need to interest them in a programme to a point where they intend to go on watching and then contrive a commercial break. It could come up at known times and be watched by positive choice. In the Italian and in other television services dependent on advertising revenue there are separate times set aside, and the separation between programmes and advertising, which was supposed to be a principle of British Commercial Television, is then something more than a fiction. But though as yet resisting general sponsorship, British Commercial Television practice is following the basic American convention, though at a much lower frequency and intensity, as can be observed from watching the number of fades and re-establishing shots in American imports shown on BBC. A whole method has followed from this: the dramatic opening sequence before the credit titles, for instance—an interesting experiment which is now commercial routine.

If 1976 is still to be the year of decision for broadcasting policy, the break is an item for the agenda. Consider the extent of the drift. Sponsored sporting events have become so natural, even on BBC, that one has to suppose a high correlation between love of horse-racing, athletics, golf, cricket or similar outdoor pursuits and directorships in beer, cigarette, razor-blade and similar companies. A belated but welcome attempt is now being made to stop a loophole on television advertising of cigarettes, but the general problem is much wider. I was watching cricket on television last week and in the close-ups of batsmen at one end was continually puzzled and distracted by the letters "pworths" apparently growing out of the caps. I eventually got the whole word in its place on the boundary fence, and realised as I did so that there have been times in watching televised football, as the moves are breaking down, when I have wanted play to move upfield so that the half-word glimpsed behind the action might be completed. I have even had some surprises, as in crosswords. So natural has this placing become, even in socialist stadiums, that it is an effort to visualise the planning, the contracts, the calculations that put them there. And it is all on the principle that since we enjoy watching a whole range of programmes and events, something else can be directly or indirectly but always profitably inserted, as if it were a natural accompaniment. I think it is still worth resisting this whole drift. It is, in any case, necessary to expose its naturalism as contrivance. And what goes, all along the line, for Commercial Television, goes also for the encroachments and contrivances that have got what is in effect advertising into public service broadcasting.

24 August 1972

Ad Hominem

The second in the series of six programmes entitled *Controversy* (BBC-2) had a promising first half but was in the end disappointing. Professors Fox and Tiger,* after yet another joke, by the chairman, about their names, presented their views on man as an animal whose evolution as a hunter has profoundly affected his modern forms of behaviour. I had recently been studying the contemporary revival of the theory known from the 19th century as Social Darwinism, and from what I gathered in the introduction I started with some feeling against Fox and Tiger. Yet if their general ideas were in this sense familiar, there was an interesting complexity in some parts of their presentation, though there was of course little time for them to develop this. Among the arranged respondents, Juliet Mitchell saw what I had taken as complexity as an attempt to have the argument both ways, and since the respondent had the advantage over the viewer in having read the book she may well have been right. A zoologist made several interesting points about the selection of animals for comparison with man: a matter that has been at issue

---

*Lionel Tiger. Social scientist and anthropologist. Author with Robin Fox of *Men in Groups* (1969).

throughout the traditional debate. A sociologist questioned the analogy with computers as a doubtful element in an argument about man's animal inheritance. A crucial point of difference then emerged. If our inheritance as hunters is in some sense determining, ought we to describe this as evolutionary or historical; and whichever it might be, but especially if it is the latter, is there any good reason for playing down the effects on our social behaviour of the historical experience of the last 5,000 years? The same point was raised, with a reference to Engels, in the first hurried intervention from the audience, and a slightly patronising reply conceded the importance of the idea of man making himself through the use of tools and by labour. By this stage, if with a certain sketchiness, a real intellectual issue had been raised. But it was not followed up.

In one contribution after another the issue was moved to Fox and Tiger's attitude to women, which had been only marginally raised but on which the people who spoke evidently had more information than the viewer. The atmosphere quickly became strained and some of the discussion was in the worst possible sense *ad hominem*. There was then an apparently planned walk-out of a demonstrative kind, which would have finished the programme off if the chairman had not kept blandly talking. What mainly emerged was the need for more time, and thus more real flexibility (allowing possible returns to the point), if issues of this difficulty are to be more than glanced at.

14 September 1972

Versions of Webster

It was interesting to see a relatively straight production of Webster's *The Duchess of Malfi* (BBC-2). When I was a student we used to read Webster and Tourneur and Ford as what, following Eliot, we called "savage farce". The extremity of some of the horrors—a brother giving his sister a dead man's hand; the dance of the madmen; the final chain of killings, like a court ritual gone wrong—was ordinarily seen in a dimension of absurdity. What happened was too bizarre to be taken quite seriously, but when it was joined to the desperate intensity of some of the verse it could be seen as a particular mode: farcical but savage, the two apparently opposite feelings conjoined in a specific emotion which had the attractive quality of distance.

That interpretation seems to me now a product of its period: not so much the period in which we inherited it, and certainly not Webster's early 17th century, but the years, say, from Wilde's *Salomé* to Eliot's "Sweeney Agonistes": the specific period of a specific social group, from the 1890s to the 1920s. The arbitrariness of the violence, the exhibited distortions of the sexual feelings, the conscious playing with the bizarre and the insane: these composed a mode, and it is easy to understand how it could be projected onto Webster and his contemporaries. Moreover, though in my own case assent to any such interpretation had long been withdrawn, there was the subsequent and very comparable fashion of what was called, in the late Fifties and Sixties, the "theatre of the absurd" and the associated "theatre of cruelty". Was not Webster ready-made for this? I remember a lively Cambridge production in which the chain of killings at the end was performed by the actors standing in a ring, each with a knife in the next man's back. It was a comment of a kind, on the arbitrariness and on the absurdity. The lively cynicism of a young man's response to this kind of world communicated very easily: the outrage modulated to a laugh. But while this was possible in a student production, what was normally happening, in the professional theatre, was an extension of arbitrary and insane horror to a practised convention.

Who then would have expected, from a contemporary television production of *The Duchess of Malfi,* anything like what we got? Think of the mad scene or the waxwork corpses or the final slaughter: would not any of twenty highly-praised directors have seen them and loved them as production numbers? There were in fact a few survivals from the past: notably a stress on incest—a frustrated incestuous love—as the Duke's motive for revenge on his sister's marriage. That kind of Freudianism is so deep in contemporary ideology that there is a certain inevitability in its abstraction from the ambiguous intensity and confusion of the responses Webster wrote for the Duke: the physical and sexual ferocity of Act II, Scene V; the calculating power and acquisitiveness of Act IV, Scene II. It is interesting that in a world like our own, which is no stranger to every kind of cruelty and confusion, habitual interpretations pick up the sexual but not the economic and political drives; or, in dividing them, fail to recognise the ways in which, in a particular social and sexual structure, they become fused or displace one another. Among the other survivals, but in a very minor way, we had Julia and the Cardinal rather self-consciously in bed, but done as if from stock, with Julia sliding out at a now practised angle, as if going for a shower. But these moments from a different sensibility stood out because the tone of James Mac-Taggart's production was so different.

Perhaps the main reason for the straightness with which it was played was that it was set in a great house, so that the realism of a social location was persistently stressed. Also, the text, with less cuts than is usual, was respected in the speaking, and there were several finely considered performances of this spoken kind. And then, as in the original, this spoken action created an active dimension within which the spectacular horrors were significant rather than instrumental or isolated. What I found myself considering, as in no other production I have seen, was the full human experience which this extraordinary play embodies. For it seems, looking back, that the fashionable revival of the Jacobean plays as savage farce, like the later period of the theatre of the absurd and the cruel, was a product of a relative security and of the kinds of indifference which that breeds. Everyone says that it was a product of insecurity—wars and the break-up of values—but much of that was in the head, and in a later generation some responses have changed: the disintegration and the suffering have gone so deep, become so internal, that they are capable of resuming their ordinary human dimensions: not savage farce but the sober recognition of anger, confusion and violence. At any rate, this is how *The Duchess of Malfi* was played, and it came through, as such, very strongly. On reflection, one could see that its specific social dimension, though stressed, had been diminished. The play ends with a moral reflection which is to ratify the bringing to power of the young Duke of Malfi. The production ended with the child staring at the intolerable ruin and turning and being led away. For my own part, I have read Webster and the others differently since I realised that Hobbes was their contemporary: what they wrote as young men, in a dramatic action, he wrote as an old man in a philosophical argument. The connections are specific: the sense of the war of all against all, the murderously destructive isolated appetites. This is redeemed in the dramatists by the conventional restoration of an innocent prince; redeemed in Hobbes, more realistically, by an absolute sovereign: in fact, redeemed by the ending of that system of absolute and irresponsible power which created both a

Duke and a Bosola and victims beyond counting.   But the confidence of that kind of analysis has been shaken in its turn: the child simply looking and turning away is now a more widely shared emotion, and the production underwrote it. Given the relative cultural prestige, among the highly educated, of television and the theatre, it seems possible that the production will get less notice than it deserves. But this is not the only occasion on which television, even with material ordinarily thought of as high culture, has shown itself significantly ahead of the theatre and other similar received institutions.

19 October 1972

Intellectual Superiority

Was it merely coincidence, or some kind of underground pro-gramme-planning, that allowed us to switch from *The Resistible Rise of Arturo Ui* (BBC-2) to *Election Night USA* (*Midweek,* BBC-1)? Brecht's satirical version of the rise of Hitler in terms of a Chicago conspiracy between capitalists and gangsters was distant enough, in historical time, from the re-election of Nixon and Agnew. But it is impossible to watch that kind of caricatured demagogy and then go across, straight-faced, to the election-day appearances and the victory interviews. Moreover, the production of *Arturo Ui* had stressed a contemporary application: with the voices of English financial speculators running under the final credits, and the conclusion: "Though the bastard's dead, the bitch that bore him is in heat again."

It was in some ways a brilliant production, with a fine perform-ance as Hitler-Ui by Nicol Williamson. But I found it, in the end, entirely resistible. It is, in any case, the flip side of Brecht. The anal-ogy of fascism with gangsterism turns an easy theatrical trick. Many others were doing it around 1941. There is a kind of political theatre which seems to come into existence to nourish the illusions of the intellectual Left. Much of the satire of the Sixties was a pale late descendant of it. Henry James once said, characteristically, that a story based on elementary passions "must be told in a spirit of intel-lectual superiority to those passions". In a period of political defeat and isolation, the Left is especially exposed to a virulent strain of this disease. Seeing fascism itself as a neurotic puppet farce was very common in the late Thirties and in war propaganda. And it is just this "spirit of intellectual superiority" that is isolating and disarming. *The Resistible Rise of Arturo Ui*: but resistible by whom? In the play the entertaining absurdity of the conspiracy is complemented by the absence of any real resistance: the only sustained opposition is from the capitalists whom the gangsters in the end double-cross. But this excludes not only the resistance of the Left: it excludes its errors and its failures. And it is in this exclusion that it becomes self-indulgent, assuming an intellectual superiority it has wholly failed to earn.

Take the final scene of *Arturo Ui*. The gangster attains power and makes a triumphal speech and procession. Behind the cheering people lining his route are the gangsters with pistols to every head. But if you believe that, you will believe anything. Political gangsters need only one point of entry, after which, as they say, they have their own methods. But that point of entry they still need, and to see it only as a conspiracy, above people's heads, is to fail to see the problem at all, and then to compound the failure in a mood of superior entertainment.

In the case of Brecht on Hitler this is now an academic point. But in any suggested contemporary application it becomes crucial. This at least was my own feeling as I switched to the election results. I have heard the strains of the flip side too often lately: the mood of amused intellectual superiority to a Nixon or an Agnew, a Heath or a Wilson; and the tune that goes with it, the liberal miming of the hard-hats who voted for Nixon, or of the English working-class people who think Enoch Powell is their spokesman. Intellectual superiority is the very last mood that can be afforded, for all these results are the failures of the Left. To see the deep social causes which are moving people that way, without pistols at their heads, with some of them, indeed, eager and insistent, is a very different matter, and needs a different political culture, from the now fashionable conversion of every symptom into entertainment. The heyday of German political satire, one remembers cautiously, preceded Hitler.

Don Taylor's *The Exorcism* (BBC-2) was that unusual phenomenon: a radical ghost story. A Christmas dinner in a converted labourer's cottage provoked the terrible return of a woman who had died there, with her children, in starvation, after her husband had been hanged for his part in a labourers' revolt. It is a feeling many of us have had, who live in old houses: that the walls might speak, ought to speak. I once watched from the stairs as a totally strange woman came up our path, opened the door with an air of familiarity, put down her bag and began taking off her hat. She had lived there, we discovered, some years before; she had temporarily forgotten not so much where as when she was. So that through all the middle scenes of *The Exorcism* I found the haunting more than conventional: it had some authentic intensity. I then lost the play in its terrible conclusion. It wasn't my sympathy that went, though there was an element in the conclusion, as in the beginning, of a displaced and ambivalent savagery. But the way it was done—within the middle-class terms Mr Taylor was offering to supersede—gave trouble. The story of the past came as through a medium from the lady of the house.

16 November 1972

Why is the BBC like "Monty Python's Flying Circus"?

The leaves will be on the trees before I watch any more British television. Yet this isn't the season for a last nostalgic look round. Perhaps people always say that television, like anything else in common experience, isn't as good as it used to be. But this autumn I have been hearing it said with conviction and persistence by a wide variety of people. At the same time, visitors from other countries, and especially English-speaking countries, insist that our television is very much better than their own home products. Of course these opinions needn't be inconsistent. But there is one feature of the visitors' praise which seems to me to point to the real situation. Every week, they say, you can find two or three really good things, usually plays. From this autumn, I find that I remember a few things like *The Duchess of Malfi* and *The Resistible Rise of Arturo Ui*, and these not just as Webster or Brecht but, in their different ways, as imaginative television. I remember also one or two interesting experiments like *The Exorcism*. That isn't much out of hundreds of hours, though there is a good deal of everyday television which can be watched, if not remembered, with interest and respect. But it may be the right way to put it now: that the reputation of British television, including its reputation abroad, rests on a few important kinds of programme, and that in much of the rest there is an evident decline.

There's always the sport and the country programmes. But in light entertainment, for example, we are in the last stages of several engaging ideas, from *Till Death Us Do Part* and *Steptoe and Son* to *Dad's Army*. There is a general air of Reappearing by Enormous Popular Request, and considering the run of the competition, that is easily explained. The liveliest contemporary comedy comes from *Monty Python's Flying Circus,* and in a way this underlines the point about the general situation. The show still has moments of its own kind of grotesque and exuberant fantasy, but mostly it is playing on strained nerves: an inevitable and unstoppable laughter somewhere on the far side of a general breakdown of meanings. This is why it is so often congenial. And watching it this autumn, I noticed how much of the breakdown of meanings had to do with the conventions of current television. Within its half-hour the interval globe appears and reappears; a familiar announcer, straight-faced, reads a news item only slightly more preposterous than some we have been hearing; men-on-the-spot relay their urgent day-old reports; bombastic historical titles appear episodically, gathering their costumed skirts around them. It is far too accurate, as a mood, to be other than achingly funny. I wonder, each time, when the credits have rolled and the flying circus starts again, how Presentation will ever recover control. It can't even say, any longer: "And now for something completely different." And so to *Midweek*: that jigsaw of faces led by Nixon (someone has his priorities right) and the seeping impression, well conveyed by two of its regular studio-men, of an ungovernable weariness at the problems of the world.

This, I believe, is the mood that matters. Television is now so pervasive that we project onto it many of our feelings about quite other things. Yet in its standard uses in this kind of society it is clearly part of the problem rather than part of the solution. We can recognise in its presentation of the world a characteristic one-way system, which we depend on (for there is not now much else) as a means of social orientation, but which succeeds in making much of everyday reality external and, crucially, intransitive. In its political and documentary uses, it only participates in a problem which is evident everywhere, and it is most honest when it admits this.

But there are more confident people about, in the middle ground. There are the tireless agents of smooth commercials, from the man who shows us how to count up to four with a headache pill to that endless incorporated miming, in song and dance about drinks, of what were once the authentically lively sounds and movements of the Sixties. But that is specifically bought stuff. What is more to the point is what is offered as new and serious—"major new series"—and then has that unmistakable middle-aged spread which can be called, politely, our heritage. *Colditz,* for example: it isn't that it's badly done—it's just preposterous that after a book and a film it's being done at all. A couple of years ago I estimated the historical centre-point of BBC Television as the mid-1920s. Perhaps we can call it progress that it is now so evidently the 1940s. But it's the level that matters: think of those escaping officers, or of *The Commanders.* Similarly, the police serials have become preoccupied with problems of promotion and command, leaving *Dixon of Dock Green* with the crimes. A portrait of a certain kind of man (but it must be a group) emerges through the central hours: all his meanings and interests in the past; a contemporary world realised only as careers and prospects. Within a general social deadlock, this kind of man has been inching his way into power everywhere. In television, he has been assisted by two developments: the idea of the package serial, with one eye on overseas markets, and the effects of cost accounting and management consultancy on the employment of creative people, many of whom have gone over to part-time work or have been lost to broadcasting altogether. The programming formulas that follow from these developments are a recipe for expensive mediocrity. Even *War and Peace,* for all its intrinsic and in a way indestructible power, is being pressed into something it is not, for if, as Tolstoy said, it is not a novel, it is certainly not a romantic serial. The visual gaping at the country houses and palaces mixes oddly with the inexorably suburban emotional style, and only Anthony Hopkins's interesting performance as Pierre keeps the historical and philosophical dimension alive.

In a situation like this, every experiment deserves praise: the two hours of BBC-2's *What did you learn from school today?,* with men as able as Dr Halsey* contributing to it but having to say, as the misunderstandings and muddles accumulated, "We're talking too fast"—the just observation on most discussion as it is now so mechanically organised. Or *Full House* (BBC-2), or the safety-valve of *Up Sunday* (BBC-2).

14 December 1972

*Dr. Albert Halsey. Director of Department of Social and Administrative Studies, Oxford University. Author of studies on education and social class.

The Top of the Laugh

"Well, finally—and I'm sorry to have to hurry you on this but we're almost out of time so can you answer very briefly, in fact you have just 20 seconds: is Britain really on the edge of disaster?"

That got said, almost verbatim, on television last week. In isolation it is an effective caricature of crisis broadcasting. Timings, for linkmen, are of course inexorable, but the internal priorities of the system as a whole express a different kind of rigidity. The only considerable virtue of these dark weeks is that some fundamental questions are being posed, by events, with unusual clarity and force. It is not easy to say that too little broadcasting time has been spent on them, though the early responses—notably BBC-2's *The Energy Crunch* and an excellent edition of *Weekend World* (LWT)—were significantly more alert than anything within the packages of the weeks of Christmas and New Year. Towards the end of New Year's week you could almost sense the relief of news editors that there was international terrorist conspiracy, or what passed for one, to take priority in the bulletins. But the very local signs are even more significant. The linkmen, the intermediaries, the interviewers—the defining figures of current affairs television—have become, in most cases, even more peremptory, impatient, inflexible than their ordinary role requires. Within this kind of systematised presentation, the fundamental question, or what sounds like it, may indeed be genially (or what looks like it) asked, but the mechanics of presentation still take priority over its answer, and the counting of seconds never manages to include the taped musical bombast and miscellaneous visual assertion of each programme's signature titles.

These deserve, incidentally, some separate study: *Pebble Mill at One* and *Nationwide* are classic specimens of the type, which is a hybrid of public service commercialese—the striking visual and musical assertion of nothing very much—and the emphatic personalisation of linkmen rather than links, interviewers rather than issues. Presentation holds its priorities, even when it is supposedly admitted that fundamental questions must be asked. And indeed that sorts well with some of the inner qualities of the crisis, in which, in an area much wider than broadcasting, presentation is trying to assert itself, against a hard real sequence of events.

That's television, they still say in the corridors, as elsewhere they still say that's business or that's politics. The point is, I suppose, that

within the systems of television or business or politics there is a residual confidence in routines of crisis-management which events may
have shaken, but which cannot be given up without other changes
which, within the systems, cannot be contemplated. Perhaps the most
important thing, over the next few months, is to see that the questions remain as clear and powerful as, in spite of the systems, they
now are.

Enough gloom, they say, at predictable points in the programming. Let's have something to cheer us up. A new series of *Till death
us do part* (BBC-1) started. Weakened by surprisingly poor technical
production, it was in any case no kind of comic relief. Who could go
on laughing at Alf Garnett as the only truths he knew almost shook
him to pieces, while his wife pinched his breakfast and his son-in-law
tossed over bits of chewed liberal newsprint? I found I could laugh at
Warren Mitchell, whose superb acting energy simply takes one over
at times. Or at Michael Bates, doing his Indian bearer turn in the
new comedy series *It ain't half hot, Mum* (BBC-1). But again, for me,
it was laughing out of context. It takes more than a couple of good
character-actors to make real comedy out of a British holding depot
in the last days before Indian independence. When the laughter turns
outwards, at a Rangi Ram calling other Indians "natives" and
"coolies", we need, I would have thought, a stronger balance of pay-
ments than we are ever now likely to have. The contrast with *Dad's
Army* (BBC-1), by the same authors, is striking. There the top of the
comedy was another group of fine character-actors, an Arthur Lowe
or a Clive Dunn who, like Eric Morecambe, can make walking into a
room hilarious. But the real base of that comedy was the fundamental incongruity and overlap between a persistent civilian world and
the spare-time military routines. The top of the laugh is always less
lasting than basic comedy like that. Or, again, we had just seen
Michael Bates in the brilliant *Last of the Summer Wine* (BBC-1),
where the humour was elderly retirement released to be boyhood
again, with all the consequent incongruity.

If it is indeed a time of national self-examination, it's as well to
read the rubric and especially, I think, the social experiences that,
within programming as a whole, now seem imaginatively preoccupy-
ing. There's this persistent return to the last war: the old films,
World at War (Thames), *Dad's Army*, *It ain't half hot, Mum*,
M*A*S*H (BBC-2) and of course *Colditz* (BBC-1) coming up again
with fanfares. There's the group from the period just before what

was called affluence: *Coronation Street* (Granada), *Steptoe and Son* (BBC-1), *Till death us do part*. Then in what they call prestige productions the long Tudor Festival is resting, but there is a well-dressed interest in the late Victorians and Edwardians: after the *Forsyte Saga, Upstairs Downstairs* (LWT), *Vienna 1900* (BBC-1), *Pygmalion* yet again. They are all interesting periods, but the ones that don't get in much are significant: the Twenties, for example, which have some connections, or 1780-1830, the blind spot in orthodox English perceptions of the past, but years which now really bear in on us. All that in residual terms, but the really striking fact is how little, beyond discussion, we are entering our contemporary world. In comedy, at least, only *Monty Python* (BBC-2) seems to have a style for it. Perhaps we could bring back *Mogul* or *The Troubleshooters,* for a laugh.

One small and memorable programme: *The Camera and the Song* (BBC-2). There were Philip Bonham-Carter and Jake Thackray in the Yorkshire Dales, then Nigel Walters and Max Boyce in the Neath valley. In the Welsh programme there was a strange contrast between camera and song. The camera seemed to weep over that blasted valley, and one of the songs—"*Duw* it's hard"—joined it. But mainly there was the perky lilt of "the factory 'neath the mountain that makes outside halves for Wales". And that kind of vigorous autonomy—does one need to add?—is also, and thankfully, an essential part of the crisis.

10 January 1974

Isaac's Urges

There was a fine production of Middleton and Rowley's *The Changeling* in *Play of the Month* (BBC-1). This was not the first time that television has shown its capacity to perform Jacobean and Caroline tragedy. The plays are moving towards interiors, in setting as much as in theme and character. The small screen can hold their inward-turning intensity. Stanley Baker and Helen Mirren as De Flores and Beatrice had the physical attributes that make the deception and violence plausible, and Antony Page's direction, shadowed, insinuating, dressed in blacks and whites, had fine judgment, pace and control. A brief experiment in the visual imagery of nightmare was a convincing extension of some of the direct imagery of the language and the implicit imagery of the action. The flexibility of such conventions is one of several good arguments for seeing our television service as a real repertory.

The rest of the week was rather different. Pwsllab on a wet night is no place for a beauty contest: not because the girls will not be beautiful but because in Pwsllab, as in its twin-town Llaregyb, the game is more important than the rules, and fantasy and petty sin more important than either. *Perils of Pendragon* (BBC-2) is a curious example of that Anglicised form of Welsh and Irish comedy which has had some success in television. And with the state of the nation, whichever way you spell it, a *pwsllab,* most things do for a laugh. Last week's episode, *A Fête Worse than Death,* was played with obvious enjoyment by some skilful Welsh actors, and it had its moments, especially Isaac Glanwy's "touch of the urges". But it resumed, in my mind, an old line of thought, about how the Welsh and the Irish have adapted themselves to a dominant English culture. I write from Cambridge, some of whose Medieval citizens took out insurance against killing a Welshman, and where, to this day, if somebody speaks to me in the street, I know it is either a close friend or an Irishman. Our private version is that we play the English on a very short line: before they have even noticed their hangup, the quicksilver exuberant Celt is beyond them and away. This may warm sad hearts but it is less than convincing. Our countries are poor and still in most ways dependent: the manners follow from that. Yet it has been so long a process that the tones are complicated. When Synge, back from Europe, wrote *The Playboy of the Western World,* he could add high romance to the petty fantasy, and the mediation was successful. Dylan Thomas, in London and New York, added a mourning despair to the same petty fantasy, and the blend was again powerful. Succeeding generations have simplified the mixture, especially in forms that are intended to be popular. *Perils of Pendragon* draws most of the jokes and extracts all the sadness from *Under Milk Wood.* I don't know its immediate provenance, and I prefer both Dylan Thomas and Gwyn Thomas straight. But as a mode it belongs to a late stage of farcical self-presentation, where the Free Wales Army throws cabbage and the lusts of Isaac are spread as schoolboy glue. From hard, sad, serious, affirmative but dependent peoples this is always, I suppose, a possible move, though it relies on the assumption that the English will accept us as fantastic, ridiculous, charming, eloquent, hopeless people and make nothing more of it. I've long doubted that, and the tradition of amused and tolerant English superiority now has so much less in the bank that I wouldn't count on any harmless joke lasting.

The Pallisers, after Trollope (BBC-2), is a very different kind of history replayed as a different kind of farce. It would be easy to say that this is a machine-made successor to *The Forsyte Saga,* and in some recess of Planning, with the ordinary reflex to an earlier, more affluent, more leisured time (that lie that works better than a truth), some such assumption may well have been made. But when you call your bourgeois family "Forsyte" you show respect as well as a sense of limitation and postponed, accumulating life. And because this is still a bourgeois society, the adaptation was made and played with a connecting inner seriousness. The Duke of Omnium and Plantagenet Palliser and Lady Glencora M'Cluskie exact plushy gestures but less reasoned identity, and so characterisation and presentation keep slipping between well-dressed solidity and late-night parody. It may hold at some level, by sheer extent, but it will not be the smoothness of Trollope, who could combine a fascination with the mechanics of power and convenience with a more fundamental, if still edgy, deference than you can now expect from actors and writers and directors. They have after all come in from the streets; they may enjoy the clothes and the mansions and they are professional enough to sketch almost anything; but to take the ideas and the feelings at their full seriousness—that, and it is much to their credit, is beyond them.

31 January 1974

Part III

An Interview with Raymond Williams

Television and Teaching

In your books on Television *and* Marxism and Literature,[1] *you develop a critique of consensus programming and the narrowing aesthetic range of programme forms. What changes in the broadcasting institutions would be necessary to counter these tendencies? Do you see it as an institutional question?*

Yes, it is; and it has been considered typically in terms of defining the functions of the large broadcasting organisations. But I think that these otherwise useful organisational definitions have themselves played a part in producing precisely what we are now criticising. The competition for the same audience and requirements like balance have brought about tendencies towards concentration and duplication, formal programming and so on. One therefore has to look towards the different institution of independent production companies—I mean genuine production companies, of course, not the so-called production companies which constitute the basis of the Independent Broadcasting Authority. This sort of solution would remove a lot of the present managerial bureaucratic elements; but the problem is then the relation of those companies to the major networks. I think the notion of the Open Broadcasting Authority still has some point—as long as the element of production by independent companies is a real one in it, and not just marginal. Indeed, I would see that as essential.

Then there should be general pressure for increasing the regionalisation of public broadcasting, which would also reduce the distance between the decisions about production and programming. These are not meant to be ideal solutions—I'm not thinking of the conditions of socialist television production—but what you could reasonably move towards within the terms of this kind of social order and with, I would have thought, a significant range of support. Even under present conditions, the break to independent production companies is always being attempted.

I am sceptical about the possible success of the OBA or of indepen-
dent production unless the massive domination of the BBC and the
programme companies is broken. Both in the Netherlands and West
Germany, with similar social orders, there does seem to be a much
more open and pluralistic structure of broadcasting and a real meas-
ure of democratic accountability, although combined with a
restricted range of programmes. Have you considered these different
modes of organising broadcasting?

I suppose I share that sense of the prospects for the OBA while the
present cultural policy is pursued and while the BBC and the programme companies retain that position of importance. One of the
basic problems is that there has never been an attempt to work out
cultural policy in broadcasting at a true political level. There have
been the usual "independent" official or semi-official enquiries, but
one of the great faults of politics is that responsibility for broadcasting and its relation to general cultural policy is so dispersed. It is not
clear whether broadcasting is subject to government decisions or not.
That it should still come under the Home Office is ludicrous. This
uncertainty means the big organisations do tend to control the nature
of initiatives in the field.

The point about the German and Dutch methods is that they are
based on *political* decisions. They have been taken at the level of an
argument between the political parties and so on, with the notion of
a more plural cultural policy. The British solution is always to
assume that the kinds of body set up to represent the public interest
are neutral and that this in itself is plural. (Of course, although these
vary at different periods, one cannot accept their definition as neutral.) This whole structure of public bodies—a kind of semi-official
centralised organisation—depends on the very particular cultural
homogeneity of the English ruling class. It's assumed that if *they* are
represented, then really the wider social interest is represented. In an
earlier stage this had some advantages, like getting conceptions of
public broadcasting as against straight market broadcasting. But later
there have been disadvantages, because what is actually a rather narrow homogeneity is taken to be very open and plural. Unless this
becomes a political argument at the level of governmental decision,
there is no way in which you can reshape the essential institutions.

One problem in forming a general socialist broadcasting policy in
Britain as against other countries seems to be that Marxist intellectu-

als have greater difficulty in dealing with broadcasting than with, for example, cinema. Why should television be so recalcitrant to handling by Marxists in theoretical terms?

I think that many of the other new forms have been as recalcitrant for well known theoretical reasons. The many mixed forms of organisation appear particularly difficult to define in simple received terms. There's no problem about describing the press as a capitalist press. There is really quite a set of problems about the definition of television or broadcasting as capitalist, although they undoubtedly occur within a bourgeois state which is governed by the capitalist form of production. Because those differences are at the institutional level, some of that has been sorted out. It is more that much of the received theory has been in terms of the individual producer in relation to the market. The theoretical background of Marxist thinking has really been concerned with the reintegration of these individual producers into the collectivity, through the notion of the integrated artist. But because all the significant new forms are inevitably forms of *collective* production, you arrive very quickly at one of the great divides in Marxist thinking. One strand thinks in terms of selfmanaging collectives; the other thinks in terms of the centralised state which expresses and sustains the dominant class influence. Although both strands have been active, it has tended to be the latter which has issued into organisation.

I can remember when I was first writing on problems of cultural policy, everyone on the Left assumed there was no problem, that you simply nationalised the broadcasting institutions. But there *is* a problem. Very few people would now think that was the only solution, although they might think it practicable.

Another problem has been the very openness, in certain situations, of these bureaucratic centralised institutions to contribution by people whose cultural affiliations and principles have really belonged quite elsewhere. In the Sixties there were many people who felt that, despite the difficulties, television was a relatively open medium just because it is insatiable. It took the Seventies to show that this was highly structurally limited.

Facing the size of institutions like the BBC or the ITV companies, it's difficult to see any institutions on the Left in which strategies and programmes can be organised. One is quickly led back to one or two names within a political party—Tony Benn, for example—but not to a body of ideas or thinkers. Given the weakness and dispersal of the Left in Britain, how could this serious lacuna be overcome?

We cannot exclude from this discussion the fact that the British labour movement has been extraordinarily resistant to initiatives of this kind, except in purely defensive questions. I have only once really co-operated with a union in this field. That was with the Musicians' Union in the argument about radio policy following the success of the pirates. (This was a very complex cultural question, because this really was a new audience wanting something new, and yet the ways in which it was being produced were potentially very dangerous.) I have also been involved with the print unions, but usually when a particular newspaper faces closure. Organisations like the Free Communications Group have also tended to become preoccupied by simply defensive battles.

Another constructive initiative, in the early Sixties, was Arnold Wesker's Centre 42. He got the TUC* to accept Resolution 42, that they should play a part in cultural policy in order to change the class relations of culture and society. Although there were mistakes in its presentation and elements of simple idealism in it, at the level of the resolution it got through. But the resistance was there. This wasn't a major part of the labour movement's perspective; it has, in general, been very slow to recognise that issues of cultural policy can be as crucial as issues of economic and political policy. When this has been talked about again at the TUC, it's been as a result of consequences forseeable when the original argument was being put forward. The unions get a dreadful press, or a critical industrial situation is given a dreadful treatment on television, and they say, we must do something about it.

So far, then, it has only been possible to bring together the constructive thinking of people whose primary concern is cultural production and cultural policy with the important union organisation in these fields in order to defend and maintain, for understandable local reasons, the character of an existing institution. Opportunities exist for a much more significant political intervention, but that would need a long-term association. While it remains so difficult to introduce new institutions—and of course this reflects the general situation of the Left in this country—a group of Left intellectuals can do

---

*Trade Union Congress. Established in Manchester in 1868, it is the co-ordinating body for trade unions in Britain.

only a limited amount. They must have really active contact not only with other organisations in the field but with the actual union organisations which, within the division of labour, can all too easily claim that their jobs are simply the *conditions* of this different kind of production, the transmission rather than the original production. While that gap remains, the effectiveness is limited. It is not an argument against working, because unless people with experience and interest in production work out some very detailed proposals, then you wouldn't get much past general goodwill.

In the present situation, doesn't the range of questions posed by new technology in the newspaper industry, the debate about the fourth television channel and the allocation of the ITV franchises demand more than simple defensive responses? What kind of ideas, carefully followed through, could be productive?

There is a need for that sort of programme, but I would say above all it needs to be done in terms of general cultural policy and not only broadcasting policy. There is also a very real need now for the emergence of some kind of research and proposal organisation. It would need to be rather general, even if it subsequently divides into specialist groups, because the relations between these groups are changing. This is one of the consequences of our technology. For example, if cassettes or even the hated "pay-TV" system were instituted in television, that would have certain advantages in providing a material base for independent companies. I am sure that more direct relations could also be introduced into book and magazine publishing. Even though they have been preoccupied with defence— after some false optimism in the Sixties that things were going the Left's way—the experiences of the Seventies have really underlined the need for these changes.

A different kind of initiative, clear in your books on Communications[2] *and* Television, *has been the movement for widespread education about television. Within this field, there are now sophisticated formal means of studying different types of programmes, as well as the sort of institutional analysis you have outlined. The problem really seems to be how to hold these two aspects in balance and show how they work on each other.*

There has been this absolute efflorescence of intellectual analysis which, although it has been very valuable, is also related to the practical blocks on production. Many people doing analysis would have been doing production in different circumstances. This has had positive and negative effects. Positively, we do have a much more serious body of analysis than I can ever remember. On the other hand, it can become a self-sufficient activity—it can become theoreticist, because it has its own pleasures and it also reflects a certain situation within the educational institutions.

The trouble with the thinking about institutions has always been finding ways of connecting it with the ordinary political system. When I wrote *Communications* in the early Sixties, there seemed to be a connection because it contained the sort of transitional reforms people felt a Labour government could undertake. In practice, once the Labour government was in office, they entirely dropped that connection. Although people have gone on working and managed to get certain initiatives taken up from time to time—at the level of manifestos or policy documents—the transition hasn't occurred.

So then yes, it may be right to show what real connections there are between certain types of work and certain types of organisation. Increasingly this is being shown in analysis of political news and opinion. I would say it is also true in terms of a lot of the drama and magazine programming, where the concept of the large audience is significantly flattening the range—that's another analytic job that very much needs to be done. But the critical moment of connection would be between that sort of analysis and the proposals for new kinds of institution justified not only by abstract principles— accountability or self-management or democratisation—but by showing that different kinds of work could be done. Here it would be important to gather together—I don't know that this has yet been done effectively—positive examples of the initiatives from outside the consensus that have found their way into the existing programming structure. One often finds the Left arguing about the merits of this or that innovation rather than trying—while retaining a proper critical interest in whether each was successful—to group them in the direction in which a policy could go. Attempts at community programming and community reporting, different kinds of drama and even attempts at reporting outside the typical professional style—all these have found their way in at the edges of some of the programme channels. If these could be grouped together to show how social relations fit into the forms and how there have been at least provisional attempts to find forms which are different not only internally but in terms of the work's relation to its audience, then I think the case would become more convincing because more concrete.

I find increasingly now if I say to people in these different fields that we need these institutional changes, they say that we need the present institutions because the crucial interaction between social relations and performance hasn't been sufficiently demonstrated. I am not a determinist in the hard sense on this. Although there is always a strong correlation between social relation and form, the whole cultural history of these connections is of forms managing to go at least some way beyond the predominant social relations—they are not merely or totally their reproduction. So every case when someone has pushed the use of a form beyond the predominant social relations does more than mark the limits; it should be cherished as a kind of victory. By gathering these examples together, the case becomes more substantial. Otherwise, many producers can become so preoccupied with what they want to produce that they would rather fight their way through the jungle alone in the hope of getting some part of it done than involve themselves at a difficult time with this much more general reform.

To what extent could teaching about the media in schools and colleges contribute to building the political basis of such an initiative?

I'm sure it can. If people have learned, as it can be learned, that it is not just the content of a programme but its form—often its deep form—that is telling you something, then you have an emerging public opinion which would be crucial in the very tough battle which would quickly occur if the Left did make really viable initiatives in these fields. One knows immediately how this would be greeted by the established organs—over the range from STATE GRAB to FURTHER BUREAUCRATISATION to THOUGHT CONTROL and so on. Of course, the Left is carrying unwanted baggage on its back in all those respects, so it goes into that battle with a certain disadvantage.

If you have people who have learned as a matter of ordinary education that it matters very much where somebody sets up a camera or where the reporter stands in relation to a confrontation in the street or what happens on a picket line, they will understand that it isn't what is said that is the only question. To take one example that

I think is repeatedly relevant, the normal situation of the camera and reporter is behind the police who are dealing with pickets or demonstrators. This puts the viewer in a situation where he or she too is invited to see them as *objects*; the viewer is, as it were, identified with this position. Now if you show how that is so or if you show what happens when the reporter or interviewer or chairman of discussion intervenes to set the terms of discussion between people who could certainly set their own terms of discussion, all that kind of learning builds up the beginning of a necessary public opinion. The long-term advantage of this education would not just be critical awareness. This was the *Scrutiny* position, that critical awareness in itself would make the significant difference. Well, it does to some extent, but it is critical awareness as a basis for really being able to understand and participate in the typical social argument and indeed social struggle that the new institutions would involve.

What sort of teaching have you done in this area?

Since the War, I suppose I have spent half my time in adult education and half my time inside Cambridge, and the contrast between the two is very sharp. Whereas in adult education I could initiate this teaching and did a great deal of it, within the university the opportunities are much harder to come by. In adult education, I did classes on newspapers and advertising and on films; these were both critical and sociological analyses, often the two together. It works extremely well in something as unspecialised and unstructured as adult education because you can always speak to a direct body of interests. That is work I very much miss. Within the university, I have done some film courses which have been concerned very much with analysis of forms and also, really, finding methods of analysis. You are dealing with students who have a very developed—they sometimes themselves think over-developed—capacity for linguistic analysis, which is thoroughly integrated in the school curriculum, but who, although intensely involved in the other media, find you can't simply transfer linguistic analysis to forms like film. So there is a discovery of terms, and also seeing what is available from earlier kinds of analysis; I particularly teach a lot about conventions.

The latest example of this teaching was a collaborative course with Stephen Heath and Colin MacCabe on *Police Fiction*. This happens to be a good central point, both because there is so much of it and because so many of the questions can be raised from different approaches. I began by talking about the evolution of police fiction as fiction, as in the novel, and tried to distinguish the stages that the detective, the criminal, the unofficial policeman, the unofficial detective and so on went through, to show how certain social relations got into particular forms.

Then we looked at different examples of current police or crime television; we tried to do an analysis, at once formal and sociological, of the positioning of the viewer in relation to the crime. What emerged was an evolution of the law-keeper from the highly respectable police figure, through the cultivated amateur who sold a certain social style along with the detection, to this very interesting development in which the distinction between the law-keeper and the law-breaker is purely nominal in terms of manifest behaviour. You are told who is the criminal and who is the cop, but at most ethical and practical levels there is little to choose. In this work, the social analysis follows the formal fairly clearly because these are different *perceptions* of the nature of law and crime. It's also a social analysis of the production of the stereotypes on which these peceptions operate. We ended the course with Tony Garnett showing us a rough cut of one of his *Law and Order* films, which led to a great argument about whether that was the way to do the counter-work.

That sort of work I have very much enjoyed, but it has had to be set up purely in the margins because the structure of ordinary university specialist courses hasn't room for it. I also work with postgraduate research students—on television as an election process, for example, on comparative analysis of newspaper treatment of certain issues, on general communications theory. Again, these are in the margins.

I'd like to ask about your time as an adult education tutor. During the Twenties and Thirties—certainly up until the Second World War—there was a rich working-class education coming directly from the labour movement in a way that no longer exists. Could this history help us today to build an education with an assignable class content, to say what is a working-class education rather than simply a state or a bourgeois education?

From the beginning of adult education, of course, there was a crucial conflict between the definition of *workers'* education and the definition of *adult* education. This was already an open split before the First World War, between the Labour Colleges, which said we must have an independent working-class education providing our own teachers, and the Workers' Educational Association, which got its teachers from the universities. In spite of their theoretical differences, both sides sustained a lot of working-class education. But in the end, the initiatives for quite independent working-class education ran into inevitable problems of funding—depending on the policies of particular trade unions—and the collaboration with the universities ran into difficulties over this problem of the definition of content and the teacher's responsibility to the institution. For example, to get a proper university adult class—the tutorial class, as it was called—you had to have the required duration and you had to have regular written work. Now this requirement of written work is a wholly knowable and predictable obstacle to the full participation of working-class students. When I did a class directly for active trade unionists, I had to forget all the forms recognisable as educational in university terms because I was discussing how to write minutes or a report of a meeting, the problems of preparing material. All these were at a much simpler level than the sort of essay which was still the model in the university classes.

One must remember that those generations included significantly larger numbers of people of very high intelligence simply deprived of educational opportunities which have since been enlarged. But it's also a matter of the cultural ambience into which this kind of study comes. We had to learn what our illusions were. For example, if you do a class in economics, as my colleagues did, and you start talking about averages and percentages, it takes quite a long time before there is an admission that those concepts need teaching, that they are not things you can simply assume are known. It's a very complicated teaching problem. The most significant moments in working-class education came precisely when people were willing to declare in a situation of trust that even these most basic intellectual tools had to be learned—but learned in a nonpatronising way.

In this context, what political effect do you think an institution like the Open University is likely to have in the long term?

The Open University is obviously very welcome; but there is a crucial disjunction between it and the adult education tradition which needn't have happened. What the Open University is highly efficient at is its collaborative course making, the often brilliant technical presentation of material—especially in the course units. This is typically done by small, specially assembled course staffs who work in more collaborative ways than most university teachers; in that respect it has advantages. But equally it is done much more centrally.

What the Open University does not yet have is the kind of properly based tutorial organisation which the adult education movement already had, where you would have not merely an educational counsellor who could help you with the problems of study, but specifically a tutor who could help sort out your intellectual problems. Education can never be the transmission of even the most brilliantly prepared material without all the follow-up. I greatly regret—it is perhaps not irreparable—that there wasn't more continuity with the adult education method. That, incidentally, was a marvellously self-organised and democratic sort of institution. Classes really did choose their own syllabuses and their own tutors—often under persuasive suggestion, but they had this right and often exercised it. This is so different from being a consumer of even the best Open University programme; there is a crucial difference in social relations. That opportunity was missed and ought to be regained.

Could the current thinking about adult and workers' education inside the trade union movement help in defining what working class education in schools should be like? There is an interesting discussion going on within the TUC Education Department about shop stewards' education, about the extent to which it should be concerned only with practical information about negotiating techniques and so on.

This argument about what shop stewards' education is, which I saw quite closely in some of its early stages, is a very good case of the definition of workers' education. On the one hand, there is the purely technicist solution: these are shop stewards, they have to do a job of negotiation, they must learn the rules of negotiation, they must learn how to read a balance sheet, and so on. That seems to me a reduction from the earlier forms of adult education, in which you learned these things in the way that I was trying to help people learn minutes and oral reports, but in which you were also doing economics. What sort of education is it anyway that prepares you for a successful negotiation with a capitalist without teaching you the whole range of issues involved?

On the other hand, that didn't go unchallenged by people wanting to combine a version of the academic study of economics with precisely these practical questions. This is clearly the correct solution;

a definition of working-class education would explicitly have to include the facts of work and the social relations of work which, except for certain directly professional subjects, have been excluded from received liberal definitions of education. It is where those join that is the crucial issue.

That is a very important area of argument which has implications for the study of film and television. This shouldn't simply be training more appreciative consumers, which is what film appreciation clubs did, or encouraging the "mystique of making" by giving people glimpses of the studio, but, within a more general body of cultural studies, admitting the social relations which have been excluded from education into the context of the organisation. This is what working-class education would be.

Some of the terms in which you were talking about the institutions of television—the need for democratic, accountable, decentralised management—sound suspiciously like some of the terms in which the populist Right talks about education. Problems like accountability and professionalism seem much more ambiguous when applied to education.

I'm sorry about the coincidence, if it is one, of phrases like "accountability" and a populist rhetoric. But when the received centre ground thinks in terms of centralised and either capitalist corporate or state corporate institutions, then what the Left says in response to this situation does sometimes sound like what part of the Right is saying. Self-management could never be compatible with populist rhetoric because it is only significant if it includes all the people concerned, not if it's just a technique of management through what are inevitably selected and privileged relations.

If there are to be any intiatives within education, though, the class organisations which are much more extended would have to be quite centrally involved—the class demands for certain general conditions could never be, as it were, subcontracted to other forms of self-management. But if demands are only in the direction of more centralised state institutions, they are actually running *with* the currents of the established society and against the opportunities of including and liberating more general resources. But, I agree, the harder, more unreceived the terms of the discussion of these relations become, the better. We are slowly learning how to work in terms of self-management and collectives at a very local level, but all the real social problems in that movement come when you start thinking about how collectives and self-managing institutions link up, as in any complex society they are bound to, and how general social decisions can be made without violating these first principles. At the moment it seems easier because these institutions live in the margin of the corporate institutions, but if you are talking about the essential social principle, then most of the social thinking still has to be done.

In the last year or two there seems to have been a retreat by many parts of the Left from the sort of social thinking in the late Sixties and early Seventies which accepted the political importance of cultural questions, a retreat from notions like Gramsci's hegemony into a "straightforward politics" in which the state is seen as central and everything else very much as subordinate. In a general socialist strategy for Britain today, what do you see as the place of cultural struggle?

My position hasn't changed much. I think that a political strategy which doesn't take account of cultural questions is living in the past. This does not imply that they should take priority over all the other kinds of struggle: the problem is precisely that they are seen as separate sectors—the "economic wing", the "political wing" and the "cultural wing". Only when they are *not* seen as sectors can the effect of the important cultural arguments come through: that there is none of these sectors that does not immediately involve the others; that a lot of the major economic and industrial disputes are about cultural institutions; that culture is involved in politics in quite a new way, especially in the involvement of the media; and conversely that all the questions about culture involve hard economic questions and questions of political institutions. Whenever there's a move to concentrate on just one sector, it's often understandable in the context of the time, but it's always theoretically wrong.

Screen Education, Summer 1979

Notes

1 R. Williams. *Television: Technology and Cultural Form* (London: Fontana 1974); *Marxism and Literature* (Oxford: Oxford University Press 1977).

2 R. Williams. *Communications,* 2nd edition (Harmondsworth: Penguin 1968).

Bibliography

1. Television materials by Raymond Williams not included in this book.

"Arguing about television." Review of *Television and the Child,* by Hilde T. Himmelweir. *Encounter* 12 (June 1959), 56-59.

"The Magic System." *New Left Review* no. 4 (1960):27-32. Reprinted in Williams, *Problems in Materialism and Culture* (1980).

"Television in Britain." *The Journal of Social Issues* 18, 2 (1962), 6-15.

"Raymond Williams gives his views on how television should be run." *The Listener* 80 (11 July 1968), 1, 34-35.

"Crisis in communications: a new mood of submission." *The Listener* 82, 31 July 1969, 138, 140. Reprinted in Williams, *Problems in Materialism and Culture* (1980).

"Teletalk." Review of *The new priesthood: British television today,* by Joan Bakewell and Nicholas Garnham. *Guardian* (5 November 1970), 9.

"Raymond Williams thinks well of the Open University." *The Listener* 86 (14 October 1971), 507-508.

"Open-circuit television." Review of *Television and the People: A Programme for Democratic Participation,* by Brian Groombridge. *Guardian* (27 April 1972), 14.

Television: Technology and Cultural Form. (London: Fontana, 1974). U.S. edition (New York: Schocken, 1975). Italian edition, *Televisione: Technologia e forma culturale* (Bari: De Donato, 1981).

Communications. 3rd edition. (Harmondsworth: Penguin, 1976).

"Legal? Decent? Honest? Truthful?—an argument about advertising." *The Listener* (16 December 1976), 331-332.

"The growth and role of the mass media." *International* Vol. 3, No. 3 (Spring 1977), 3-6. Reprinted in C. Gardner (Ed.) *Median, politics and culture: A socialist view* (London: Macmillan, 1979), 14-24.

"A lecture on realism." *Screen* 18, 1 (Spring 1977), 61-74.
"Realism and non-naturalism." *Official programme of the Edinburgh International Television Festival* (1977).
"Television and the mandarins." Review of *The Future of Broadcasting,* the Annan Report. *New Society* (March 1977), 651-652.
"The book of governors." Review of *Governing the BBC,* by Asa Briggs. *Guardian* (29 November 1979), 10.
"Isn't the news terrible?" Review of *More Bad News,* by the Glasgow University Media Group; *The Whole World is Watching,* by Todd Gitlin. *London Review of Books* 2, 13 (July 1980), 14.
"Gravity's Python." Review of *From Fringe to Flying Circus,* by Roger Wilnut. *London Review of Books* 2, 13 (July 1980), 6-7.
"Foreword." In A. Hunt, *The Language of Television: Uses and Abuses* (London: Eyre Methuen, 1981), vii-x.
"Foreword." In J. McGrath, *A good night out: Popular theatre: audience, class and form* (London: Eyre Methuen, 1981), vii-xi.
How to be the arrow, not the target." *Irish Broadcasting Review* No. 15 (1982), 16-21.
"This sadder recognition." Interview about *So that you can live,* a television production based on *The Country and the City,* by Raymond Williams. *Screen* 23, 3-4 (1982), 144-52.
Towards 2000. (London: Chatto & Windus, 1983).
"An interview with Raymond Williams." By Stephen Heath and Gillian Skirrow. In Tania Modelski (Ed.) *Studies in Entertainment: Critical Approaches to Mass Culture* (Bloomington and Indianapolis: Indiana University Press, 1986), 3-17.

2. Related material by Raymond Williams on Radio and policies for Arts.

"Just what is Labour's policy for radio?" *Tribune* (18 February 1966), 8.
"What happens after the 'pirates' walk the plank?" *Tribune* (7 October 1966), 9.
"Commercial radio: the thin edge of the wedge?" *Tribune* (2 August 1968), 6-7.
Mayday Manifesto 1968 (Ed.) Raymond Williams. (Harmondsworth: Penguin, 1968).
"The arts council." *Political Quarterly* 50 (1977), 151-157.
"Lecture." In *The Arts Council: Politics and policies* (London: Arts Council, 1983), 9-16.

"State culture and beyond." In L. Appignansi (Ed.) *Culture and the State* (London: Institute of Contemporary Arts, 1984), 3-5.

3. Selected discussions of Raymond Williams's television writings.

Rick Altman. "Television/Sound." In Tania Modelski (Ed.) *Studies in Entertainment* (Bloomington and Indianapolis: Indiana University Press, 1986), 39-54.

Briggs, Asa. "TV Guides." Review of *Tubes of Plenty: The Evolution of American Television*, by Erik Barnouw and *Television: Technology and Cultural Form*, by Raymond Williams. *Partisan Review* 45 (1978):478-481

Ellis, John. *Visible Fictions: Cinema, Television, Video* (London: Routledge and Kegan Paul, 1982), 117-126.

Franco, Jean. "Go with the flow: Books on television." *Tabloid* 3 (Winter 1981), 35-41.

Grossberg, Lawrence. "Strategies of Marxist Cultural Interpretation." *Critical Studies in Mass Communication* 1 (1984), 400-402.

Himmelstein, Hal. *On the Small Screen: New Approaches in Television and Video Criticism* (New York: Praeger, 1981), 88-89.

Hood, Stuart. Review of *Television*, by Raymond Williams. *Guardian Weekly* (8 June 1974), 21.

Modelski, Tania. "The Rhythm of Reception: Daytime Television and Women's Work." In E. Ann Kaplan (Ed.) *Regarding Television* (Los Angeles: American Film Institute, 1983), 67-75.

Motterhead, Chris. Review of *Television: Technology and Cultural Form* in *Screen Education* No. 14 (Spring 1975), 35-38.

O'Connor, Alan. *Raymond Williams: Writing, Culture, Politics* (Oxford, New York: Basil Blackwell, 1989).

Slack, Jennifer Daryl. *Communication Technologies and Society* (Norwood, New Jersey: Ablex, 1984), 75-76.

Williams, Raymond. *Politics and Letters: Interviews with New Left Review* (London: NLB, 1979), 233-34.

Index

Printed in Canada